Kate Chopin, Edith Wharton and Charlotte Perkins Gilman

Kate Chopin, Edith Wharton and Charlotte Perkins Gilman

Studies in Short Fiction

Janet Beer
Professor of English
Pro Vice Chancellor / Dean of Humanities, Law and Social Science
Manchester Metropolitan University

palgrave
macmillan

First published 1997

First published in paperback 2005 by
PALGRAVE MACMILLAN
Houndmills, Basingstoke, Hampshire RG21 6XS and
175 Fifth Avenue, New York, N. Y. 10010
Companies and representatives throughout the world

PALGRAVE MACMILLAN is the global academic imprint of the Palgrave Macmillan division of St. Martin's Press, LLC and of Palgrave Macmillan Ltd. Macmillan® is a registered trademark in the United States, United Kingdom and other countries. Palgrave is a registered trademark in the European Union and other countries.

ISBN 0–333–54542–7 hardback (outside North America)
ISBN 0–312–21095–7 hardback (in North America)
ISBN-13: 978–1–4039–4276–0 paperback
ISBN-10: 1–4039–4276–5 paperback

This book is printed on paper suitable for recycling and made from fully managed and sustained forest sources.

A catalogue record for this book is available from the British Library.

Library of Congress Cataloging-in-Publication Data
Beer, Janet, 1956–
Kate Chopin, Edith Wharton, and Charlotte Perkins Gilman : studies in short fiction / Janet Beer.
p. cm.
Includes bibliographical references and index.
ISBN 0–312–21095–7 (cloth)
ISBN 1–4039–4276–5 (pbk)
1. Short stories, American—Women authors—History and criticism.
2. American fiction—Women authors—History and criticism.
3. American fiction—20th century—History and criticism.
4. American fiction—19th century—History and criticism.   5. Women and literature—United States.   6. Chopin, Kate, 1851–1904–
–Criticism and interpretation.   7. Wharton, Edith, 1862–1937–
–Criticism and interpretation.   8. Gilman, Charlotte Perkins,
1860–1935—Criticism and interpretation.   9. Short story.
I. Title.
PS374.S5B44 1997
813'.4099287—dc21   97–34098
                                                              CIP

10   9   8   7   6   5   4   3   2   1
14   13   12   11   10   09   08   07   06   05

Printed and bound in Great Britain by
Antony Rowe Ltd, Chippenham and Eastbourne

For David

Contents

Preface to the 2004 Reprint   ix

Acknowledgements   xi

1   Kate Chopin, Edith Wharton and Charlotte Perkins Gilman:
    Studies in Short Fiction – An Introduction   1

2   "dah you is, settin' down, lookin' jis' like w'ite folks!"
    Ethnicity Enacted in Kate Chopin's Short Fiction   24

3   Without End: the Shape and Form of Desire in
    Kate Chopin's Short Fiction   40

4   Kate Chopin's Short Short Stories – on the
    Verge(s) of Narrative   66

5   Edith Wharton and the Coherence of the
    Novella: From Initiation to Disillusion   91

6   Edith Wharton, Literary Ghosts and the Writing of
    New England   116

7   The Means and Ends of Genre in the Short Fiction
    of Charlotte Perkins Gilman   147

8   Charlotte Perkins Gilman's Analogues – Reiterating
    the Social Health   174

9   'The Yellow Wallpaper' on Film – Dramatising
    Mental Illness   197

Conclusion   214

Bibliography   216

Index   220

Preface to the 2004 Reprint

Between 1997 and 2004 significant critical works have been steadily added to the valuable and groundbreaking work on the short stories of the three writers who are the subjects of this book. Gilman, in particular, has been the subject of a number of outstanding essay collections, stimulated by two international Gilman conferences, one at the University of Liverpool in 1995 and the other at Skidmore College in 1997. The centenary of the publication of Chopin's novel, *The Awakening*, was celebrated in a special conference at the University of Glasgow in 1999 and her work was significantly represented at the 'New Orleans in Europe' conference held at the University of Warwick in 1998. Latterly the Edith Wharton Society moved to the United Kingdom for its 2003 international conference 'Edith Wharton in London' where discussions of the short stories featured prominently on the programme. The recording of this academic activity provides a mere snapshot of the kind of debate, intellectual engagement and sheer enthusiasm that is generated by the work of these three writers, an enthusiasm which shows no sign of waning.

There are a few editions or studies published between 1996 and 2004 which are worth highlighting here, either because they are of general interest to the Chopin, Wharton or Gilman scholar or have a specific contribution to make to study of the short stories. Pamela Knights' edition of *The Awakening and Other Stories* has an excellent introduction in which the short stories are discussed in detail and Nancy Walker gives an overview of both the early and post-*Awakening* stories in her new *Literary Life* of Chopin. The most important book to be published in Wharton studies in the last few years is George Ramsden's *Edith Wharton's Library*, a catalogue of the surviving books from the writer's library with a Foreword by Hermione Lee and an Introduction by Ramsden himself. The book provides vital and inspiring information for the Wharton scholar eager to know not only which books Wharton owned but also the kind of marks and annotations she made in them. Also discernible in many of her books are clues to the relationships she had with other writers as demonstrated in their flyleaf dedications to her. Ramsden's Introduction and his helpful notes throughout the catalogue describe the history of the library, its particular strengths in terms of subject areas, the provenance of the books, for example, which of them come from Walter Berry's collection and which from her father's 'gentleman's library', whilst also making cross references between Wharton's own writing and the marks on the printed pages she owned and loved. He closes the book with a set of extracts from Wharton's works which concern books and libraries and it is clear from the catalogue that the relationship between the writer and her books was absolutely central not only to her professional life but to her personal life, so much of her investment in the printed page is visible in the books she owned. Ramsden includes an extract from a letter sent from Wharton to Sally Norton in 1901 in the Introduction: 'I send you back the little book with a faint scratch here and there to show you the detached things that struck me... this is the nearest approach to talking over a book together'—and this sense of 'talking [it] over' is powerfully communicated to the reader in the detail of her book collection. Also proving invaluable to Wharton scholars is Sarah Bird Wright's *Edith Wharton A–Z* which supplies answers to questions of publication, location and provenance; the *A–Z* is particularly informative on the short stories.

In *'The Yellow Wallpaper' and the History of Its Publication and Reception* Julie Bates Dock provides an illuminating and meticulously compiled publication history of the short story, knocking more than a few myths about the reception of the text on the head and giving details of the extensive print record of the story, published and re-published in a range of different anthologies, especially tales of the macabre. All the most important Gilman scholars are represented in three essay collections published since 1998, two of them edited by Val Gough and Jill Rudd and one by Catherine Golden and Joanna Schneider Zangrando; the short stories are the subject of a significant number of the essays. Details of all these texts can be found in the Bibliography.

Janet Beer, 2004

Acknowledgements

A version of Chapter Two, ' "dah you is, settin' down, lookin' jis' like w'ite folks!" Ethnicity Enacted in Kate Chopin's Short Fiction', first appeared in *The Yearbook of English Studies*, Volume 24, 1994 and a portion of Chapter 5, 'Edith Wharton and the Coherence of the Novella: From Initiation to Disillusion', in the Virago Press Edition of *Madame de Treymes*, London, 1995.

Grateful acknowledgement is made to Syracuse University Press to reproduce material from Kessler, Carol Farley *Charlotte Perkins Gilman: Her Progress Toward Utopia with Selected Writings* (Liverpool University Press, 1995). Grateful acknowledgement is also made to Associated University Presses for permission to reproduce material from Knight, Denise D. (ed.) *'The Yellow Wallpaper' and Selected Stories of Charlotte Perkins Gilman* (London: Associated University Presses, 1994). Extracts from 'The Storm' and other stories are reprinted by permission of Louisiana State University Press from *The Complete Works of Kate Chopin*, edited by Per Seyersted, copyright 1969 by Louisiana State University Press.

Extracts from Kate Chopin's Account Book are authorised by the Missouri Historical Society, St Louis. Excerpts from 'Bewitched' are reprinted with the permission of Scribner, a division of Simon and Schuster, from *The Ghost Stories of Edith Wharton*, copyright 1925 by Pictorial Review Co.; copyright renewed 1953 by the Hearst Corporation. Excerpts from 'All Souls' and the Preface are reprinted with the permission of Scribner, a division of Simon and Schuster from *The Ghost Stories of Edith Wharton*, copyright 1937 by D. Appleton-Century Co.; copyright renewed 1965 by William R. Tyler. Excerpts from 'Friends' and 'The Angel at the Grave' are reprinted with the permission of Scribner, a divison of Simon and Schuster, from *The Collected Short Stories of Edith Wharton*, edited by Richard W.B. Lewis (New York: Scribner, 1968). Excerpts from 'The Young Gentlemen' were reprinted by permission of William B. Tyler and the Watkins/Loomis Agency.

I would like to acknowledge the help of a number of people and organisations in the research and writing of this book and must begin with Sister Bernadette Porter and the Society of the Sacred

Heart, the providing body for Digby Stuart College of the Roe-hampton Institute, who both helped in the funding of a visit to the Missouri Historical Society in St Louis and extended the most wonderful hospitality whilst I was there. In particular Sister Mary Byles was the perfect guide to old and new St Louis. I am very grateful to my employer, the Roehampton Institute, and all my colleagues in the Department of English for allowing me leave to work on this book. I would also like to say how much the professional and personal support of Linda Thomas, Joanna Thornborrow, Shân Wareing and Ishtla Singh has meant to me; I have always felt very privileged to be an honorary linguist in their company.

I want to give special mention to my colleague, Kevin McCarron, whose clear insights into many and varied texts, genres and problems of composition have been of inestimable help throughout the last four years of teaching and writing. He is, and I hope will always remain, a very good friend. The encouragement and support of Ann Thompson and Elaine Showalter have also been a great and exceptional privilege during the period in which I was working on this book. I would also like to express a debt of gratitude to the dramatist, Maggie Wadey, for her time and patience, to Lionel Kelly for his continuing kindness and for the opportunities he has extended to me, to Lesley Cassie for succour both intellectual and emotional, to Kay and Robert Burns for their unfailing warmth and hospitality on visits to the United States and to Katherine Joslin whose clarity of thought and incisiveness on electronic mail never cease to amaze me. My children, Tom and Helena, throughout the composition of this book, have been interested commentators on my various moods and activities and I would like to pay tribute here to their resilience, their good-nature and to tell them how much I love them.

1

Kate Chopin, Edith Wharton and Charlotte Perkins Gilman: Studies in Short Fiction – An Introduction

The three authors who are the subjects of this book, Kate Chopin (1850–1904), Edith Wharton (1862–1937) and Charlotte Perkins Gilman (1860–1935), were prolific and innovative short-story writers. All three wrote short stories throughout their professional lives and were also practitioners in other genres; all wrote poetry, for private and public consumption, both Gilman and Wharton wrote novels, criticism, autobiography, essays and cultural critiques, Wharton wrote travel books and Gilman had a long and distinguished career as a sociologist, lecturing and writing outside the academic establishment to a wide range of different audiences. Chopin, the most dedicated short story writer of the three, wrote a few minor articles and was the author of three novels: one, *Young Dr Gosse*, was destroyed after she failed to find a publisher for it, another, *At Fault*, was published at her own expense in 1890[1] and her third and best known, *The Awakening*, was published in 1899, toward the end of her life.

In this book I will be looking at the work of these writers only in their short fiction but as this short fiction comes in a variety of shapes and guises I will be ranging between discussions of Kate Chopin's micro-narratives, stories of less than a thousand words, and Edith Wharton's novellas, *Sanctuary*, *The Touchstone* and *Madame de Treymes*. The chapters are all discrete, all explore separate aspects of the writers and, although there are many grounds for comparison between them, my central concern here is not to sustain the analogous qualities of their work. In each chapter I take an aspect of the short fiction of the individual writer and focus closely on subject and style, engaging in detailed readings of a range of texts which support notions of thematic and generic coherence, coherences which are largely undisturbed by other development and change in the work of each writer over the course of her professional life.

In an article published in *The Times Literary Supplement* in June 1995, Elaine Showalter makes the point that in the 1890s 'the best work of the decade was in the short story not in the novel.... Women writers in the 1890s found the short story a suitable form for the new feminist themes of the decade: the exploration of female sexuality and fantasy, the development of a woman's language, and the critique of male aestheticism.'[2] These claims are certainly exemplified in the careers of Kate Chopin, Edith Wharton and Charlotte Perkins Gilman, all experimenting during the decade and beyond with both subject and technique in the genre of the short story. Whilst Kate Chopin wrote of sexuality and desire in the lives of both men and women with a frankness rarely before seen, Charlotte Perkins Gilman and Edith Wharton sought to change and renew the subject and the structure of fiction to reflect the wider cultural dislocations of the *fin de siècle*, and, especially, the implications of social and technological change for women. Gilman never desisted from critiquing that which she termed 'The Man-Made World',[3] seeking to impress upon her readers the pervasive and destructive nature of existing divisions into gendered lives, whilst Wharton, in all her works of fiction and non-fiction, undertook the task of establishing herself as a writer with her own distinct voice, subject and artistic ambition, despite the criticisms of those who would dismiss her as a 'Literary Aristocrat',[4] playing at being a writer, or as a mere imitator of Henry James who could have nothing new to offer.

In May 1890, Edward Burlingame of *Scribner's* accepted Wharton's 'Mrs Manstey's View' – an imaginative leap into the life of a working-class widow in a New York boarding-house – for inclusion in the magazine and she thus published a work of prose fiction for the first time.[5] Kate Chopin began 1891 with rejection; her story about syphilis and its legacy, 'Mrs Mobry's Reason' became in that year, as Emily Toth tells us in her biography, *Kate Chopin*, the writer's 'most rejected story'.[6] Unlike Gilman and Wharton, Chopin was already a well-established writer in 1891, but this did not stop editors throughout the magazine publishing world from refusing this particular piece. *Century, Scribner's, Arena, Belford's, Lippincott's, Atlantic, New York Ledger, Cosmopolitan, Inland Monthly, Harper's,*

Kate Field's Washington, Two Tales, New England Magazine, and *Vogue*[7] – the last named usually to be relied upon to take material from which other magazines shied away – all these declined to publish. The story eventually saw the light of day in the *New Orleans Times-Democrat* in April 1893,[8] two years after it was written, and such a delay between writing and publication is actually not exceptional in the publication history of Chopin's work. In 1892 Gilman's 'The Yellow Wallpaper' was published in the *New England Magazine,*[9] but only after its now famous rejection by Horace Scudder, the over-scrupulously sensitive editor of the *Atlantic Monthly*: 'Mr Howells has handed me this story. I could not forgive myself if I made others as miserable as I have made myself!'.[10]

It was not only rejection that Chopin and Gilman shared: the subject of venereal disease was one which would preoccupy Charlotte Perkins Gilman in her later work and I discuss the fictions which have the effects of sexually transmitted diseases as their narrative imperative in Chapter 8 of this book. She wrote repeatedly about the social and medical effects of the disease and the secrecy surrounding its very existence, but she obviated the need to obtain the approval of a timid editor for her subject by publishing her stories in her own magazine, *The Forerunner,* between 1909 and 1916. As she details in her autobiography, *The Living of Charlotte Perkins Gilman,* posthumously published in 1935, there were a modest number of editors who were willing to publish her writing, especially early in her career, but she was not willing to compromise her principles by pandering to the prevailing tastes in magazine fiction and she defiantly refused offers from William Randolph Hearst to write for *Good Housekeeping* or *Cosmopolitan.* Her sense of purpose was always more powerful than her desire for either financial or critical success:

> As years passed and continuous writing and speaking developed the various lines of thought I was following, my work grew in importance but lost in market value. Social philosophy, however ingeniously presented, does not command wide popular interest. I wrote more and sold less.
>
> Theodore Dreiser, then on the *Delineator,* as I remember, looked gloomily at me over his desk, and said, 'You should consider more what the editors want.' Of course I should have, if I had been a competent professional writer. There are those who write as artists, real ones; they often find it difficult to

consider what the editor wants. There are those who write to earn a living, they, if they succeed, *must* please the editor. The editor, having his living to earn, must please his purchasers, the public, so we have this great trade of literary catering. But if one writes to express important truths, needed yet unpopular, the market is necessarily limited.

As all my principal topics were in direct contravention of established views, beliefs and emotions, it is a wonder that so many editors took so much of my work for so long.[11]

All three writers felt the constraints of what was deemed acceptable by the magazine editors and sought to find ways and means to accommodate the strictures of the censoring eye of those in charge at the journals and publishing houses whilst remaining in control of their own discursive practice. But, in being dismissive of any writing which did not aim at the achievement of the radical reform of the existing social order through the power of polemic, whether in the form of fiction or sociology, Charlotte Perkins Gilman did not, at any point, accede to either the censorship of the magazine editor or the imposition of a subject, for to have done so would have invalidated her work entirely. She was briefly the editor of a radical magazine, the *Impress*, in 1894 in San Francisco,[12] for which she wrote reviews, articles, poetry and editorials, but the magazine failed after a short period and until she established *The Forerunner* in 1909 she did not publish any more fiction, concentrating instead on writing works of social theory: *Women and Economics* was published in 1898, *Concerning Children* in 1900, *The Home: Its Work and Influence* in 1903 and *Human Work* in 1904.

Despite the apparent unanimity of the editorial establishment as regards appropriate themes and subjects for the magazine audience,[13] all three writers knew that there were differences between editors and exploited these in so far as they could by submitting and resubmitting stories to different journals. Chopin, the writer most affected by the apparently arbitrary power of the editors, offers the following commentary in her essay series, 'As You Like It':[14]

But editors are really a singular class of men; they have such strange and incomprehensible ways with them.

I once submitted a story to a prominent New York editor, who returned it promptly with the observation that 'the public is getting very tired of that sort of thing.' I felt very sorry for the public; but I wasn't willing to take one man's word for it, so I clapped the offensive document into an envelope and sent it away again – this time to a well-known Boston editor.

'I am delighted with the story,' read the letter of acceptance, which came a few weeks later, 'and so, I am sure, will be our readers.' (!)

When an editor says a thing like that it is at his own peril. I at once sent him another tale, thinking thereby to increase his delight and add to it ten-fold.

'Can you really call this a story, dear madam?' he asked when he sent it back. 'Really, there seems to me to be no story at all; what is it all about?' I could see his pale smile.

It was getting interesting, like playing at battledore and shuttlecock. Off went the would-be story by the next mail to the New York editor – the one who so considerately gauged the ennui of the public.

'It is a clever and excellent piece of work,' he wrote me; 'the story is well told.' I wonder if the editor, the writer, and the public are ever at one.[15]

This description of the business of submission and the claims made by the editors both for authority and authenticity as regards the taste of the reading public are, characteristically, made the occasion of much sarcastic comment from Chopin in her essay. However, there are serious points which arise from her account of this specific incident or series of incidents which go some way toward adumbrating the terms of my enquiries into the work of all three writers in this book. Chopin raises the matter of editorial presumption where public taste is concerned and throws it into disrepute; she ventilates the argument of what constitutes a story and shows it to be a matter of some dispute and she also demonstrates the fallaciousness of any easy alignment of editor, writer and reader as consonant in their needs. These are all factors of some significance both in the working lives of these writers and in the manner in which their texts are received by an audience. Despite the radical ideological differences between Kate Chopin and Charlotte Perkins Gilman – Chopin's total, self-declared abjuration of any moral intent for her fiction and Gilman's refusal to write anything which did not have the express intention of reform – they both had a clear and cogent sense of artistic purpose, as did Edith Wharton. All three writers stretched and manipulated generic conventions and boundaries in order to disrupt expected contiguities of structure and theme and they variously contracted and expanded the limits of the short story to accommodate their particular thematic. Each writer made different responses to the requirements of the moral and pecuniary marketplace as well as to the dictates of their own imperatives as creative artists, but Gilman must, for interpretative as well as straightforward biographical reasons, be considered as distinct from Chopin and Wharton in the steps she took in order to disengage from the necessity to sustain the goodwill of the magazines.

Kate Chopin wrote to earn a living; she kept records of submissions, transactions and monies earned; her account book details all payments received for published writing and tells us, for instance, that 'Mrs Mobry's Reason' earned her $5.[16] Gilman subsisted for much of her professional life on the earnings she made from her lectures and writings, her fiction did not provide her with a steady or lucrative income and, as she says in her autobiography, she 'never got a cent for ['The Yellow Wallpaper'] till later publishers brought it out in book form, and very little then'.[17] Edith Wharton lived on a very much grander scale than Chopin or Gilman, but, like them, she earned her own living and made shrewd financial decisions and advantageous deals with her publishers. As R.W.B. Lewis recounts in his biography of Wharton, her literary earnings in 1905, the year in which her novel, *The House of Mirth*, became a bestseller, were more than $20,000,[18] a sum undreamt of by Chopin and Gilman. Chopin's December 1899 entry in her account book, 'Royalties on The Awakening' is for $102, with subsequent sums of $35 and $10.15 recorded in 1900 as joint income from the novel and her short story collection, *A Night in Acadie*, published in 1897.[19] Although the differences between them were enormous in terms of both what they expected to earn and what they actually earned, the fact remains that all three relied, if not entirely, then substantially on their incomes from their writings to maintain their chosen lifestyles; to cite the extremes: for Wharton that involved the maintenance of large, servanted country houses and for Gilman travelling expenses between accommodation which might be offered by those sympathetic to the causes she espoused.

Whilst the short story served an important role in the continuing artistic development of all these writers, Edith Wharton might easily be assumed to be the least focused upon it as a form since she worked in so many different genres and was a prolific novelist. However, as I shall discuss in the context of the novellas, her experimentations in short fiction were excellent preparation for the business of the construction of longer works although this does not mean that her short stories are, in some way, to be construed as inferior to her novels. Barbara White, in her *Edith Wharton: A Study of the Short Fiction,* comments on the immediate proficiency of Wharton as a writer of short stories: 'her early stories cannot really be considered apprentice work. As a writer Wharton sprang full-grown, as it were, from the head of Zeus.'[20] There is no sense in which Wharton's short stories are to be considered as anything other than texts in which she was able to do different things than in her novels and also, and more importantly, in and around the writing of short stories she found a medium in which to theorise her craft. Wharton regarded the short story as the most accessible of literary modes and the one in which she felt most competent and assured; in her oft-quoted letter to Robert Grant, written in response to his comments on her novel, *The Fruit of the Tree,* published in 1907, she says: 'As soon as I look at a subject from the novel-angle I see it in its relation to a larger whole, in all its remotest connotations; & I can't help trying to take them in, at the cost of the smaller realism that I arrive at, I think, better in my short stories. This is the reason why I have always obscurely felt that I didn't know how to write a novel. I feel it more clearly after each attempt, because it is in such sharp contrast to the sense of authority with which I take hold of a short story.'[21] That 'sense of authority' is given expression not only in her stories but in her writing about the short story genre, particularly in her 1925 book, *The Writing of Fiction* where she talks with confidence about the responsibilities of the writer in the construction of the tale: 'One of the chief obligations, in a short story, is to give the reader an immediate sense of security. Every phrase should be a sign-post, and never (unless intentionally) a misleading one: the reader must feel that he can trust to their guidance.'[22] The importance of paying attention to detail, to the 'smaller realism', is the consistent theme of Wharton's writing about the short story but her dominating concern is always with the establishment of an intimate rela-tionship between writer and reader. In her Preface to *Ghosts*, the collection published in 1937, she says 'But when I first began to read, and then to write ghost stories, I was conscious of a common medium between myself and my readers, of their meeting me halfway among the primeval shadows, and filling in the gaps in my narrative with sensations and divinations akin to my own.' It is also in this Preface that she makes the statement: 'for reading should be a creative act as well as writing',[23] and in the composition of her short stories and novellas Wharton was as much preoccupied with the achievement of a consonance of form and content, which would ensure that her readers were given the opportunity to be active in the construction of meaning and effect, as she was with the mechanisms of the plot.

There is always a distinct morality on offer in Wharton's fiction and, whilst taking it as given that all three women wrote because they wanted to write, felt the imperative to create, to leave their mark on the world of letters, they had distinctive positions as to their purposes as writers. Chopin absolutely refused any imputation of moral intent to her fiction, as will be seen in my discussions of her short short stories and the tales which deal with sexual desire, but both Gilman and Wharton expressed opinions to the effect that to have any value – aesthetic or otherwise – fiction must have a moral purpose. For both these writers the shared morality or indeed, in Gilman's case, the actual act of sharing a new and radical morality with her readers, was an intrinsic part of the design and point of the fiction. In a letter written in December 1905 to Dr Morgan Dix, the rector of Trinity Church in New York, Wharton says:

> I could not do anything if I did not think seriously of my trade; & the more I have considered it, the more it has seemed to me valuable & interesting only in so far as it is "a criticism of life." – It almost seems to me that bad and good fiction (using the words in their ethical sense) might be defined as the kind which treats of life trivially & superficially, & that which probes deep enough to get at the relation with the eternal laws; & the novelist who has this feeling is so often discouraged by the comments of readers and critics who think a book "unpleasant" because it deals with unpleasant conditions, that it is a high solace & encouragement to come upon the recognition of one's motive. *No* novel worth anything can be anything but a novel "with a purpose," & if anyone who cared for the moral issue did not see in my work that *I* care for it, I should have no one to blame but myself – or at least my inadequate means of rendering my effects.[24]

The novellas which are the subject of my discussion in Chapter 5, all of which ran serially in *Scribner's* magazine before publication in book form, share a concern, at some level, with issues of both social and aesthetic morality. Whilst they are important for all sorts of reasons they emphatically establish her as a writer embarking upon a quest for the ways and means to create a fiction which will 'get at the relation with the eternal laws.' Wharton wanted to tell compelling tales, but these tales, in order to be aesthetically as well as morally cogent, had to express some profound 'bearing' on ' "the old woe of the world" '[25] as she says in her autobiography, *A Backward Glance*, when reflecting upon her novel, *The House of Mirth*. Additionally, my bringing together in Chapter 6 of the stories, written throughout the course of her career, which are set in New England, reflects upon Wharton's enduring commitment to exploring the topography of the moral life of a culture. As ever in Wharton's work, aesthetic issues are also ethical issues; the New England stories are alike in their communication of the sense of a past whose values are being refused or distorted by subsequent generations.

At the beginning of her writing career Wharton relied upon the advice of Edward L. Burlingame and William Brownell of *Scribner's* as well as her close friend, Walter Berry, who provided a good deal of support by both suggesting revisions and assisting with matters of organisation and style. As Wharton says in tribute to Berry in her autobiography, *A Backward Glance*: 'The instinct to write had always been there; it was he who drew it forth, shaped it and set it free. From my first volume of short stories to *Twilight Sleep*, the novel I published just before his death, nothing in my work escaped him, no detail was too trifling to be examined and discussed, gently ridiculed or quietly praised.'[26] Notwithstanding the elegiac nature of her tribute to Berry in the context of an autobiography which has a generally ameliorative tone, the advice Wharton received from both editors and friends was an enabling principle in her development as an artist; she sought the company of artists and men and women of letters, the literary world was her chosen milieu and the practice of her art was intimately bound up with her social life and the people with whom she chose to associate. Wharton's background and income gave her access to the kind of international culture of letters unavailable to Chopin, primarily for reasons of money and location. Whilst Kate Chopin's personal and professional network was therefore naturally more restricted than Wharton's, she did actively avoid participation in the kind of 'literary set' which St Louis had to offer. Chopin was always vigilant in defending herself against any charges of literary preciousness; both in her public and private writings she established a persona for herself which pretended to humility whilst actually ironising the pretensions of those people who belonged to the kind of improvement 'Clubs' which were proliferating in the 1890s. An essay Chopin wrote for the *Century* magazine, entitled 'In the Confidence of a Story-Writer', published in 1899 without the author's name, makes plain her disdain for any intellectual or artistic affectation: 'I hurried to enroll myself among the thinkers and dispensers of knowledge, and propounders of questions. And very much out of place did I feel in these intellectual gatherings. I escaped by some pretext, and regained my corner, where no "questions" and no fine language can reach me'.[27]

So, whilst Edith Wharton can be said to have taken up a position of almost total immersion in the business, the practice and the social life of what she called the 'Land of Letters',[28] Chopin engaged only selectively with the literary establishment. This is not to say that she did not take an avid interest in current developments in European and American literature and her work as a reviewer delineates a very definite set of opinions about a variety of writers. But Chopin's chief interest was in the development of her own work to a point where she could both accommodate the strictures of the magazine editors – strictures which will be more fully discussed in Chapter 3 of this book – whilst allowing free rein to her own distinct style and subject matter. Her two published novels, coming at the beginning and end of her most productive period of writing, the 1890s, are interesting indicators of her growth in both capability and stature. *At Fault* has some of the hallmarks of Chopin's later, better work; for example, she experiments here with unconventional themes and characters: one of the central players is a female alcoholic, matters at issue include divorce and remarriage, law and order, racial tension and contrasting attitudes between North and South. This early novel did not, however, achieve the consonance of theme and language which is so marked a feature of Chopin's short stories and which is extended to brilliant effect in *The Awakening*.

In a letter written in October 1894 to Waitman Barbe, a West Virginia editor and poet, Chopin outlined her working methods and also her estimation of the comparative value of the short story and the novel: 'It is either very easy for me to write a story, or utterly impossible; that is, the story must "write itself" without any perceptible effort on my part, or it remains unwritten. There is not a tale in "Bayou Folk", excepting the first, which required a longer time than two, or at most three sittings of a few hours each.... My first efforts in literature took the form of two novels of fifty and sixty thousand words. They were written in 1890. The novel does not seem to me now [to] be my natural form of expression. However should the theme of a novel present itself I should of course try to use it. I do not consider one form of more value than the other.'[29] This response to a set of questions about the practice of her craft is in many ways typical of Chopin's extant comments on the process of fiction making. She habitually talked about herself as a creative artist without a moral purpose, without a routine or even regular place to work in, without any kind of principles, either compositional or ethical.

Although most of Chopin's observations on the subject of the craft of fiction as she practised it are heavily inflected with irony, she does express, chiefly in reviews of other writers, a discernible set of artistic tenets, although they are, substantially, articulated negatively. It is plain from her comments on Mrs Humphrey Ward, on Emile Zola, Thomas Hardy and Hamlin Garland, amongst others, whom she criticised for their overt moralising and creaking novel structures, that she abhorred fiction with a purpose, the only kind which her contemporary and moral antithesis, Charlotte Perkins Gilman, ever thought worthwhile. Chopin, as she says in her letter to Barbe, rarely revised her own fiction, but on occasions she did respond to criticism and indeed, knew when to seek it out. The story 'A No-Account Creole' – first a 30 000-word novella, reduced to a 10 000-word story on the advice of her friend, Dr Kolbenheyer, and finally revised along lines suggested to her by R.W. Gilder, editor of the *Century* magazine, wherein it was published in 1894 – earned the author $100, a not inconsiderable sum.[30] Chopin was an intensely private writer and usually resisted any invitation to be serious – 'I am completely at the mercy of unconscious selection'[31] – when talking about the business of composition or, indeed, its social incumbencies. She also refused membership in any confederacy of artists – either literal or ideological. The only writer to whom she pays direct, profuse and regular homage is Maupassant, attributing her own artistic awakening – 'It was at this period of my emerging from the vast solitude in which I had been making my own acquaintance, that I stumbled upon Maupassant'[32] – to his example and influence.

In terms of her family background and education Kate Chopin was heir to a world set aside from Anglo-Saxon pruderies, its character significantly different from the childhood worlds of Wharton and Gilman, both so full of New England or Old New York interdictions and inhibitions. Warner Berthoff in an essay which introduced an edition of *The Awakening* in 1970 and which is reprinted in his *American Trajectories: Authors and Readings 1790–1970*, expresses her difference thus: 'Except for a scattering of immigrant sojourners like Crèvecoeur in the late colonial period or Lafcadio Hearn a century later, Kate Chopin is the first consequential figure in American writing whose birthright consciousness and literary taste were formed outside the Protestant, Anglo-Scottish matrix of our older cultural history. We have, really, to look no further for the outward sources of those qualities in her work – the casually secure freedom of mind and feeling, the easy grace of form, the relative indifference to Grundyite prohibitions – that set her apart from the capable run of dialect-writers and local-color realists filling the magazines in her day'.[33] Chopin's reputation as a writer has benefited immeasurably from the relaxation of the prescriptive canon which would exclude her from consideration as a serious artist because of the classification of the majority of her work as local colour.[34] Berthoff's estimation of her as capacious rather than narrowly focused, cosmopolitan rather than provincial, sophisticated rather than naïve in terms of form, re-orientates our reading of her work in the broader context of European as well as American literature, establishing her in a relationship with French culture which, in specific post-colonial terms, I will be discussing in the context of her portrayal of ethnicity in Chapter 2 of this book.

A concomitant part of the marginalisation of Chopin's work in local colour has been a reluctance to engage with the complexities of her writing about race. Whilst the ideological terrain of the critical debate about texts like Mark Twain's 1894 novel, *Pudd'nhead Wilson* is much-contested and ever-changing, Chopin and her work have been treated as if stuck in a pre-civil war ideological rut. Individual stories like 'Désirée's Baby' have been allowed by some critics to transcend the perceived limitations of an author who was, although only a child, on the confederate side in the civil war, whose family owned slaves and who was married to a man who was a member of the 'Crescent City White League',[35] but discussion of ethnicity across the body of Chopin's work is rare. One of my reasons for focusing on her portrayal of race is to redress this imbalance. That Chopin changed her opinion during her adult life about the value of marriage, that she lost her religion, that she became more broad-minded about sexual expression as she grew older, that she became in every way more liberal, no-one has had any trouble crediting these changes to her account in discussion of her life or her fiction. The people she mixed with in St Louis – her close friend William Schuyler for one – were generally holders of liberal opinion; Schuyler, according to Emily Toth, 'made one of the first serious studies of the spirituals sung by southern blacks'[36] and he was responsible for writing a profile of Kate Chopin, published in *The Writer* in August 1894, which emphasises her 'delicate and sensuous touch and the love of art for art's sake'.[37]

Where scholars working on Charlotte Perkins Gilman – myself included – have very obvious reasons for avoiding discussion of her views on eugenics and on race, plainly stated as they are in both her fiction and her non-fiction, and prefer instead to examine the radical agenda she set out on the subject of women's emancipation, there is no consensus of view on the subject of Chopin and race; neither is there any evidence of her espousal of the white supremacist views of her husband or anyone else. In her book, *Tomorrow is Another Day: The Woman Writer in the South 1859–1936*, Ann Goodwyn Jones provides a sensitive and insightful survey of the portrayal of race in Chopin's fiction, and it is this discussion that I would like to renew and extend. Whilst Goodwyn Jones approaches Chopin on the subject of race largely in the context of the thematic and structural 'connections between blacks and women',[38] noting that the story, 'La Belle Zoraïde', which I discuss in detail in Chapter 2, 'complicates the issue of race and shows even more clearly that Chopin is using blacks as an objective correlative for her feelings about oppression',[39] she also explores the contingencies of Chopin's capacity to use and then undermine the stereotypical in her fiction.

I would argue that the same kind of exegetical attention which is paid to her portrayal of sexual relations should be paid to Chopin's depiction of ethnicity. In discussion of the work of George Washington Cable and the reception of his work in her book *Gender, Race and Region in the Writings of Grace King, Ruth McEnery Stuart and Kate Chopin*, Helen Taylor notes that his example, having 'divided his work into two parts, writing anodyne sentimental fiction to make a living, while using lectures and tracts as the medium through which to expose southern racism...demonstrates the powerful proscription by northern editors from the 1880s onwards of overtly political southern fiction that did not present an idealized, harmonious view of the South and the race question'.[40] Even if Chopin's intentions had been polemical – as Cable's clearly were – she would also have known that the constraints of the marketplace were such that she could not afford to be transparent in the depiction of either race or sex, both were controversial subjects. In a fiction which always withholds the moral judgement but which flirts with endorsing the radical, the rebellious, Chopin correspondingly withholds the ideological. Her work, however, only requires close reading to yield signification vastly beyond the easy categorisation into homilies of local colour which some of her stories have suffered; she is careful to write good and bad into black and white and not to fall unawares into the abyss of absolutist Manichean allegory. Chopin transcended the limits of her age in the depiction of race relations just as she transcended her age in the portrayal of sexual relations and in order to illustrate this claim I shall discuss briefly here the way in which she deconstructs the dominant social mores in her story 'The Godmother', a late piece which seems to me to be indicative, indeed paradigmatic, of her treatment of the dominant social attitudes toward slavery, Christian morality and the accepted limits of sexual conduct.

The story, published in the St Louis *Mirror* in December 1901,[41] not only exposes the distortion of Christian notions of the proper role and duties of the godparent, it also puts on display, through revelation of the unthinking responses of this particular society to crime and criminals, the outrageous injustices of a system which operates only for the benefit of the white population. The title of the story, as noted by Per Seyersted in his edition of *The Complete Works of Kate Chopin*, changed from 'The Unwritten Law'[42] to 'The Godmother' before publication. Thus attention is switched from the law – of whatever variety – to the official role of such as Tante Elodie, the central character, as 'Godmother', the votary of the Christian law, who goes out to hide the evidence of homicide dressed 'like a nun'.[43] There are clearly a number of unwritten laws in this society; there is the natural law, the law of instinct and feeling which puts Tante Elodie's love for Gabriel Lucaze, her godson, above the due course of the civil law; and there is the law which operates on behalf of the ruling class outside the civil law to keep the underclass in its place; lynch-law is a less than subtle undercurrent here as we are told that any suspects will do as long as they are black and can be blamed for the white man's death. There is also the law of the Christian church which exhorts god-parents to take responsibility for the moral well-being of their charges.

From the outset the injunction to all godparents to sustain their godchildren in Christian conduct is contradicted by Tante Elodie's indulgence of Gabriel, to the extent that she takes active respons-ibility not, as she should, for the clearing of his conscience, but for the means by which his crime is concealed. Even when Gabriel expresses the desire to confess his sins, she prevents him: "The best thing is to go give myself up, I reckon, and tell the whole story like I've told you. That's about the best thing I can do if I want any peace of mind." "Are you crazy, Gabriel! You have not regained your senses. Listen to me. Listen to me and try to understand what I say."[44] Whilst the burden of guilt is too much for Gabriel to bear and he ultimately destroys himself with reckless living, Tante Elodie is always certain that she knows best and has right on her side. At the beginning of the story Chopin carefully prepares us to understand the basis of Tante Elodie's morality: 'She was one, also, who considered the emancipation of the slaves a great mistake. She had many reasons for thinking so and was often called upon to enumerate this in her wordy arguments with her many oppon-ents.'[45] She is unsentimental, looking back on her past with the certainty of always having made the right choices, and her shrewd assessment and execution of the necessary steps to conceal the truth of the murderer's identity puts on display her talent for ruthless action. Her first question to Gabriel, after the immediate shock of his revelation, is 'Was it a negro?' and this is clearly of central moment to her in formulating not only her plan of action but in estimating the likely response of the townspeople to the murder. If the deceased had been black then clearly the energy expended upon seeking out his murderer would have been minimal and Gabriel would have been certain of safety from pro-secution.

Additionally, with the murder of the white man the automatic response of the forces of the civil law is to apportion blame to the black community: '"Mr Ben's got about twenty darkies from

Niggerville, holding them on suspicion," continued Fifine, dancing
on the edge of her chair. "Without doubt the man was enticed to
the cabin and murdered and robbed there. Not a picayune left in
his pockets!"'[46] Unimportant when victims, but of crucial
importance when a villain is needed, members of the local black
population are not even dignified here by Gabriel with the status of
proper suspects or even individual identity: '"I'll never say
anything unless some one should be falsely accused"'.[47] Whilst
the 'labor of love' undertaken on Gabriel's behalf turns Elodie from
godmother into demon: 'She felt like some other being, possessed
by Satan. Some fiend in human shape, some spirit of murder'[48] it
also exposes the entire community as complicit in the perversion of
laws both civil and religious. The writing in 'The Godmother' puts
on display Chopin's ability to undermine the apparent certainties
of her protagonists by irony and understatement. It is not her style
or her intent to bludgeon her audience with an overt morality or
message but the signs of her discontent with the value system of
her society are discernible through close reading. The forces of
convention are arrayed against the underclass in this society not
by the overt means of the Christian or civil law but by the
'Unwritten Law' which privileges Gabriel Lucaze above all
enscribed laws and which also, by its very indulgence of him,
ultimately destroys him and brings the system which supports him
into irredeemable disrepute. The guests at a wedding watch 'a man
who was coming down the street, distributing, according to the
custom of the country, a death notice from door to door'.[49] There
are no houses, no places of celebration which are spared the news
of the death of Gabriel, and those who receive the news, locked into
the distorting position of the fixed point of view, can only see Tante
Elodie's reception of the information through the falsifying prism
of 'romance'. The community attributes her love for Gabriel to the
failure of her engagement to his father, but early in the story
Chopin disabuses the reader of any such sentimental notion:

> There was a romance connected with her early days. Romances
> serve but to feed the imagination of the young; they add nothing
> to the sum of truth. No one realized this fact more strongly than
> Tante Elodie herself. Whilst she tacitly condoned the romance,
> perhaps for the sake of the sympathy it bred, she never thought
> of Justin Lacaze but with a feeling of gratitude towards the
> memory of her parents who had prevented her marrying him

thirty-five years before. She could have no connection between her deep and powerful affection for young Gabriel Lucaze and her old-time, brief passion for his father. She loved the boy above everything on earth.[50]

Nostalgia, whether expressed through Tante Elodie or ideas of the old South, appears in its most sinister form as the ideological imperative which tacitly justifies the exclusion of the black from the protection but not the persecution of the law, but it also features in the constant misreading of the present through a spurious backward envisioning of the 'romance' of the past. The community seeks to comprehend the relationship between the godmother and godson in the light of her 'romance' but no-one is more aware than Tante Elodie of the falseness of this perspective. The story ends not only with the image of Gabriel's corpse, a sacrifice to her feudal mentality and ruthless partiality, 'down on the plantation', but with a wider sense of what is gone: 'She thought of her own place down there beside Justin's, all dismantled, with bats beating about the eaves and negroes living under the falling roof'.[51] With the end of Gabriel comes the realisation of what else is dead within her hitherto unchallenged cultural certainties: the decaying 'place' is the haunted house of a decadent civilisation. The plantation is no longer a part of a humanised landscape; abandoned to the 'bats' and those who were once accommodated in order to serve the feudal overlords but now barely hang on to the edge of civilisation, it is as derelict as her ideological certainties and as dangerous to seek shelter in. The simple story of 'The Godmother' and her misplaced devotion to her young charge is a thinly spread surface over a picture of the wider dislocations of this society, dislocations which even Gabriel comes to see when he realises the part Tante Elodie has played in his escape from suspicion: 'She seemed to his imagination, less a woman than a monster, capable of committing, in cold blood, deeds, which he himself could only accomplish in blind rage.'[52] Tante Elodie, 'The Godmother', is not the last representative of the gentility, spiritual grace and secular charm of the old South, but the monstrous proof of its enduring power to pervert and distort the course of both justice and retribution as well as the lives of its individual members.

Kate Chopin is a complex and skilful technician in the medium of the short story and perhaps nothing is more worthy of close critical attention than her refusal to support the dominant social mores and morality even whilst exploiting a tradition, that of local colour, whose conventions apparently support the status quo. Clearly the regional tale has been used by a number of writers, in Michael Davitt Bell's words: 'as a subset of American realism'[53] which is particularly concerned with the depiction of women's lives; but in the case both of Chopin and Wharton the shape and content of local colour was modified, made to serve the distinct purpose of expressing the otherwise inexpressible through the regional. In Edith Wharton's work local colour really only comes to life in the ghost story, tales of real or imagined terrors which haunt the landscape of New England, whereas Chopin's total immersion in Louisiana meant that the topography of her fiction is at once more mundane and more subversive in its use of the quietly dissenting voice. Of the three writers discussed in this book Chopin has been the most widely trivialised in terms of both form and subject and if my claims for her technical and artistic expertise in the short story seem extravagant then that is because they are extravagant. From the smallest, single-paragraph tale, to the ambitious sweep of *The Awakening,* her prose and the formal construction of her work is worthy of the closest attention and, whilst she has not suffered from the same type of dismissal as Charlotte Perkins Gilman – that is, dismissal on aesthetic grounds from serious consideration as a writer of fiction with only one work to her credit as an artist – Chopin still stands in need of the kind of attention which will allow her to rise above the mass of local colourists and into the foreground in any consideration of the short story in late-19th-century America.

In a letter to her future husband, Houghton Gilman, dating from November 1898, Charlotte Perkins Gilman talks about her immediate work plans: 'Now I am contemplating an 18 months tour of the world. a. Lecturing on an impressive scale; b. Newspaper letters with deep inner purpose; c. a book of stories to carry on my work from its plane of mere argument into the popular imagination; and d. a play for the first young actress in America. Um! If I'm not a genius I'm very near a fool I guess.'[54] In the agenda she sets for herself her stories are not only placed alongside all her other professional endeavours and ambitions but they are firmly expressed as designed to extend the possible audience for her social theories. Gilman was the author, as Ann J. Lane reports, of 490 poems and 186 pieces of fiction,[55] but her claims for her work were always modest in terms of their artistic merit; she was interested only in their potential to change her readers' perceptions of their everyday world. It is often repeated, indeed, has been until recently almost a critical truism, that the only 'real' work of art Charlotte Perkins Gilman produced is 'The Yellow Wallpaper' as if all her other fiction is only read under sufferance because she once rose above the quotidien and produced a small but perfectly formed masterpiece.

The reasons why fiction with a distinct and overt moral purpose – that is, the only sort of writing which Gilman felt to be worthwhile – is often disregarded by the critically judicious reader is an issue worth exploring in some detail in the context of work like Gilman's. The differences between received notions of high and low culture are so often communicated in terms of aesthetic values which are privileged above moral or indeed, any other significance, that fictions which have clearly discernible messages end by being denigrated as obvious or technically inept. I would argue that Gilman's moral tales, for surely all of her tales, including 'The Yellow Wallpaper', are moral, are all the more interesting for being written to a purpose and it is this that should be at the forefront of any critical investigation of her work, not her failure to conceal her purpose. The formulaic nature of the majority of Gilman's writing and the explicitness of her ideological standpoint are what make her fiction exciting, interesting and outstanding. The didactic intent, inscribed as it is in the structure, language and theme of all the short stories she wrote, actually show Gilman to be an expert manipulator of generic convention and form. She was concerned above all things to estrange her audience from the usual subjects and style of fiction in order to make them think anew about the culture in which they lived and so she adopted a variety of different but entirely recognisable genres, defamiliarised the content and thus modified the form.

I want, in this study, to direct critical attention away from 'The Yellow Wallpaper', not because I underestimate its power and complexity, but in order to create a space where her other work in short fiction can receive undivided attention. However, not content to exclude consideration of 'The Yellow Wallpaper' from any book which has Gilman as one of its central subjects, I have taken this opportunity to discuss the way in which the story has been adapted for television, treating the dramatisation as a worthy and revitalising extension of Gilman's desire to use art to change society at large, and specifically here, the treatment of women with psychological disorders. As she describes it in her autobiography, the possible effects which the story might have upon its readership is its *raison d'être*: 'But the real purpose of the story was to reach Dr S. Weir Mitchell, and convince him of the error of his ways. I sent him a copy as soon as it came out, but got no response. However, many years later, I met some one who knew close friends of Dr Mitchell's who said he had changed his treatment of nervous prostration since reading "The Yellow Wallpaper". If that is a fact, I have not lived in vain'.

Edith Wharton, whilst a self-declared moralist, did not often write with transparent ethical purpose; she did not scruple, however, to write blatant anti-German propaganda into her fiction during the war, as her novella, *The Marne*, published in 1918[57] amply demonstrates. Gilman never wrote without an overt pedagogic intent but she put this intent to a variety of uses in a variety of forms, substantially in forms of popular fiction like the utopian, the detective novel and the romance. These particular genres all fall within the remit of Anne Cranny-Francis's powerful exposition of the cultural work of different literary forms in her book, *Feminist Fiction: Feminist Uses of Generic Fiction*, an exposition which is as applicable to the work of Charlotte Perkins Gilman at the beginning of the 20th century as it is now: 'Feminist writers are now performing a complex aesthetic/ideological manoeuvre; utilizing their relegation as inferior or mass culture producers in order to show the legitimating processes in operation; using generic forms in order to show the ideological processes (of patriarchy) in (textual) operation.'[58]

Gilman was performing similar pyrotechnics with both message and medium; she did not make what she would have seen as concessions in her writing to suit the tastes or purposes of any editor; she occupied a position as regards the literary marketplace which was absolutely uncompromising, writing to please no-one but herself but with no less an ambition than the improvement of the human race. Gilman's fiction is ideologically driven, opposition is the energising factor in her writing and her work a ceaseless onslaught against the status quo. She was more usually to be found in a settlement house than a literary salon; her sense of her purpose and high duty to the improvement of the human race kept her out of literary circles but, fortunately, not out of active intervention in both the generic conventions and means of production of the short story.

The work of Chopin, Wharton and Gilman in the short story is perhaps more highly esteemed in contemporary critical opinion than ever before, a re-orientation that can substantially be attributed to the influence of feminist revisions of literary history and which is particularly significant in the case of Gilman, whose fiction did not reach so wide an audience as the others during her lifetime. Whilst the political opinions of the three were drawn in definite contradistinction, their interpellations in the stylistic and thematic conventions of the short story establish adherences between them which can only, or such is my hope, illuminate their congruity as well as their diversity and demonstrate the unique, innovatory contribution that each made to the tradition of the short story.

Notes

1.   Toth, Emily *Kate Chopin* (London: Century, 1990), p. 189.
2.   Showalter, Elaine 'Smoking Room', *Times Literary Supplement*, 16 June 1995, p. 12.
3.   Actually the title of a book by Gilman, *The Man-Made World; or, Our Androcentric Culture* (New York: Charlton Co., 1911).
4.   From the title of an essay, 'Our Literary Aristocrat' by Vernon L Parrington, *Pacific Review*, June 1921.
5.   Lewis, R.W.B. *Edith Wharton* (London: Constable & Co., 1975), p. 61.
6.   *Kate Chopin*, p. 198.
7.   *Kate Chopin*, p. 198.
8.   *Kate Chopin*, p. 414.
9.   The publication date of the story is the subject of some confusion among scholars. In her book, *The Captive Imagination: A Casebook on 'The Yellow Wallpaper'* (New York: The Feminist Press, 1992), Catherine Golden explains the reasons for the misdating of the story's first publication and arrives at January 1892 as the true date of its appearance in the *New England Magazine*. See also Julie Bates Dock *et al.* in ' "But One Expects That": Charlotte Perkins Gilman's "The Yellow Wallpaper" and the Shifting Light of Scholarship', *PMLA*, Vol. 111, 1, January 1996, pp. 52–65, for a scathing appraisal of the inaccuracies – textual and otherwise – that have dogged the critical treatment of Gilman's tale.
10. Gilman, Charlotte Perkins *The Living of Charlotte Perkins Gilman*, 1935 (Madison: University of Wisconsin Press, 1990), p. 119.
11. *The Living of Charlotte Perkins Gilman*, pp. 303–4.
12. See Ann J. Lane's account of the *Impress* in her biography of Gilman, *To Herland and Beyond: The Life and Work of Charlotte Perkins Gilman* (New York: Meridian, 1991), Chapter VII.

13. See Larzer Ziff's discussion of the ideological imperatives of those in charge at the literary magazines at the turn of the century in his *The American 1890s: Life and Times of a Lost Generation* (London: Chatto and Windus, 1967), pp. 123–4.
14. A series of six undated essays published in the St Louis *Criterion* between February 13 and March 27 1897, reprinted in *Complete Works*, pp. 706–20.
15. Chopin, Kate *The Complete Works of Kate Chopin* (Baton Rouge: Louisiana State University Press, 1969), pp. 717–18.
16. Chopin, Kate Account Book, Kate Chopin Papers, Missouri Historical Society, St Louis, Mo.
17. *The Living of Charlotte Perkins Gilman*, p. 119.
18. *Edith Wharton*, pp. 151–2.
19. Kate Chopin, Account Book.
20. White, Barbara A. *Edith Wharton: A Study of the Short Fiction* (New York: Twayne Publishers, 1991), p. 28.
21. Lewis, R.W.B. & Nancy Lewis (eds). *The Letters of Edith Wharton* (London: Simon and Schuster, 1988), p. 124.
22. Wharton, Edith *The Writing of Fiction* (London: Charles Scribner's Sons, 1925), p. 37.
23. Wharton, Edith *The Ghost Stories of Edith Wharton* (New York: Charles Scribner's Sons, 1973), p. 2.
24. *The Letters of Edith Wharton*, pp. 98–9.
25. Wharton, Edith *A Backward Glance* (New York: 1934; rpt. London: Constable & Co., 1972), p. 207.
26. *A Backward Glance*, p. 116.
27. *Complete Works*, p. 704.
28. *A Backward Glance*, p. 119.
29. Seyersted, Per & Emily Toth (eds) *A Kate Chopin Miscellany* (Natchitoches: Northwestern State University Press, 1979), pp. 120–1.
30. *Kate Chopin*, pp. 177–8 & 203–4.
31. *Complete Works*, p. 722.
32. *Complete Works*, p. 700.
33. Berthoff, Warner *American Trajectories: Authors and Readings 1790–1970* (University Park: Penn State Press, 1994), p. 70.
34. See Helen Taylor's discussion of local color and its contingencies in her book, *Gender, Race and Region in the Writings of Grace King, Ruth McEnery Stuart and Kate Chopin* (Baton Rouge: Louisiana State University Press, 1989), pp. 15–22.
35. *Kate Chopin*, pp. 133–6.
36. *Kate Chopin*, pp. 243–4.
37. *A Kate Chopin Miscellany*, pp. 115–19.
38. Jones, Anne Goodwyn *Tomorrow is Another Day: The Woman Writer in the South, 1859–1936*, (Baton Rouge: Louisiana State University Press, 1981), p. 153. See also Ryu, Chung-Eun 'The Negro as a Serious Subject in Kate Chopin's Fiction', *English Language and Literature*, Vol. 36, (4), 1990, pp. 659–78 for a discussion of the differences in relations between black and white in Chopin's Louisiana as

compared to other Southern States and how these differences are reflected in the fiction.

39. *Tomorrow is Another Day*, p. 151.
40. *Gender, Race and Region in the Writings of Grace King, Ruth McEnery Stuart and Kate Chopin*, p. 21.
41. *Kate Chopin*, p. 420.
42. *Complete Works*, p. 1028.
43. *Complete Works*, p. 604.
44. *Complete Works*, pp. 602–3.
45. *Complete Works*, p. 598.
46. *Complete Works*, p. 607.
47. *Complete Works*, p. 609.
48. *Complete Works*, pp. 604–5.
49. *Complete Works*, pp. 613–14.
50. *Complete Works*, p. 599.
51. *Complete Works*, p. 614.
52. *Complete Works*, p. 612.
53. Bell, Michael Davitt *The Problem of American Realism: Studies in the Cultural History of a Literary Idea* (Chicago: University of Chicago Press, 1993), p. 171.
54. Hill, Mary A. *The Journey from Within: The Love Letters of Charlotte Perkins Gilman, 1897–1900*, (Lewisburg: Bucknell University Press, 1995), p. 196.
55. Lane, Ann J. *To Herland and Beyond: The Life and Work of Charlotte Perkins Gilman* (New York, Meridian, 1991), p. 289.
56. *The Living of Charlotte Perkins Gilman*, p. 121.
57. See my discussion of Wharton's war writings in my book, *Edith Wharton: Traveller in the Land of Letters* (Basingstoke: Macmillan, 1990), Chapter 3.
58. Cranny-Francis, Anne *Feminist Fiction: Feminist Uses of Generic Fiction* (London: Polity Press, 1990), p. 6.

2

"dah you is, settin' down, lookin' jis' like w'ite folks!" Ethnicity Enacted in Kate Chopin's Short Fiction

The cultural norms which are established, inscribed and valorised in Kate Chopin's earliest stories are those of a Europe which is populated by people who are artistically sensitive, gifted and well-educated, some of whom have found their way to America, or, to be more specific, to Louisiana or into the Creole community of St Louis. This elite, featured in stories like 'Wiser than a God', published in the *Philadelphia Musical Journal*, and 'With the Violin', published in the *St Louis Post-Dispatch*,[1] both in 1889, comes endowed with values which are transcendent in the formation of the larger culture of the New World. The dedication of Paula Von Stoltz to her piano, or the proof of access of even such lowly working men as Papa Konrad to the finest music, makes the point that the higher things are derived from Europe and that such foreignness is positive, aesthetically sophisticated, civilised and civilising. As a result of this, however, those who do not derive from European society, that is, the enslaved, have no right of access to the values intrinsic in all things from the old country(ies) of the white population. So these early stories, at times awkwardly written with the stilted, self-conscious language which is typical of Chopin when not quite at her ease with her material, nevertheless set the tone, more than the tone, set the social structure within which her fiction operates. Chopin speaks of a society where absolute values are enshrined in European culture, the culture of the slave has had to be denied a separate existence because the system of bondage demanded the deculturation and, to a certain extent, the dehumanisation of the black population and the denial of the separate history of their countries of origin.

24

The transcendence of such European values means that there are particular tensions operating within the society that Chopin portrays which make it distinct in its social organisation and structure. There are tensions between Louisiana and its sister states in the Union, tensions between the population which is heir to European culture and the population which originated elsewhere, and tensions between Europe and America. Moreover, Louisiana as depicted here is, in spirit if not in fact, a colony in the French-dominated New World not a part of the United States. There is no movement toward homogeneity, there is no virtue placed upon becoming a member of Crèvecoeur's 'new family of the United States'.[2] It is not an act of defiance towards the equalising ideology of the civil war which keeps Louisiana separate, it is, as Chopin never fails to demonstrate, a simple matter of cultural confidence, of powerfully felt conviction in the superiority of its own distinct social organisation. The Creoles, and members of the other ethnic groups who remain separate in this society but who come together to express the certainties which make their co-existence so apparently harmonious, are unperturbed by the questions which agitate the wider post-war world. The Creoles, the 'Cadians, the Blacks, the few Anglo-Americans and fewer Native Americans continue as before, accepting the same easy classifications and stereotypes and operating within a version of a feudal system which is indistinguishable from that of slavery.

In their study of 'Theory and Practice in Post-Colonial Literatures', *The Empire Writes Back*, Ashcroft, Griffiths and Tiffin argue for a definition of the term post-colonial as appropriate 'to cover all the cultures affected by the imperial process from the moment of colonization to the present day. This is because there is a continuity of preoccupations throughout the historical process initiated by European imperial aggression'.[3] In this chapter I propose to demonstrate that Chopin's Louisiana is a post-colonial rather than an American post-bellum society; that it bears a complex of relationships both within and without itself that mark it equally as a continuing post-colonial society in its position as regards the United States as well as Europe and, additionally, a post-colonial society in its own internal power structure. There is a case made for the inclusion of the United States as post-colonial in *The Empire Writes Back*: 'perhaps because of its current position of power, and the neo-colonizing role it has played, its post-colonial nature has not been generally recognized. But its relationship with the metropolitan centre as it evolved over the last two centuries has been paradigmatic for post-colonial literatures everywhere. What each of these literatures has in common is that they emerged in their present form out of the experience of colonization and asserted themselves by foregrounding the tension with the imperial power, and by emphasising their differences from the assumptions of the imperial centre.'[4]

Chopin's fiction is, in fact, written on the cusp of this change between America as post-colonial and America as coloniser and this is powerfully illustrated in the picture of Louisiana as Chopin draws it. Chopin's Louisiana, in the post-civil-war welter, is caught in the act of trying to retain its special relationship with Europe, and in particular with France, by adumbrating the significant cultural 'differences' as differences with America rather than Europe. The definition, 'local color', beloved of Northern editors as a means of classifying and distancing Chopin's fictional territory was, as Sandra Gilbert points out in her introduction to *The Awakening and Selected Stories*, actually an enabling principle in her work, allowing her to 'tell what would ordinarily be rather shocking or even melodramatic tales in an unmelodramatic way, and without fear of moral outrage'.[5] This does not only apply to the plots and themes of Chopin's stories, it also applies to the territory itself; the adherence of Chopin's Louisianans to their *locale*, to their particular form of the post-colonial social organisation, is as subversive and seditious as any offence against conventional Christian morality or mores perpetrated within the fictions. Her writing, in its portrayal of life in Louisiana, expresses the hegemony of the Creole; in its concerns, its cultural assumptions and its value system it expresses Europe; and in its form it expresses the American post-bellum – the new position of submission and reluctant resignation to the laws of the Northern States.

This nexus of cultural inter-dependencies can be simply illustrated by looking briefly at Chopin's 'La Belle Zoraïde', written in 1893 and published in *Vogue* the following year.[6] Chopin tells this story in the standard English of her audience but places a Louisiana frame around it. Thus the story is translated for the reader from 'the soft Creole patois, whose music and charm no English words can convey'[7] and ends with a glimpse of this other language: 'But this is the way Madame Delisle and Manna-Loulou really talked to each other: "Vou pré droumi, Ma'zélle Titite?" "Non, pa pré droumi; mo yapré zongler. Ah, la pauv' piti, Man

Loulou. La pauv' piti! Mieux li mouri!"'.[8] The story told here is one of slavery, of the absolute control over life and health of the slave by the master/mistress and, in her own position of subservience, the status of Manna-Loulou, the story-teller, is indistinguishable from the subject of the story, Zoraïde. We are given details of the way Manna Loulou prepares Madame Delisle to receive her tale: 'The old negress had already bathed her mistress's pretty white feet and kissed them lovingly, one, then the other.'[9]

Chopin is clear here on details of colour, on what makes a mistress and what a slave or servant; the story is about colour – shades of colour, the significance of colour to both black and white and the tragedy of colour. It is a particularly Louisiana setting and story of colour with the exchanged intimacies between dominated and dominating and the difference in the usual master-slave boundaries illustrated in the relationship between Madame Delarivière – 'who was...godmother as well as...mistress,'[10] to Zoraïde. The United States is another nation or nations to these Louisianans; le beau Mézor is 'sold away into Georgia, or the Carolinas, or one of those distant countries far away, where he would no longer hear his Creole tongue spoken, nor dance Calinda, nor hold la belle Zoraïde in his arms'.[11]

So, the story expresses the post-colonial relationship of Louisiana to the United States in its recognition of the necessary steps which must be taken in order to mediate the tale to the audience, it expresses the post-colonial relationship to Europe, specifically to France, in language and in details of religious practice, and the post-colonial organisation of Louisiana itself in the enduring nature of the ante-bellum social hierarchy. The story is concerned explicitly and overarchingly with the massive hubris of the master in the construction of the master-slave relationship. Madame Delarivière is playing God in her wish to dispose the affections and loyalties of her slaves and in seeking to erase Zoraïde's child from its existence as a daughter. The story concerns human desire and human preference and the folly of trying to line those up with colour.

Chopin's narratives engage with the pressures of cultural stereotypes, they engage with the interconnections and dependencies that individuals, communities and nations must sustain in order to survive both psychically and physically. There is one way of reading the story of 'La Belle Zoraïde' which says that Zoraïde goes mad because she has been privileged beyond her capacities, that in seeking to choose her own husband she is stepping outside the boundaries of her abilities and therefore madness is the inevitable result. As ever with Chopin, there are other, more complex readings, readings which transcend the time and place and the predictable Louisianan or North American reading. Another is that Zoraïde is driven mad because she is confronted for the first time in her human life with the fact of her powerlessness to express a preference, even so basic a preference as to be a mother to her own child.

Chopin's fictions, and particularly her short stories, are subversive documents. There are a number of levels on which the stories work; the blacks have subversive voices as they apparently say what the master wants to hear, as in the case of 'Old Aunt Peggy' in the story which bears her name. But there is always a cost, as I discuss in detail in Chapter 4; something may be gained but it cannot equal what has been lost. Aunt Peggy may know the best means of flattery to ensure herself a comfortable old age but if she is abandoned by those who were once her masters she has no other resources – the children, the possessions which might have accrued to her old age have been disallowed by the conditions of slavery as she has experienced them. The narrative organisation is often the main subversive instrument, with the surface meaning apparently conventional, apparently moving toward closure and a restoration of the accepted social order but actually, as in the story, 'Athénaïse', published in the *Atlantic Monthly* in 1896,[12] being undermined by the processes of revelation that have occurred throughout the tale. This technique is typical of Chopin's short fiction and is made explicit in, for example, 'The Story of an Hour', published in *Vogue* in 1894, where the machinery of the twist in the tale, the easy explanation, is exposed in all its spuriousness as a mode of interpretation.

In his important essay, 'The Economy of Manichean Allegory: The Function of Racial Difference in Colonialist Literature',[13] Abdul JanMohamed discusses the dominance of the Manichean allegory in the ideological structure of colonialist fiction; the 'Economy' of his title being 'based on a transformation of racial difference into moral and even metaphysical difference'.[14] In her short stories Chopin plays upon and with the susceptibilities of a society that is actually structured upon what JanMohamed calls the 'central trope'[15] of post-colonial fiction, the easy division of black and white into 'good and evil, superiority and inferiority, civilization and savagery, intelligence and emotion, rationality and sensuality, self and Other, subject and object'.[16] Chopin entertains all those too facile divisions and, crucially, shows them in process, both in forming and in dissolving, her vision encompasses the complicity of all constituents of the rich ethnic mix of Louisiana in the perpetuation of the mores of a post-colonial civilisation.

Chopin, in her fiction, is never the moralist. Indeed, her perceived amorality, her failure – in the eyes of her contemporaries – to put the conventional moral view, meant that *The Awakening* stirred the kind of condemnation which revealed the discomfort felt by her readers at the unmediated, apparently unguarded nature of her portrait of Edna Pontellier. Her picture of Louisiana is not informed by a simple ideology nor any kind of moral message; Chopin's characters are denizens of Louisiana, they are all, as Houghton Mifflin's advertisement for her first published collection *Bayou Folk* vaunted, 'semi-aliens',[17] as far as the rest of the United States is concerned. The location for her fictions is primarily the state of Louisiana, occasionally she tells a Missouri story in a Missouri language or glances towards St Louis – her home for the greater part of her life – or even to Paris, but the narrative landscapes which predominate are New Orleans and Natchitoches Parish, the scenes of her short married life. The smallest voice, the only literal ethnic minority in Chopin's Louisiana is the American. The White Anglo-Saxon Protestant rarely speaks in Chopin's text, the American spoken language is absent from this particular Babel of tongues, although, of course, the mediator of the culture, Chopin herself, speaks the standard English of her readership. There is no national, whole-cultural normalising pressure in Chopin's fiction; assimilation into the larger community of the United States is not a concern here, rather Louisiana's foreignness is emphasised to the reading public. The stranger, the alien within the culture of Louisiana is the American; American practices and influence are there only to be resisted and, as is illustrated in a story published in 1895 in the *Youth's Companion* – 'A Matter of Prejudice'[18] – the racial is apparently, but only apparently, less problematic in this society's prejudices than the cultural. There is a distinct and unique version of America adhered to by the community and another, equally distinct, abjured.

This story concerns the softening in attitude of one Madame Carambeau toward the alien American; at the outset she is 'a woman of many prejudices – so many, in fact, that it would be difficult to name them all. She detested dogs, cats, organ-grinders, white servants and children's noises. She despised Americans, Germans and all people of a different faith from her own. Anything not French had, in her opinion, little right to existence'.[19] Madame Carambeau's French America is divided by colour but in its own distinct way; the institutionalised racism on display in Louisiana is a domesticated racism, one which – in Chopin's fiction – obtains complicity from the black population in order to sustain alterity from the rest of the American nation. Chopin portrays a society in what JanMohamed calls 'the hegemonic phase' of development; here, if one substitutes European Americans for colonisers and African Americans for natives – 'The natives accept a version of the colonizers' entire system of values, attitudes, morality, institutions, and, more important, mode of production. This stage of imperialism [relies] on the active and direct "consent" of the dominated'[20] – it is possible to correlate the roles of black and white in the maintenance of the ante-bellum power structure in Louisiana with the situation in lands more straightforwardly colonized. Where the black servant, here in the story 'Mamouche', published in *Youth's Companion* in 1894, asks the question: ' "Is you wi'te o' is you black?...Dat w'at I wants ter know 'fo' I kiar' victuals to yo in de settin'-room." '[21] then social and even psychological subjection to the role of either servant or master has come to be central to personal and cultural identity, dangerously central in a society so enmeshed in miscegeny, as can be easily borne out by the most superficial reading of 'Désirée's Baby'.

The narrative present of Kate Chopin's short stories is of a society where slavery no longer exists and yet its class structure is absolutely determined by the power-relations of the old, pre-war South. There is, enshrined within this social organisation, a quantifiable, at times tangible, distinctive Southern morality, the terrible, tragic nature of which is stripped down and exploited by Chopin in the construction of her narratives. Where the prevailing values of a society can be simply described in terms of black and white, with the black always wrong, always negative, always evil or simple or cowardly or cunning then any picture of that society is susceptible to portrayal in terms ironic or parodic and this is Chopin's picture.

Chopin's prose is multivalent; she runs off into meaning and signification at any number of levels and she is never more complex than when she seems to be simple. The stories she apparently turned out so effortlessly [22] are more than inclusive of the sting in the tale she learned from Maupassant, her French master in the art of short story telling. There are multiple stings: a story like 'Athénaïse', an apparently straightforward account of the fulfilment of the woman's natural role as mother, contains within it not only the delineation of an episode shaming to human dignity in the memory of an incident in the history of slavery but an unequivocal and ungainsayable denial of the socially accepted idea of marriage:

> At no time did Cazeau make an effort to overtake her until traversing an old fallow meadow that was level and hard as a table. The sight of a great solitary oak-tree, with its seemingly immutable outlines, that had been a landmark for ages – or was it the odor of elderberry stealing up from the gully to the south? or what was it that brought vividly back to Cazeau, by some association of ideas, a scene of many years ago? He had passed that old live-oak hundreds of times, but it was only now that the memory of one day came back to him. He was a very small boy that day, seated before his father on horse-back. They were proceeding slowly, and Black Gabe was moving on before them at a little dog-trot. Black Gabe had run away, and had been discovered back in the Gotrain swamp. They had halted beneath this big oak to enable the negro to take breath; for Cazeau's father was a kind and considerate master and every one had agreed at the time that Black Gabe was a fool, a great idiot indeed, for wanting to run away from him.
>
> The whole impression was for some reason hideous, and to dispel it Cazeau spurred his horse to a swift gallop. Overtaking his wife, he rode the remainder of the way at her side in silence.[23]

Unable to bear a physical position in relation to his wife that is in any way reminiscent of his father's to his slave, Cazeau tries to place himself by her side. Unlike his father he does not wish for the title of 'master', he realises the dangers in dependence upon such a self-definition when the woman who allows you to realise the definition is, like Black Gabe, restless and seeking to escape. The common view, that which said that Athénaïse Miché needed a man in order to know what it was she wanted, what it was she was meant to be: 'Marriage they knew to be a wonderful and powerful agent in the development and formation of a woman's character', also holds that Black Gabe is a fool for not appreciating such a Master as Cazeau Senior. This Southern discourse allows of no alternative view; where 'every one' as a term of inclusiveness excludes the black population then the dependence in society upon the absolutes offered by simple division into full humanity for the white and a debased, predictable humanity for the black offers no grounds for disputation. Black Gabe is, without doubt, 'a fool'; Athénaïse is, without demur, a woman awaiting the completion of a man: 'a master hand, a strong will that compels obedience" '.[24] However, Cazeau's refusal to play such a part alters the story entirely from its apparently simple existence as documenting the process of hormonal change for Athénaïse Miché, a change which happily coincides with the generally accepted idea of what the function of marriage is in society, to the story of humanity's enduring struggle to gain and keep power over its fellows. The story within a story here, the tale of Black Gabe, renders the tale of Athénaïse not at all as it was before, it belies and negates the conventional ending as Athénaïse's all-encompassing maternity reaches out for the crying child, any crying child, black or white, and takes us back to her original 'sense of hopelessness, an instinctive realization of the futility of rebellion against a social and sacred institution'.[25]

Chopin's narratives modulate between the portrayal of such 'futility', as in 'The Story of an Hour', where the only freedom from the unwanted proximities of marriage which can be envisaged by the central protagonist is in her own death, and the more subtle depiction of the means by which people maintain sufficient autonomy to be able to endure within the 'institution'. I would like to use the story 'A Dresden Lady in Dixie', written in 1894 and published in the *Catholic Home Journal* in 1895,[26] to demonstrate Chopin's ability to pinpoint and dissect the power and value structure of her society. This story is a paradigm of the post-colonial fiction; it is set on a plantation, slavery is no longer a fact of life but the class structure which places poor whites, in this case the Bedaut family, above all blacks, and the family headed by 'the planter', the Valtours, at the top, is still firmly in place. The plot rests on the theft of a Dresden china figurine. The ornament, in itself, speaks of European culture and aesthetic value, of manufacturing brought to an advanced stage of development, but it also carries the weight of many memories, in this case, the prior attachment of 'A baby's lips that were now forever still'. The exclusivity of the whites' relationship with such an object is thus doubly reinforced: its monetary value derives from its origination in European culture and its sentimental value derives from the luxury of grief for the lost child, not a privilege afforded to the black under the system of slavery, where the lost child was never the parent's own to grieve for. Enter Pa-Jeff, the trusty, loyal retainer, so oblivious to his rights in the wider world that he went 'all through the war with "old Marse Valtour"' serving the family in their fight with the emancipator as faithfully as he had served them before and since. 'Pa-Jeff's uprightness and honesty were so long and firmly established as to have become proverbial on the plantation.'[27] His name has thus become a watchword for universally accepted human virtues but this does not save him from being regarded as inescapably representative of something other than himself and his virtues: 'He would sit there courting the sunshine and blinking, as he gazed across the fields with the patience of the savage.'[28] For such as Pa-Jeff the definite article will only ever be attached to a universally accepted 'truth' about his apparently inescapable nature – 'the savage'. Monsieur Valtour is 'the planter', he comes from 'the family', the truths expressed here indicate his status. His character, whilst partly defined by his elevated position, will not bear so simple an act of definition as Pa-Jeff's.

Pa-Jeff, however, is not allowed by Chopin to rest so easily within the categorisations of this society. She has him reclaim his full humanity in decisive action, in taking responsibility for making something happen in Agapie's life: 'He sat very still watching her disappear; only his furrowed old face twitched convulsively, moved by an unaccustomed train of reasoning that was at work in him.' So, it may have fallen into disuse, not being required too often of him in his socially preordained role, but Pa-Jeff has the capacity for 'reasoning' and not only for reasoning, as it turns out, but for invention, for story-telling and, above all, for empathy. Pa-Jeff locates himself within the given culture; he participates in the Manichean ideology of the ruling class, employing their oppositions to embrace the contradictions inherent in his own position when placed alongside that of Agapie: "She w'ite, I is black", he muttered calculatingly. "She young, I is ole; sho I is ole. She good to Pa-Jeff like I her own kin an' color". This line of thought seemed to possess him to the exclusion of every other. Late in the night he was still muttering. "Sho I is ole. She good to Pa-Jeff, yas." He recognises that the only way to restore the status quo is to use the terminology which is supposed to be his; to employ the language of guilt and shame, that which Agapie cannot bring herself to use and which is not supposed to apply to her – 'its neva been no thief in the Bedaut family'[29] – in order to fulfil all the simple truths about the foolish, morally suspect but harmless old negro he ought to be. Pa-Jeff self-transforms into the necessary fiction which supports the entire social order. Any prescribed idea of what his race simply is or is not, according to Chopin, has to be courted and embraced, Pa-Jeff becomes a stereotype voluntarily, employing along the way the system of oppositions which have been waiting all his life to define him in spite of his life and his known character.

Thus, Pa-Jeff's heroism, the grand act of self-denial undertaken so as to free a young life from restriction and pain, renders him up to his society as evidence of its organisational and social validity. He proves his unworthiness to participate in the higher culture: the Dresden figurine, emblem of the European cultural hegemony, becomes a 'li'le gal.... She do look mighty sassy dat day, wid 'er toe a-stickin' out, des so; an' holdin' her skirt des dat away; an' lookin' at me wid her head twis'[30] as she plays her part in the "nigger yarn" he spins. He denies his ability to participate in the finer feelings, an aesthetic appreciation of the ornament or the sentimental association it has for his mistress and becomes the creature of his masters' imaginations, the sensual, the simple, the uncontrolled. The motivating factor of his great empathy for Agapie's situation is denied by the means – the language – which he must use in order to persuade 'the family' of his guilt. He has recognised Agapie's partial transcendence of the confines of the social order 'She good to Pa-Jeff like I her own kin an' color' and responds by relocating himself within its limits to reward her.

Agapie, however, knows better than to believe the simplicity of the Manichean allegory; she knows that black and white cannot be lined up with good and bad, for not only did she steal the figurine but after he tells the lie that saves her 'somehow she could not look into his face again'. The fact of his senility and whole-hearted embracing of the allegory in his dotage cannot alter Agapie's knowledge of the fiction at the heart of the society which supports her. Pa-Jeff 'confused, bewildered, believed the story himself',[31] the story, that is, not only of the Dresden Lady in Dixie but of the fatally flawed morality of the 'ole fool-nigga'[32] he makes himself out to be. Chopin puts the Manichean allegory to work in the story, making literal what is unspoken in the culture, that in order to perpetuate the class system encoded by slavery, white and black must be susceptible to the simplistic and unthinking correlatives of good and evil. Pa-Jeff tells his tale of the struggle betwixt temptation and righteousness as a battle between 'Satan' and 'De Sperrit' with Satan triumphant in round one and the Spirit in round two. The story of Pa-Jeff's 'temptation and fall' enlarges as it and he grow older, both in terms of his embellishment of the tale and in terms of his trusting audience. But there is not a single detail in the larger story which lets us rest easy with the publically admitted view. As the ultimate arbiters of what is and is not morally acceptable the Valtours are predominant, and whilst 'Agapie grew up to deserve the confidence and favors of the family',[33] without Pa-Jeff's intervention she would have been exiled from both their esteem and that which they have to endow as benefactors. Agapie, a white, is given the chance to remake herself as good even though she has fallen; the black is confined forever within stereotype.

People are shown in Chopin's fiction, through the exceptional or even the unexceptional events of their everyday lives to be more than their single, isolated acts; their inter-relationships and dependencies are more than can be contained within the trope, the Manichean trope, which so often expresses this civilisation. Chopin, ultimately cynical, ultimately unable to allow anyone to rest within stereotype without revealing a degree of discomfort, uses the resources of her culture to expose its own strengths and weaknesses.

The stock characters of her region's fiction, are, as has already been noted with regard to Chopin's use of the umbrella of local colour, revelatory of whole-cultural weakness, of fallacy and, often, of tragedy. In her book, *Kate Chopin*, Barbara C. Ewell notes that 'Afro-American loyalty' is a 'quintessentially Reconstruction theme'.[34] This is undeniably so, and Chopin herself exploits the theme in a number of stories besides 'A Dresden Lady in Dixie'; for example, in 'For Marse Chouchoute', and 'Beyond the Bayou' both published in 1891, 'The Bênitous' Slave', published 1892, 'Tante Cat'rinette' in 1894, 'Neg Creol' in 1896, and 'Aunt Lympy's Interference', published in 1896, such loyalty is at the heart of the story. However, other stories, like 'Odalie Misses Mass', published in 1895 and 'Ozème's Holiday' in 1894, show the other side of the relationship as mutual dependence and loyalty are illustrated by the enduring commitment of the white to the black. Chopin takes the assumptions of her culture and exposes them to the type of scrutiny that only the stereotype can bear; the story of Pa-Jeff sacrifices the old man in making him into what JanMohamed calls 'generic being'[35] in order to save Agapie; other stories show people destroyed by stereotype, their fellows unable to rise sufficiently above the accepted view to keep them from a tragic end.

As with Pa-Jeff in 'A Dresden Lady in Dixie', Désirée, in the story 'Désirée's Baby', written in 1892 and published in *Vogue* in 1893, is shown in the process of becoming a stereotype, here, the tragic mulatta whose only recourse is to throw herself into the river if she is to prevent her baby being taken away from her into slavery. Straightforwardly enthralled as she is to the name and the will of her husband she cannot believe that there may be an alternative version of the story which seems to suggest that she is solely responsible for the portion of the child's colour which condemns him in the eyes of Armand. This is not to simplify what is an extraordinarily complex tale and, as Ellen Peel discusses in her illuminating essay 'Semiotic Subversion in "Désirée's Baby"', 'Whether or not Désirée is black, the impossibility of knowing her race reveals the fragility of meaning more than Armand's knowable race does.'[36] Again Chopin does not allow us any certainties. Armand, as much a victim as Désirée of a social organisation that valorises racial purity and practises miscegeny, is apparently the villain of the piece, the fairy-tale prince turned bad; but, in this world of absolutes, he is destroyed by the final utterance more surely than Désirée herself. The Manichean allegory here is so powerfully in place that its contiguities can destroy love, can eliminate feelings both of passion and paternity: 'Moreover he no longer loved her, because of the unconscious injury she had brought upon his home and his name'.[37] It is absolutely necessary to Armand's sense of self that his wife should be of his kind – or what he thinks of as his kind – and not comparable to 'La Blanche' or any other of the women over whom he has *droit de seigneur*. When he believes that she has been revealed to be other than like him he must hate the thing he formerly loved in order to re-establish his difference, his mastery. In this post-colonial society Armand's status as master is wholly dependent upon his colour and his mother's letter thus reveals to him his own inauthenticity. The handsome Southern prince is inevitably tainted, Chopin indicates, not, and I repeat not, by the 'one drop' rule or any other such colour classification, but by the iniquities and contingencies of the system itself.

There can be no certainties in this ante-bellum or in any other post-bellum tale; as Peel emphasises, Désirée herself 'disrupts signification'[38] by the simple fact that no-one ever knows her origins. Like a slave she is given her master's name but is then, unlike a slave, refused its continuation. Unable to continue in her married life Désirée is seemingly also unable to return to her adoptive home; her idea of her place in the world has been destroyed and, as has already been noted, she takes the route of the tragic mulatta, betrayed by the false promises of the master, to the bayou. The only person to rise above simple classifications is Madame Valmondé: ' "My own Désirée: Come home to Valmondé; back to your mother who loves you. Come with your child" '.[39]

In his essay JanMohamed argues for the division of the post-colonial fiction into two types – the 'symbolic' and the 'imaginary' – whereby the 'dialectic of self and Other' is admitted in the former but the latter 'tends to fetishize a nondialectical, fixed opposition between the self and the native'.[40] It is the presence of such as Madame Valmondé in the story of 'Désirée's Baby' that marks Chopin's work as a 'symbolic' rather than 'imaginary' post-colonial text, using JanMohamed's terminology which he, in turn, derives from Lacan: 'The "imaginary" is a preverbal order, essentially visual, that precedes the "symbolic", or verbal, order in the development of the psyche'.[41] The difference between the writers who practise these two versions of the post-colonial fiction is crucial when looking at Chopin's work because her use of stereotype could mark her out as 'imaginary' – the straightforward practitioner of the Manichean allegory. However, the structural ambiguities she contains within her fictions, again in the words of JanMohamed, 'admit the possibility of syncretism, of a rapprochement between self and Other'.[42] Chopin's stories rise above and beyond the confines of her own culture, reflecting all its constituents as so much more than their socially ascribed roles. La Belle Zoraïde, Athénaïse, Pa-Jeff and Désirée, in being compromised by their culture into madness, maternity, senility and indeterminacy of colour, turn into that which they are supposed to be as a result of their inferior or predisposed status. It is a measure of Chopin's genius that she never allows us to forget at what cost such people change from the individual to the generic.

Notes

1. Toth, Emily *Kate Chopin* (London: Century, 1990) p. 414.
2. de Crèvecoeur, J. Hector St John *Travels in Pennsylvania and New York* (1801).
3. Bill Ashcroft, Gareth Griffiths & Helen Tiffin, *The Empire Writes Back: Theory and Practice in Post-colonial Literatures* (London: Routledge, 1989), p. 2.
4. *The Empire Writes Back*, p. 2.
5. *The Awakening and Selected Stories*, introduced by Sandra Gilbert (London: Penguin Books, 1984), p. 16.
6. *Kate Chopin*, p. 416.
7. Chopin, Kate *The Complete Works of Kate Chopin* (ed. Per Seyersted) (Baton Rouge: Louisiana State University Press, 1969, repr. 1993), p. 304.
8. *Complete Works*, p. 308.
9. *Complete Works*, p. 303.
10. *Complete Works*, p. 304.
11. *Complete Works*, p. 306.
12. *Kate Chopin*, p. 418.
13. JanMohamed, Abdul R. 'The Economy of Manichean Allegory: The Function of Racial Difference in Colonialist Literature', *Critical Enquiry* (12, 1985, 1), pp. 59–87.
14. 'The Economy of Manichean Allegory: The Function of Racial Difference in Colonialist Literature', p. 61.
15. 'The Economy of Manichean Allegory: The Function of Racial Difference in Colonialist Literature', p. 61.
16. 'The Economy of Manichean Allegory: The Function of Racial Difference in Colonialist Literature', p. 63.
17. *Kate Chopin*, p. 223.
18. *Kate Chopin*, p. 416.
19. *Complete Works*, p. 282.
20. 'The Economy of Manichean Allegory: The Function of Racial Difference in Colonialist Literature', p. 62.
21. *Complete Works*, p. 268.
22. See Emily Toth's discussion of Chopin's writing habits in *Kate Chopin*, pp. 206–7.
23. *Complete Works*, pp. 432–3.
24. *Complete Works*, p. 434.
25. *Complete Works*, p. 432.
26. *Kate Chopin*, p. 417.
27. *Complete Works*, p. 345.
28. *Complete Works*, p. 348.
29. *Complete Works*, p. 349.
30. *Complete Works*, p. 350.
31. *Complete Works*, p. 351.
32. *Complete Works*, p. 350.
33. *Complete Works*, p. 351.

34. Ewell, Barbara C. *Kate Chopin* (New York: The Ungar Publishing Company, 1986), p. 123.
35. 'The Economy of Manichean Allegory: The Function of Racial Difference in Colonialist Literature', p. 64.
36. Peel, Ellen 'Semiotic Subversion in "Desiree's Baby"', *American Literature* (Vol. 62, 2, June 1990), p. 233.
37. *Complete Works*, p. 244.
38. 'Semiotic Subversion in "Désirée's Baby"', p. 224.
39. *Complete Works*, p. 243.
40. 'The Economy of Manichean Allegory: The Function of Racial Difference in Colonialist Literature', pp. 65–6.
41. 'The Economy of Manichean Allegory: The Function of Racial Difference in Colonialist Literature', p. 86.
42. 'The Economy of Manichean Allegory: The Function of Racial Difference in Colonialist Literature', p. 73.

3

Without End: the Shape and Form of Desire in Kate Chopin's Short Fiction

Kate Chopin wrote often about sexual attraction; physical desire frequently propels the narrative in her fiction. When asked, in 1898, by the *St Louis Post-Dispatch*, to write an article in response to the question ' "Is Love Divine?" ', this formed part of Chopin's answer: 'I am inclined to think that love springs from animal instinct, and therefore is, in a measure, divine. One can never resolve to love this man, this woman or child, and then carry out the resolution unless one feels irresistibly drawn by an indefinable current of magnetism.'[1] Chopin does not try to define or find the source for this 'indefinable current of magnetism' in her fiction but she writes again and again of the effects of powerful emotion and the consequences of its arousal. For a woman writing in the 1890s and seeking to sell her stories in the carefully regulated world of magazine publishing Chopin had to be cognisant of the restrictions which prevailed as regards the portrayal of the erotic. Therefore, before she could write stories about sexual attraction and its effects, she had to find ways in which she could deflect the magazine editors – upon whom she depended for an important part of her livelihood – from focusing on the often radical content of her stories. Emily Toth has discussed in detail the liberal regime at *Vogue* magazine[2] which allowed Chopin to publish material likely to be refused by other journals, but there are other means by which Chopin managed to avert the censoring eye of the editor. It is these means that I intend to address in this chapter in the context of stories which treat, in some measure, the erotic, particularly where the erotic expresses the otherwise inexpressible about the lives of women. My discussion will culminate, however, in consideration of 'The Storm', written in 1898,[3] which, by necessity, must be approached on slightly different terms, not least of which is to make an attempt on the question of why Chopin might want to write a story she could and would not expect anyone to publish.

In general it is the tension which is maintained between style and content that generates the most complex readings of Chopin's work. As I discuss in the context of ethnicity, Chopin was able to use what might elsewhere be regarded as the limitations of her Louisiana settings or local colour to screen her subject matter. Wherever the story was set her concern in her writing was always to communicate 'human existence in its subtle, complex, true meaning, stripped of the veil with which ethical and conventional standards have draped it',[4] as she says in her description of the proper province of art in the report she wrote on 'The Western Association of Writers', published in *Critic* on July 7, 1894. When looking at the stories which are most powerfully concerned with physical desire, however, it can be seen that many are without specific location and do not fit neatly into the category of local colour. When dealing with sexual attraction Chopin did not necessarily use the regional mode as the most germane to her needs although it is, for obvious reasons, the genre that dominates in the stories which treat ethnicity and the post-colonial.

Writing about sex was actually one of the ways in which Chopin could distance herself, as an artist, from the pieties of the age. Just as she put herself at a remove from her fellow inhabitants of Natchitoches Parish, New Orleans or St Louis in order to transform herself into the authorial voice that could mediate a particular topography to the rest of North America, so in writing about sex she had to locate a means by which to communicate a sense of the profound importance of the erotic in the lives of both women and men. This, I believe, she found in story structures which allowed her to exploit conventional form and narrative in order to accommodate controversial material. There are strategies at work in the fiction which gave Chopin licence to rove whilst still keeping a watchful eye on the fine line marked out by the magazine editors and it is those strategies I will seek to scrutinise here.

Although she never attempted to find a publisher for her most explicitly erotic story, 'The Storm', Chopin did expect to see stories like 'Her Letters' and 'Two Summers and Two Souls' in print and, of course, was at her most candid in her depiction of sexual attraction and marital infidelity in *The Awakening*. Stories she wrote throughout the 1890s have sexual attraction, sexual repulsion and sexual fulfilment as their subject: Chopin portrays discontented wives, husbands and wives who are attracted to women and men other than their spouses, casual sex, straightforward lust and obsessive love which can be beyond both reason and endurance. There are no limits to her respect for the many and various forms of desire but neither does she shy away from telling the stories of those in desperate need of escape from the unwanted physical proximity of a lover or a husband, as in 'In Sabine', 'A No-Account Creole', 'The Story of an Hour' or 'Athénaïse'. Even where there is no third party involved in the breakdown of the marriage, the subject of the dysfunctional relationship could be as difficult for the writer of the time to mediate as illicit passion. The whole-cultural imperatives of Chopin's time and place were in favour of the indissolubility of the marriage contract and the containment of women's sexuality within its boundaries. In her fiction Chopin examines the breaches in those boundaries, made from within and without; always suspicious of absolutes, she seeks to problematise and complicate the business of courtship and marriage by bringing into the foreground the exigencies of desire.

As Richard Fusco points out in his discussion of 'In Sabine', in his book, *Maupassant and the American Short Story: The Influence of Form at the Turn of the Century*, Chopin effectively distracts her readers from the serious business of the end of a marriage by the manner in which the story is told: ' "In Sabine" exploits sentimentality in a manner typical of 19th-century melodrama, progressing linearly to the happy conclusion that the audience wants. Consequently, the assault upon the then-popular notion of the inviolable sanctity of marriage becomes just one point integrated within a fictional continuum.'[5] As the story proceeds Chopin is careful to include details of Grégoire and 'Tite Reine's different destinations – there is no suggestion that they are running away together – but nevertheless her central female character is being aided in an escape from a marriage and, indeed, just such an escape is the ending the reader is led positively and hopefully toward. As in Fusco's account of the 'fictional continuum' which carries the reader past the controversial aspects of 'In Sabine', the events of Chopin's story, 'Athénaïse', and in particular their resolution, divert attention away from that which might be considered as tendentious within the narrative. As has been recognised in recent, detailed discussions of the story,[6] 'Athénaïse' is above all else a cogent account of the oppressive nature of the marriage contract but Chopin structures her fiction so that the narrative impetus

toward the happy ending, the successful reconciliation of this particular husband and wife after times of early misery and incom-
patibility, carries the story forward.

'Athénäise' is one of only four stories that Chopin managed to
publish in the prestigious *Atlantic Monthly* over the course of her
writing career. They did not publish it without editorial intervention, however, as Emily Toth notes: '*The Atlantic* gave
"Athénäise" a subtitle, "A Story of Temperament", as if to suggest
that the story's problem was just a matter of individual peculiarities'.[7] This attempt to direct and control the response of the readership is in many ways typical of editorial conduct at the literary
magazines and in particular, at *The Atlantic*. Ellery Sedgwick, in his
study, *A History of the Atlantic Monthly 1857–1909: Yankee Humanism
at High Tide and Ebb*, tells how Horace E. Scudder, editor of the
journal from 1890 until 1898, yoked his personal morality to that of
a projected reading public which was deemed to have scrupulous
standards in order to argue for a fiction that abjured didacticism
but nevertheless adhered to recognised moral principles. In a letter
to Madame von Teuffel in 1895 Scudder wrote: ' "So sensitive has
the better class of the public become that, with or without reason,
both publishers and authors are held to a pretty strict account as
regards the tendency of the fiction produced. Very fine distinctions
are not made, but the question insistently put requires a categorical
answer. Does or does not this book tell for restraint, conformity to a
recognised social order, an unselfish sense of honor and high
principle?" '.[8] The story of 'Athénäise', it will be seen, seems to
conform to Scudder's criteria for acceptibility in its resolution, but
along the way it effectively and ruthlessly undermines the basis for
that resolution. The ending, Athénäise's return to her home, in fact,
becomes the least important development in a narrative which
testifies to the fact that Cazeau, the son of slave-owners and a man
widely expected to 'master' his wife, will never again allow such
expectations to put him in a position where he must be responsible
for the coercion of another human being in the name of marriage.

Chopin positions her readers here, and elsewhere, so that they
are sensitive to the conditions of existence for her protagonists, but
this is not an exercise in creating partisanship. At the beginning
Cazeau is more of an object of pity than the absconding Athénäise,
misled and confused as he has been by her pre-marital attentions:
'He could not comprehend why she had seemd to prefer him above
all others; why she had attracted him with eyes, with voice, with a

hundred womanly ways, and finally distracted him with love'.[9] Awaiting our notice as readers, as the narrative proceeds, are Chopin's apparently incidental references to the monstrous exigencies of the 'social and sacred institution'[10] of marriage that would take a girl and put her in intimate contact with a grown man without due warning of the physical consequences, and take a grown man and put him in close proximity to a girl who has been taught to flirt and to beckon but not to know what to expect when faced with his unmediated reality. The story of 'Athénaïse' is driven in linear terms in turn by the forces of revolt and reconciliation enacted by the title character; her escape from and final return to the marriage determines the course of the narrative. However, it is a greater force of revulsion, that which is experienced by Cazeau, that determines his non-intervention in the action and thus the nature of the final resolution. He is repelled by the idea that marriage puts him in the same relation to Athénaïse as his father was to his slave and his radical refusal to resort to the force that another father, Monsieur Miché, approves, allows the narrative to draw to the conventional conclusion that Scudder's intended readership would approve.

Athénaïse is able to express the disgust which she feels: 'It's jus' being married that I detes' an' despise. I hate being Mrs Cazeau, an' would want to be Athénaïse Miché again. I can't stan' to live with a man; to have him always there; his coat an' pantaloons hanging in my room; his ugly bare feet – washing them in my tub, befo' my very eyes, ugh!'.[11] and if the possible consequences of such enforced intimacy were not so tragic, this expression of aversion would be comic in its effects. However, the closeness which engenders such distaste in Athénaïse is serious because it approximates to physical threat; marriage is a hazardous business for young girls brought up for that end and no other. Whilst Athénaïse is fortunate in the decency of the man to whom her parents are glad to consign her – her father talking in terms of being 'rid' of her, of Cazeau being a man with 'a master hand, a strong will that compels obedience'.[12] – and also in the restraint shown by Gouvernail, others in Chopin's tales, like 'Tite Reine, are not so happy in their choice. Marriage puts women at risk because it is seen as the end, the completion of the woman, not something which has to be lived or endured. All Chopin's unhappily married women are in revolt against endings, against the idea of them as finished or completed in the act of marriage. Her stories are full of women who have been misunderstood or misread as entirely known and therefore closed. It is in too close a concentration upon the end that mistakes are made – as in the last words of 'The Story of an Hour' – and so it is by dismantling the mechanism of the end that I will attempt to locate Chopin's means of writing about desire.

'Her Letters', published by *Vogue* in 1895,[13] is a psychological drama which treats its two protagonists, a husband and wife, in separate parts of the story in order to demonstrate how little they really know of each other whilst apparently living in an intimate relationship. The beginning of the story discloses the secret life of the woman as Chopin reveals, without ever saying so directly, that she has had a passionate affair with a man other than her husband. The erotic charge carried by the description of her enactment of a ritual communion with her lost love is almost palpable as she reprieves his letters from being thrown into the fire:

> With feverish apprehension she began to search among the letters before her. Which of them had she so ruthlessly, so cruelly put out of her existence? Heaven grant, not the first, that very first one, written before they had learned or dared to say to each other "I love you." No, no; there it was, safe enough. She laughed with pleasure, and held it to her lips. But what if that other most precious and most imprudent one were missing! in which every word of untempered passion had long ago eaten its way into her brain; and which stirred her still to-day, as it had done a hundred times before when she thought of it. She crushed it between her palms when she found it. She kissed it again and again. With her sharp white teeth she tore the far corner from the letter, where the name was written; she bit the torn scrap and tasted it between her lips and upon her tongue like some god-given morsel.[14]

This unholy ecstasy of communion, as the symbolic presence of the beloved, in the form of the letters, is received into the body of the woman, is the climax of the episode in which the woman and her capacity for love are revealed to us. The letters, 'encircled in her arms' are the only things which communicate life in the story. They give the unnamed woman her only means of sustenance and the metaphoric language which dominates in the text is that which expresses spiritual nourishment: 'That was four years ago, and she had been feeding on them ever since; they had sustained her, she believed, and kept her spirit from perishing utterly.'[15]

Chopin negotiates a number of dangerous areas here; not only is she describing extra-marital love but she is using the rituals of the Christian church to express sexual ecstasy. She is able to use such scandalous content and style, however, because of the limits she sets for it in the narrative as a whole. The structure of the story – allowing three parts out of the four to an account of the husband's mental breakdown – means that the woman's story becomes – to all intents and purposes – the introduction to the real business of the narrative which is to show the path to destruction of the man whose complacencies have been destroyed. To take an examination of the structure further, perhaps the first part of the story could be considered as the sub-text of the whole, rather than a preface, in that its content underlies, extends and gives meaning to the linear narrative of the subsequent three parts. Instead of allowing us to guess, along with the husband, the content of the letters, Chopin makes explicit for her readers the extent to which a one-sided account of a marriage can be completely false by beginning with the picture of the sensual life of the woman and following it with her bereaved husband's estimate of her nature: 'She had never seemed in her lifetime to have had a secret from him. He knew her to have been cold and passionless, but true, and watchful of his comfort and his happiness'.[16]

In the opening scene of this story Chopin arrests conjecture by her direct and audacious treatment of the adulterous woman and the risks she takes in order to sustain a living sense of her own physical and emotional nature. The unfaithful wife is a given, there is no moral comment, no intervention in the text which would suggest that the narrator had any opinion at all about the woman's conduct. The existence of her erotic life is predicated as separate from any form of judgement, moral or otherwise, unlike the secret life which her husband imagines for her. Through the annexation of the language of organised religion, Chopin reinforces the aesthetic distance of the narrative from all the grounds for judgement that might normally be called upon to operate in such a case. The enclosed room, the separation from other members of the household, the ritualised nature of the encounter with the letters, all these serve to mark off the account of adultery from the space that is occupied by the marriage as it is subsequently revealed to us. It takes place in a different, a distinct sphere where the physical and the spiritual are gratified and the woman is autonomous.

Throughout her writing life Chopin often drew similarities between the feelings engendered by the rituals of the church with those of sexual arousal, stories like 'Two Portraits', written in 1895 and 'A Vocation and a Voice', written the following year, turn crucially on the contiguities of the two forms of ecstatic self-abandon. In 'Her Letters' Chopin identifies the primitive side of human nature with the enactment of the rituals of worship just as she positioned the 'divine' as interchangeable with 'animal instinct' in her essay on the question of 'Is Love Divine?'. She gives us a picture of a calm, well-organised, level-headed woman, who issues instructions to servants, locks doors, makes plans to destroy incriminating evidence, but who is reduced to a trembling creature with 'pained and savage eyes' when the paraphernalia of her ceremony of worship is threatened. Chopin is shameless in her borrowings, not only does the woman's memory of the affair take shape in a parody of the sacrament but the transubstantiation: 'This man had changed the water in her veins to wine, whose taste had brought delirium to both of them.'[17] is made to signify not spiritual but sexual fulfilment. As she has gone outside marriage for this consummate experience so she must impose her own shape or form upon the memory of the affair; within her locked room she enacts the ceremony which has kept her alive; its physicality, its ecstasy are contained by the worship of the relics of her passion.

The pace of the story and the points at which information is communicated are of central importance to the way in which Chopin manages to keep her audience in suspension of judgement. The woman talks of 'one man and one woman' as authors of the letters, she talks of 'one, above all, who was near to her, and whose tenderness and years of devotion had made him, in a manner, dear to her' and again to 'that other one' and the 'very one'. Until she is about to disappear in person from the story the word 'husband'[18] is not mentioned and even then it only appears in the instructions she leaves him to destroy the package of letters unopened. We are not certain until she writes the note that the person she damned with faint praise earlier as being only 'in a manner, dear to her' is her husband and by then it is too late, we know too much about the real centre of her life. The balance of her husband's existence is fatally deranged by the request she makes of his 'loyalty and his love', but the 'perfect faith' she has in his sense of duty, which she expresses and he enacts in the story, shows her to have been accurate in her assessment of his character. Where her passion is dramatised in the rituals which recall her love affair, his existence is quickened and his emotions aroused only by 'the man-instinct of possession'.[19]

His behaviour is that of the jealous man, seeking the tell-tale signs of infidelity, looking for the clue that will prove his suspicions to be well-founded. As in Maupassant's, 'Les Bijoux', where the widower in the story discovers that his wife's jewels, which he had always believed to be paste, were real and therefore spoke of the profitable but immoral life she led apart from him, the posthumous revelation of unknown depths of deceit or depravity destroys not only the past but the future. Where Maupassant leaves his readers to make their conjectures along with the husband, Chopin ensures that her readers are fully aware of both the folly of complacency and the impossibility of certainty where the secrets of the human heart or even the human body are concerned. As with Armand in Chopin's 'Désirée's Baby' the basis upon which identity has been formed is revealed to be false; for the loyal husband here, since 'the darkness then had closed around him and engulfed his manhood',[20] there is no peace except in death. The realisation that the woman he called 'wife' was not contained within that word, was not circumscribed by the status he gave her, also means that he loses what he has understood as his 'manhood' because his notion of such is constructed upon women being entirely knowable, without secrets and without passion.

Although less obvious in terms of their structure or exegesis, there are other stories which are concerned with the refusal of endings, the refusal of the interpretation of a woman which has been made by the man involved in the action or, crucially, by the reader of the tale. Two such are 'A Shameful Affair', published in 1893 by the *New Orleans Times-Democrat*, after nine rejections from other publications,[21] and 'A Respectable Woman', published by *Vogue* in 1894. The first story is concerned with the workings of shame, Chopin treating shame as a cultural phenomenon which regulates the acknowledgement of desire, but, in contradistinction from guilt, shame is also shown to open the way for transcendance over some forms of social control as a more individual and personal morality is developed. Whilst Mildred is concerned to bring herself to the attention of Fred Evelyn she takes every opportunity afforded to her by propriety to attract his notice and when propriety fails she forces its limits by initiating contact with him. She makes it known that he will be permitted to drive her to church, she watches his comings and goings, she follows him to the riverbank in order to watch him fish, she demands the use of his rod and when the bait is finally taken her eyes 'gleamed for an instant unconscious things into his own'.[22]

The first part of the story charts the beginning of desire, the second the partial fulfilment of desire and the third the conflict engendered between pleasure and shame. Even when she receives the letter which tells her that the object of her infatuation belongs to her own social class she is sufficiently self-aware to know that this information is irrelevant. What attracts her to him is not his background, wit, charm or intelligence: 'He was young and brown, of course, as the sun had made him. He had nice blue eyes. His fair hair was dishevelled. His shoulders were broad and square and his limbs strong and clean. A not unpicturesque figure in the rough attire that bared his throat to view and gave perfect freedom to his every motion.' The description of Fred Evelyn as he appears to Mildred is noticeably monosyllabic in contrast to the pretentious, prissy language in which she gives an account of herself: 'She...who had come to seek in this retired spot the repose that would enable her to follow exalted lines of thought.'[23]

Everything about Fred is clear-cut and crisp except his hair, 'dishevelled' as it is by the work that makes the rest of his body so hard-edged. The last sentence of the description is interesting for its early exclusion of an active verb so that the impression given is one of an accepted truth. The account thus seems to emanate from an impartial observer of a labouring man who seems rather generic than individual. Fred is a physical type – not a particular character with distinguishable habits; nothing is known of him beyond his physical presence until Mildred receives the letter telling her of his origins and his eccentricity. After the kiss, however, he moves from the stereotype of the muscular labourer to the stereotype of the chivalrous gentleman, behaving in a conventional manner, taking the blame for any intemperance and impropriety shown and climbing rhetorical heights that speak of his education and background: 'I am the most consummate hound that walks the earth.' Fred's assumption of blame for the moment of abandon is not a controversial matter, but Mildred's equal claim to responsibility is. The basis of his conduct towards her is the acceptance of a belief that she is innocent, guiltfree and has been damaged by his action. Her simple words, by which she lifts herself out of the generic which speaks of all girls as chaste, pure-minded and susceptible to harm, are sufficient to overthrow his notions of appropriateness. She unpicks his stereotypical masculinity and renders him girlish in his reaction to her words: 'Then a sudden quick wave came beating into his brown throat and staining it crimson, when he guessed what it might be.' Both Mildred and Fred have been undone by the forces of desire. Neither of them can exist as convention would have them again because the principle upon which much of their social behaviour, and certainly the operation of shame, has been founded, no longer applies. Mildred refutes the ending which Fred, not so eccentric after all, offers her; she gives him a different perspective and thereby takes it out of the hands of her 'father, or brother, or any one' to whom he might confess his shame, taking it as her personal responsibility to reach a time when she will 'have forgiven'[24] herself.

In 'A Respectable Woman' Mrs Baroda follows the same course as Mildred in beginning her interest in a man by feeling 'piqued'[25] at his lack of interest in her. The simple fact of the physical presence of the man is again what awakens the woman's sexual interest as Gouvernail's silences and indifference seem hardly designed to attract her. Again like Mildred Mrs Baroda is confused by the difference between the social rôle she expects her guest to play and Gouvernail's actuality. Just as Fred does not respond to Mildred's invitation to flirt, Gouvernail does not register either Mrs Baroda's indifference or her imposition of her presence upon him. Without taking any action or even engaging in the social niceties, both men are the unwitting instigators of dramatic developments in the self-knowledge of others; they are catalytic to momentous change in the lives of the women they encounter. Mrs Baroda and Mildred become helpless in the face of their own physical desire; Mildred engages in pursuit and must live with the memory of the kiss, Mrs Baroda resorts to flight and refuses to have any contact with Gouvernail for more than a year. When in proximity to him she has been consumed by the conflict arising from her struggle to keep a hold on her identity as a 'respectable woman' whilst attempting to control her newly awakened 'physical being'.[26]

An ending to the story which would restore Mrs Baroda to her place as the embodiment of the title 'A Respectable Woman' is offered to the reader when the invitation to Gouvernail is once again extended: ' "I have overcome everything! you will see. This time I shall be very nice to him" '. What her husband takes as the overcoming of her dislike could also, of course, be the overcoming of her passion or, alternatively, the overcoming of the scruples which prevented her from pursuing the attraction. The two latter interpretations hang suspended as possibilities above the story. However, whatever the reading of these lines, the fact remains that the intimacy of this married couple – evidenced by their informal sharing of the dressing-room, their liking for each other's company, their 'long, tender kiss'[27] – has been and may again be threatened. There is no certainty, no stability, no emblem of a highly ordered society such as marriage, which is not susceptible to disruption by the demands of physical desire. The story allows us to lift Mrs Baroda out of her closed reading as 'A Respectable Woman' and to place her in a number of alternative situations; the possibility exists for her to continue as that woman or to use her reputation to conceal a quite different existence. We do not know what will happen but our reading of Mrs Baroda can never be quite the same again because doubt has been planted by the ambiguous ending of the story and, having already witnessed both the power of the feelings that shake her and her resolution to control them, we are forced back into the body of the story in order to suspend judgement.

There are a number of stories where the ending seems designed to demonstrate the insubstantial nature of what has gone before, the transience of desire, for instance, is explored in 'Two Summers and Two Souls' where the predictable ending, the return of the young man to fulfil the promises of love he has made to a young woman, is the ending that will lead to the falsification of his life. This story, published in *Vogue* in 1895, explodes the 'singular delusion that love is eternal'[28] with its picture of a relationship at first given expression in intemperate, passionate language: 'He talked like a mad man then, and troubled and bewildered her with his incoherence. He begged for love as a mendicant might beg for alms, without reserve and without shame, and the passion within him gave an unnatural ring to his voice and a new, strange look to his eyes that chilled her unawakened senses and sent her shivering within herself',[29] but finally articulated in the cold language of commerce: 'He simply went to her. As he would have gone unflinchingly to meet the business obligations that he knew would leave him bankrupt'.[30] Time has allowed love to grow in the woman as she makes her choice for life – probably the only choice she will ever have the opportunity to make – and to die in the man, as he resumes his business and social commitments. The terrifying zeal of his desire for her with its resistance to normal constraints has burned itself out so that nothing, not even indifference, remains. There is actually no room for such intemperance in relation to the transactions that bind people together in a society arranged around the notion of absolutes. In a world where love is freighted with the burden of eternity and women have nothing to do but wait, then even mad men are taken at their word and expected to fulfil their promises.

In 'At Chênière Caminada' Tonie Bocaze is also intemperate in the nature of his feelings but his inarticulacy prevents him from transgressing pre-existent social boundaries, of class as well as decorum. This story, rejected by *The Atlantic*[31] but published in 1893 by the *New Orleans Times-Democrat*, is a Louisiana tale, set as it is in and around the vacation resort of Grand Isle. In so far as it tells the story of a simple, local man who has never ventured far from home, whose topography is recognisable and, indeed, visible at a single glance, then this is a good example of local colour. Where the story diverges from the path of local colour, however, is in the picture of Tonie and his passion, the passion that can see its only fulfilment in his own death and that of his beloved. Louisiana whimsy, the depiction of local idiosyncracies which might illustrate the conditions of the time and place, would be inadequate to the task of expressing Tonie and the strength of his feelings, and so Chopin emphasises the anti-picturesque aspects of the fisherman from the very beginning. He is 'not' many things: she describes him in the first paragraph entirely in terms of negatives, chief amongst which is the fact that 'he had no desire to inflame' or be inflamed; and in the second paragraph in terms of an unattractive and ineffective surplus, with his 'too long' face, 'too unmanageable' limbs, 'too earnest' eyes and 'too honest' demeanour. From this account of him, however, Chopin then moves us towards an understanding that this simple and unprepossessing character is capable of such excesses and intensity of feelings of both love and hopelessness that he can see no satisfaction in life except the destruction of the woman he loves.

There are no cheerful peasants on Chênière Caminada; when Tonie 'tramped from one end of the island to the other'[33] in a state of besotted confusion some of the events he fails to register are a woman screaming, a death, and a collision with a drunk. Tonie himself is transformed by love from a strapping, healthy man to a 'wretched-hearted being' with 'haggard eyes and thin, gaunt cheeks'.[34] Hopeless love destroys life and it is only in his gladness at the death of his beloved that Tonie receives a reprieve. He is clear and unequivocal about his feelings about Claire Duvigné's death; the expression of pleasure with which he so horrifies his mother signals his passage back to 'the moving world about him.'[35] The shocking nature of his sentiments is defused by his very simplicity; in focusing on his feelings and their straightforward expression Chopin ensures that we see only from Tonie's point of view. Claire Duvigné, with her 'pose' and her 'coquetry',[36] and despite her tragic early death, is of little interest beside this man whose profound faith in the curé's words that all will be equal in heaven is sufficient to restore him to life. His passion has passed from inducing a state of physical hopelessness, compounded by his imagining of her with another man, to one of transcendant certainty: 'It is with the soul that we approach each other there.'[37]

Nancy S. Ellis in her essay, 'Insistent Refrains and Self-Discovery',[38] discusses to good effect the part played by religious music in Tonie's awakening to new and powerful feelings. The music and the atmosphere of Chênière Caminada combine to affect him in a new way for although the 'lazy, scorching breeze blowing from the Gulf'[39] is a powerful influence it is his habitual element and is more often a hostile rather than sensual or romantic presence in his life. Natural forces are those with which Tonie does battle in his work as a fisherman and in which 'his father and brothers had perished...during a squall in Barataria Bay.'[40] When his mother demands an explanation from her son for his feelings of joy at Claire's death Tonie can find no inspiration in the view: 'He looked out across the water that glistened gem-like with the sun upon it, but there was nothing there to open his thought. He looked down into his open palm and began to pick at the callous flesh that was as hard as a horse's hoof. Whilst he did this his ideas began to gather and take form.' Tonie's hand is the pivotal symbol here, not the gleaming water of the gulf; it is the hand of a working man and as such marks him as distinct from those who engage with the sea as tourists, as bathers or day-trippers. Tonie's hand is his point of reference, looking at it triggers the ability to articulate his understanding of both his present and his future, it is his true signifier.

Chopin permits local colour to enact the closure of the story: 'With misty eyes she watched him walk away in the direction of the big brick-oven that stood open-mouthed under the lemon-trees,'[41] highlighting the quaint and the romantic, the picture-postcard version of the location. Tonie's return to his rôle as dutiful, contented son and old-fashioned fisherman, is again, however, a misleading conclusion. Just as Chopin opens 'A Gentleman of Bayou Têche', another story of 1893, with a knowing reference to the popular uses of the regional: 'It was no wonder Mr. Sublet, who was staying at the Hallet plantation, wanted to make a picture of Evariste. The 'Cadian was rather a picturesque subject in his way, and a tempting one to an artist looking for bits of "local color" along the Têche;'[42] so she closes 'At Chênière Caminada' with a similarly tempting bit of local colour to cover over the extremities of emotion that have been on display. The violent desperation of Tonie's intention to plunge into the ocean with his beloved, his stalking of her every movement, the monitoring of her relationships with other men; this obsessive behaviour reaches a non-violent conclusion with her death and his expression of confidence in the heavenly consummation of his desire, but it might easily have ended another way. When Chopin wrote the story it was partly as a tribute or an act of memorialisation, a hurricane having destroyed Grand Isle on October 1 1893.[43] The story, from its quiet beginnings in the church, through the whirlwind of Tonie's feelings and his growing, destructive fixation, to its resolution in the aftermath of pointless death and devastation, imitates the calm before the storm, the storm and then the unnatural calm which follows. But the stillness of the final scene is not to be trusted; the unpredictability of the storm is an ever-present threat to the calm.

The picturesque is also apparently foregrounded in the story of 'In and Out of Old Natchitoches', published in 1893 in *Two Tales*, a Boston journal which expired after two years being, as Toth says, 'too avant garde'[44] for the tastes of the time. This piece was syndicated by Chopin with the American Press Association in 1895, along with 'In Sabine'[45] and thus both pieces reached a larger public than was usual for her work, their settings and subjects no doubt facilitating their acceptability for syndication. As I have already discussed, 'In Sabine' contains material which in the climate of the 1890s would not generally have been considered suitable for the magazine audience and similarly 'In and Out of Old Natchitoches' is positively bursting with controversial material, being at the most superficial glance concerned with the segregation of schools, gambling, the effects of unrestrained aggression and the proper limits on the conduct of single women.

In his book, *Cultures of Letters: Scenes of Reading and Writing in Nineteenth-Century America*, Richard Brodhead discusses the 'memorial function' of regional writing whereby fiction serves 'as a surrogate memory of a life now passing into the past'.[46] He notes the particular use of 'Old' as a signifier in the title of those works that seek to advertise their concern with the regional as a means to portray obsolete ways of life now beyond retrieval. In 'In and Out of Old Natchitoches' Chopin could be seen to be announcing a nostalgic project in her title, just as in 'In Sabine' she seems to be positioning the reader to hear a tale of life as it is led in 'the big lonesome parish of Sabine'.[47] However, as this story unfolds it becomes clear that Chopin is actually using geographical specificity as a diversion. The reader, like Bud Aiken, initially thinks that 'Tite Reine is 'In Sabine' for life but soon becomes distracted by the execution of her retreat back into Natchitoches and by Grégoire's crossing of the Sabine River on his way into Texas. The ending here is that rare thing in Chopin's fiction, the resolution of events; this is, however, only the case because it is the ending that endorses the destruction of the marriage and thus the anti-establishment ethos of the tale.

The ending of 'In and Out of Old Natchitoches' is a tidy resolution of the mystery of why a respectable young lady should not be seen in the street with Hector Santien, Grégoire's brother, but this is largely tangential to the number of explosive issues that are thrown up throughout the course of the story. The whimsical title, with its nursery rhythmic qualities, does not mislead in its promise of the regional, but the field of reference of 'Old' contains those who stay in the country, like old Madame St. Denys Godolph, with her adherence to the old ways, those like Santien, who have left Natchitoches, but take their pre-war assumptions of manners and mores to the city with them, as well as Suzanne, who is given no choice but to return to the past. Santien, with his melodramatic alias: 'Deroustan, the most notorious gambler in New Orleans'[48] appears to be a figure from another age with his stagey good-looks and his excessive attention to his appearance: 'He might have posed, as he was, for a fashion-plate. He looked not to the right nor to the left; not even at the women who passed by. Some of them turned to look at him.'[49] In a story which is in many ways concerned with the rites of passage of the woman into maturity and marriage it seems at first perverse that the possibilities of the erotic are communicated by this dilettantish figure and not by Alphonse

Laballière whose courtship of Suzanne, it is intimated, will be successful. The erotic here, however, is complicated by Chopin's carefully structured account of the ambiguous nature of Santien's sexuality and the part it plays in Suzanne's awakening. Where Laballière is aggressive, forceful, impetuous and insistent in his masculinity Santien is detached, calm, unruffled and maintains a 'quizzical'[50] distance; where Laballière is a man of few words, most of which he regrets, Santien is a man who 'talked incessantly'.[51] The story begins with Laballière and his masculine dynamism on display; he is 'knocking into shape a tumbled-down plantation',[52] and, when she writes of the planter, Chopin exercises a good deal of narratorial authority, leaving us in no doubt about the nature of the man: 'Laballière could have seen how charming she was, had he not at the moment been blinded by stupidity',[53] 'for there was no denying he was blunt'.[54] Indeed, Chopin also lets us know that he is incapable of concealment: 'He lifted his hat to Suzanne, and cast a quick glance, that pictured stupefaction and wrath, upon Hector.'[55] In contrast to this portrayal of Laballière as entirely open to scrutiny, Chopin's manner of communicating Santien is to cast doubt upon the sincerity of every aspect of his life. Not only does she convey a sense that his dandified appearance speaks of more than a fastidious nature – he is 'faultless', there is no 'man to equal Hector in the elegance of his mien'[56] – there is no impetuosity, only self-reflexivity. Whilst everything about Laballière is spontaneous, Santien is communicated through his manners, even his reactions are a result of the polite distance he maintains between himself and the world: 'his indignation was not so patent as she would have liked it to be'.[57]

As Chopin builds up the tension in the story by creating an enigma out of the figure of Santien, the climax of the story thus becomes the transaction between him and Suzanne which will define the nature of their relationship in the future, not the proposal of marriage from Laballière to Suzanne that is inevitable from the first page nor the revelation of Santien's other life. Santien is beyond embarrassment, beyond surprise and detached in the face of others' emotions; as Suzanne begs him to reveal himself to her, to tell the truth about himself, he responds with a gesture of what might be constructed as contempt for the business of love-making: 'He held the rose by its long, hardy stem, and swept it lightly and caressingly across her forehead, along her cheek, and over her pretty mouth and chin, as a lover might have done with his lips. He noticed how the red rose left a crimson stain behind it. She had been standing, but now she sank upon the bench that was there, and buried her face in her palms. A slight convulsive movement of the muscles indicated a suppressed sob.'[58] His distance is intact as he participates in the transaction, yet monitors its effects and controls its interpretation at the same time.

The demonstration of his knowledge of the sort of display which might be required of a lover is as beautifully put together as if it had been sincere; he knows that his action imitates what 'a lover might have done with his lips' but the use of the rose constructs an aesthetic distance. The gesture with the rose is not simply a device through which the cool head and impassive demeanour of the gambler can be revealed, it is performance which displays his command of the discourse of eroticism. He can produce a response which is controlled and yet contains within it sufficient of the erotic to show his understanding of the woman who has all but declared her love for him. This deliberate gesture is both instrumental and decadent in being accomplished as easily as any well-mannered reply to questions that are asked of him and concerns that are expressed for him. He describes himself as impervious to the charms of any woman, supplementing his 'Talk, talk', as Suzanne describes it, with arch observations; but his self-regard, expressed via the absolute perfection of his appearance, is indicative of his dishonesty. He refuses to close down the possibility of romance with a woman: 'he looked at her with a deliberation that quite unsettled her'[59] and yet also resists committing himself to an honest declaration of intent or sexual preference. When Chopin closes the story with the revelation of his notoriety as a gambler the anti-climax is almost palpable; the explanation is as mis-leadingly melodramatic as his appearance. Suzanne, on the train and at the mercy of 'the sheer force of [Laballière's] will', is exhausted and inert; sent home by Santien: 'Promise me that you will go back to the country. That will be best',[60] she is resigned to her fate, which is to remain in ignorance.

In this story Chopin puts on display both an excess and a paucity of traits identifiable as masculine; the contrast between the aggressive and physically insistent Laballière and Santien, '*un ange de bon Dieu*',[61] leaves Suzanne helpless and confused, caught between the coxcomb and the planter, between the rose and the thorns. The phallic symbolism of the 'long, hardy stem' stripped of both 'the heavy lower leaves' and of its thorns so that all that is left at its tip is the rose, enforces the distance between them which is maintained by the self-protective nature of Santien's manners. The rose, a common emblem of romance, is here re-orientated to refute the romance conceived by the 'marvelously fair'[62] Suzanne.

Chopin was unafraid to venture into areas of human desire and fulfilment which transgress propriety as the piece, 'Two Portraits', demonstrates in the most candid manner. This dual tale was refused, according to Per Seyersted in his biography of Chopin, 'by everyone, including the *Yellow Book* and the *Chap-Book*'[63] and tells of the arbitrary nature of the focus of desire, though not of the nature that will be likely to surrender to the sensual. This piece, constructed as a diptych, repeats its opening paragraph so that the life of 'The Wanton' and the life of 'The Nun' begin with the same genetic inheritance; heredity is thus shown to decree the nature of the commitment made by Alberta, environment the direction in which she focuses it. The ending of the woman is thus in her beginning as the two titles within the story give us, without equivocation, the destination of the woman/women about to be described. Here Chopin foregrounds closure because these alternative versions of Alberta are both finished – all other possibilities have been removed by the single dedication of the life either to the ecstasies of religious or sexual abandon. Thus the radical impetus of the story does not inhere simply in the sordid tale of Alberta the wanton but in the spectacle of the life of the nun circumscribed by the shadow of the brothel.

The voluptuous language of the bordello with its attendant tones of sexual violence conveys a scene that is entirely human and physical in all its expressions which is then extended and complemented through description of a woman who has been taught to subdue the body and reach out only with her soul. The spiritual is demonstrated to be inseparable from the physical and attracts a more explicit portrait of sensual abandon than that which is experienced by the wanton:

> Oh, the dear God! Who loved her beyond the power of man to describe, to conceive. The God-Man, the Man-God, suffering, bleeding, dying for her, Alberta, a worm upon the earth; dying that she might be saved from sin and transplanted among the heavenly delights. Oh, if she might die for him in return! But she could only abandon herself to his mercy and his love. "Into thy hands, Oh Lord! Into thy hands!"

She pressed her lips upon the bleeding wounds and the Divine Blood transfigured her. The Virgin Mary enfolded her in her mantle. She could not describe in words the ecstasy; the taste of the Divine love which only the souls of the transplanted could endure in its awful and complete intensity.[64]

The life of the nun and the wanton are alike in their exclusivity; they have surrendered to a singleness of purpose and to a disregard for the continuation of life on any level below the ecstatic with the final rapture of death always near at hand. As ever in Chopin's work there is no direct moral comment made upon the lives that are pictured here and so the juxtaposition of the alternative versions of Alberta's existence becomes the most speaking part of the story. The lives of the nun and the wanton interrogate each other through their inter-changeability and in the fact that the end of their lives can be witnessed in the beginning of their dedication to a single purpose. The curtailment which is imposed upon both halves of the diptych highlights the absence of real celebration and productive change from the lives of women who are above all others deemed to have only one purpose: to worship 'the God-Man, the Man-God'. The closed reading of a woman, the essentialist argument, that women are determined from birth to be one thing or the other – angel or whore – is exposed here by Chopin's portrayal of the perverseness of the process required to reach a female destination on the extreme edge of either the secular or spiritual structures in society. Both women, in being forced to the margins, come to inhabit a sort of nether-world where the sensate being can barely distinguish between life and death, with the experiences of life providing a 'foretaste of heavenly bliss'[65] and the idea of losing the charms that guarantee sexual gratification being ameliorated by the placing of 'death and oblivion always within her reach.'[66]

For an unequivocal celebration of physical and even spiritual fulfilment it is necessary to go to Chopin's 'The Storm', sub-titled 'A Sequel to "At the 'Cadian Ball"', where the enactment of a sacred rite is lyrically and sensuously intertwined with sex in a carnivalesque suspension of the rules of normal social engagement. Here Chopin describes an exciting, abandoned, sexual encounter between adulterers. This story communicates the openness to desire of both men and women; it also shows the astonishing ease with which they can move from ecstasy to the quotidien. In contrast to the sterile curtailment and always imminent closure of the nun and the wanton the final line of 'The Storm' marks the end of nothing but weather: 'So the storm passed and everyone was happy.'[67]

The story, 'At the 'Cadian Ball', published in 1892 in the Boston Journal, *Two Tales*, shares family connections as well as a publisher with 'In and Out of Old Natchitoches' in the person of Alcée Laballière, brother of the planter who is the triumphant lover in the later story. It tells of the manner in which the engagements of two couples, Alcée and his cousin, Clarisse, and Bobinôt and Calixta are accomplished. The marriages thus arranged follow lines of class but there are significant reservations about the physical appropriateness of the relationships expressed in the manner of the telling of the courtship. Alcée is pressing and spontaneous, the first Clarisse knows of his feelings is when he 'came in from the rice-field, and, toil-stained as he was, clasped Clarisse by the arms and panted a volley of hot, blistering love-words into her face'[68] which she coldly repels.

Calixta mocks Bobinôt's physical awkwardness, 'standin' *planté là* like ole Ma'ame Tina's cow in the bog'[69] and after being charmed by Alcée, cannot bear to have Bobinôt touch her despite having promised to marry him. 'The Storm' is signposted as the 'Sequel' to the story of the night of betrothals and thus is destined, in spite of the successful conclusions of courtship in the first story, to be treating unfinished business. The fact that Chopin wrote 'The Storm' undoes any resolution which might seem to occur at the end of 'At the 'Cadian Ball' – neither men nor women are closed by marriage.

According to Emily Toth, Chopin wrote 'The Storm' in a single sitting in July 1898.[70] The story is as well-structured as any of her other late pieces, and indeed, is powerfully allusive in its borrowings of language and imagery from *The Song of Solomon*. This story continues the pattern of thematic and linguistic inter-weaving of religious and sexual ecstasy in Chopin's fiction, only here it is not an imitation of ceremony or worship as an act of control over an otherwise ungovernable passion, it is an act of celebration. The irony with which Chopin sometimes maintains authorial distance is absent and perhaps the privately indulgent nature of the story can be seen in the surrender Chopin makes to an effulgent language which would not usually form a part of her lexicon. She is on the edge of cliché in this tale but the syntax which would seem most susceptible to charges of extravagance is that which derives from the *Song* and its tropes. In this way charges of cliché are defused both by the line of descent of the description and also, perhaps, an acknowledgement that the transcending of cliché is not actually possible, either when describing adulterous encounters or sheer, pleasurable, abandoned sex.

The breaking of the storm is also the breaking of the sexual tension which has been gathering, in contemporary reader time at least, since the night of the 'Cadian Ball'. The *Song* provides a motif for the tale: 'Many waters cannot quench love, neither can the floods drown it';[71] and whatever else, the sex described here is neither pornographic nor ridiculous. The words of the *Song* which reverberate through the account of Calixta and Alcée's love-making – 'pomegranate', 'lily', 'fountain', 'spring', 'breasts', 'chamber'[72] – are in some respects metaphorically tired but their familiarity becomes a part of the double indulgence of using the words and the nature of the encounter itself. Through her borrowings she can both normalise and aestheticise the encounter.

As in the *Song of Solomon*, the sexual act, as described, is there as a given, there is no arbitrating moral voice. The explicit account of their love-making is the centre-piece of the tale; it has to stand on its own because its very celebration of physical intimacy marks it off from the other aspects of both Calixta and Alcée's lives which receive attention in the five part structure of the tale. There are problems attached to their physical proximity to other people, problems which were delineated in the account of the night of their betrothal. The story opens with Bobinôt and Bibi in the village store, the second part describes the storm and the sexual encounter, the third the unexpectedly cheerful welcome Bobinôt and Bibi receive from Calixta, the fourth Alcée's letter to his wife inviting her to stay away on vacation for another month, and the fifth, Clarisse's receipt of the letter and her relief at the prolonged opportunity to 'forego' 'their intimate conjugal life'. 'So the storm passed and everyone was happy.'[73] – the sexual encounter, like the storm, has released the tensions which afflict the atmosphere in both marriages.

The story of 'The Storm' is at the heart of a network of relationships which feature regularly throughout Chopin's fiction. It features characters who appear elsewhere and whose family members have tales attached to them; it forms the sequel to a story which appeared both in a magazine and in a book – Chopin's 1894 collection, *Bayou Folk*[74] – and was, therefore, firmly in the public arena. Yet Chopin can never have expected 'The Storm' to be made public. The reading position she might have constructed for the audience for the story is thus an intriguing one and in its exegesis it is possible to see devices characteristic of her art at their most transparent because there is no consciousness of a potentially censorious audience. The story is not significantly different from Chopin's other work. The structure is clear, the plot is linear, the lower classes speak in dialect and the upper in standard English or French, there is no arbitrating moral voice or comment and what happens in the middle is more important than the end. So far, so predictable. Where in other stories the fact of change and its consequences become the centre of attention, in 'The Storm' it seems at first sight that absence of change facilitates the action. That five years have passed since they were last alone together has not lessened the powerful physical attraction between Alcée and Calixta. There is a change, however, a change on which the story turns, but also a change that would entirely prevent publication.

Chopin makes it clear that the two can only enjoy each other because they are married – to other people. Where Calixta's virginity kept Alcée in check when they were single and in Assumption together: 'Now – well, now – her lips seemed in a manner free to be tasted, as well as her round, white throat and her whiter breasts'. Marriage here is the enabling principle of the spectacular sex they have: 'And when he possessed her, they seemed to swoon together at the very borderland of life's mystery'; marriage is the factor which enables her to enjoy the physical gratification that her relationship with Alcée always seemed to promise. The woman here is not finished but begun by marriage – 'Her firm, elastic flesh that was knowing for the first time its birthright'[75] – but, it is clear, she cannot expect to find everything she needs within marriage. Whether the sexual encounter between Alcée and Calixta is ever repeated is not to be known; what considerate spouses Alcée and Calixta have both become in the first flush of their physical gratification is known and Chopin wants to communicate none of the more complicated emotions that might follow the storm to her reader.

Chopin understands the topography of desire; the 'borderland' the lovers inhabit, albeit briefly, is the territory described by Milan Kundera in *The Book of Laughter and Forgetting*: 'It takes so little, so infinitely little, for someone to find himself on the other side of the border, where everything – love, convictions, faith, history – no longer has meaning. The whole mystery of human life resides in the fact that it is spent in the immediate proximity of, and even in direct contact with, that border, that it is separated from it not by kilometers but by barely a millimeter.'[76] Chopin does not have to move her readers much more than 'barely a millimeter' from their preconceptions about other people's lives in order to bring about a huge re-orientation of their perceptions about appropriate endings. At a distance of a hundred years it is our privilege to read and enjoy whilst also subjecting her work to the kind of complex scrutiny that pays the fullest tribute to her fiction. Chopin was able to supply the editors who bought her work with appropriate endings in most cases, but, as I have, I hope, demonstrated, the endings are often the most inappropriate place to look for significance. The society in which Chopin lived was intensely bound up with the maintenance of borders, between colours, between classes, between men and women, between respectable and disreputable and between the North East of America and other regions with distinct identities; it liked to draw tidy conclusions. Chopin crossed borders all her life; she grew physically and intellectually away from the narrow certainties of her Catholic, Confederate childhood into a free-thinking, radical and courageous woman. Her fiction is transgressive, it breaks the limits of its temporal and geographical space, freeing its subjects from the confines of the expected ending and illuminating that alternative locality wherein 'human life' as Kundera has it or, to repeat Chopin's own words, 'human existence in its subtle, complex, true meaning, stripped of the veil with which ethical and conventional standards have draped it' is enacted.

Notes

1.   *Kate Chopin*, pp. 309–10.
2.   *Kate Chopin*, pp. 279–81.
3.   *Kate Chopin*, pp. 318–22.
4.   *Complete Works*, pp. 691–92.
5.   Fusco, Richard *Maupassant and the American Short Story: The Influence of Form at the Turn of the Century* (University Park: The Pennsylvania State University Press, 1994), p. 148.
6.   See especially Susan Lohafer's discussion of 'Athénäise' in Lohafer, Susan *Coming to Terms with the Short Story* (Baton Rouge: Louisiana

State University Press, 1983), pp. 115–132 and Emily Toth, *Kate Chopin*, pp. 274–75.

7. *Kate Chopin*, p. 275.
8. Sedgwick, Ellery *A History of the Atlantic Monthly 1857–1909: Yankee Humanism at High Tide and Ebb* (Amherst, University of Massachusetts Press, 1994), p. 225.
9. *Complete Works*, p. 438.
10. *Complete Works*, p. 432.
11. *Complete Works*, p. 431.
12. *Complete Works*, p. 434.
13. *Kate Chopin*, p. 417.
14. *Complete Works*, p. 399.
15. *Complete Works*, p. 398.
16. *Complete Works*, p. 400.
17. *Complete Works*, p. 399.
18. *Complete Works*, pp. 398–400.
19. *Complete Works*, p. 401.
20. *Complete Works*, p. 405.
21. *Kate Chopin*, p. 200.
22. *Complete Works*, p. 134.
23. *Complete Works*, p. 131.
24. *Complete Works*, pp. 131–136.
25. *Complete Works*, p. 334.
26. *Complete Works*, p. 335.
27. *Complete Works*, p. 336.
28. *Complete Works*, p. 457.
29. *Complete Works*, p. 455.
30. *Complete Works*, p. 457.
31. *Kate Chopin*, p. 235.
32. *Complete Works*, p. 309.
33. *Complete Works*, p. 310.
34. *Complete Works*, pp. 315–16.
35. *Complete Works*, p. 317.
36. *Complete Works*, pp. 314–15.
37. *Complete Works*, p. 318.
38. Boren, Lynda S. and Sara deSaussure Davis *Kate Chopin Reconsidered: Beyond the Bayou* (Baton Rouge, Louisiana State University Press, 1992). pp. 216–229.
39. *Complete Works*, p. 309.
40. *Complete Works*, p. 311.
41. *Complete Works*, pp. 309–18.
42. *Complete Works*, p. 319.
43. *Kate Chopin*, p. 222.
44. *Kate Chopin*, p. 216.
45. *Kate Chopin*, p. 246.
46. Brodhead, Richard *Cultures of Letters: Scenes of Reading and Writing in Nineteenth-Century America* (Chicago: University of Chicago Press, 1993), p. 20.
47. *Complete Works*, p. 325.

48. *Complete Works*, p. 267.
49. *Complete Works*, p. 266.
50. *Complete Works*, p. 266.
51. *Complete Works*, p. 260.
52. *Complete Works*, p. 255.
53. *Complete Works*, p. 257.
54. *Complete Works*, p. 259.
55. *Complete Works*, p. 263.
56. *Complete Works*, p. 260.
57. *Complete Works*, p. 262.
58. *Complete Works*, p. 265.
59. *Complete Works*, p. 261.
60. *Complete Works*, p. 266.
61. *Complete Works*, p. 261.
62. *Complete Works*, p. 255.
63. Seyersted, Per *Kate Chopin: A Critical Biography* (Baton Rouge, Louisiana State University Press, 1969), p. 73.
64. *Complete Works*, p. 465.
65. *Complete Works*, pp. 465–6.
66. *Complete Works*, pp. 463.
67. *Complete Works*, p. 596.
68. *Complete Works*, p. 220.
69. *Complete Works*, p. 224.
70. *Kate Chopin*, p. 318.
71. *Song of Solomon*, Chapter 8, verse 7.
72. *Complete Works*, pp. 594–5.
73. *Complete Works*, p. 596.
74. Chopin, Kate *Bayou Folk* (Boston: Houghton, Mifflin, 1894).
75. *Complete Works*, pp. 594–5.
76. Kundera, Milan *The Book of Laughter and Forgetting* Translated from the French by Aaron Asher 1996 (London: Faber and Faber, 1996), p. 281.

4

Kate Chopin's Short Short Stories – On the Verge(s) of Narrative

In the early 1890s Kate Chopin wrote a number of brief fictional pieces which are at first sight on the margins of consideration for the title of 'story'. The majority of these very short short stories could be relatively easily situated as fables, sketches, parables or vignettes, varieties of narrative which might be read as having some pedagogic intent in drawing a simple moral or enforcing a point. Such a designation of her fiction as didactic would be at odds, however, with the way in which Chopin constructed herself as writer[1] and with the way in which she has always been read: for instance, the absence of authorial moral comment and judgement in *The Awakening* was one of the grounds upon which the novel was attacked by its earliest readers. A profile of Kate Chopin written by her friend, William Schuyler, for *The Writer* in August 1894 makes particular mention of Chopin's attitude to the work of a fellow novelist in order to make this very point: 'She has great respect for Mrs Humphrey Ward's achievements; but Mrs Ward is, *au fond*, a reformer, and such tendency in a novelist she considers a crime against good taste'.[2] Fiction written with a didactic intent was, as will be seen in discussion of the work of Charlotte Perkins Gilman, a familiar mode in the larger field of women's writing in the 19th century. Chopin had no difficulty in distinguishing herself from those whose mode was straightforwardly moral but to embrace the sub-genres of the short story which have as their very essence the didactic intent whilst abjuring didactic intent seems somewhat perverse and thus beautifully consistent with much of what we know about the wilful and seductively dissonant authorial voice of Kate Chopin.

The sophisticated detachment of Chopin's narratorial stance is actually as much a feature of the superficially homiletic pieces as it is of any other of her works and in this likeness can be found many other grounds for comparison. The complexities involved in the maintenance of distance in stories which apparently yield to a moral reading can be used as a means by which to read a larger coherence into Chopin's work in both thematic and structural terms. The principle of reading in detail, by means of inference and interpretation, can be continued into the longer short stories and indeed, into *At Fault*, her novel of 1890, and *The Awakening*. Like the larger works the short short stories, whilst often pointing to what seems to be an obvious moral, rarely communicate any message straightforwardly. The moral, if it exists, may be the reverse of that first expected, or the ambiguities of Chopin's language may prevent the reader from drawing any simple or straightforward conclusion from the narrative. These pieces are as capable as any longer, apparently more complex, narrative of dramatising all the open-endedness of which the short story as a genre is capable and, indeed, the very imminence of the ending alerts us to the dangers of reading the whole text as if closed.

Susan Lohafer, in her book *Coming to Terms with the Short Story*, describes the short story as the most 'end-conscious'[3] of genres and thus its readers as concomitantly alert to impending closure. Short short stories like those Kate Chopin wrote are predicated on the calculation of the effect of abbreviation and ending. However, even the primary fact of their apparently foreshortened appearance on the page invites the reader into the position of inference rather than that of the expectation of revelation. Despite the dangers to which Lohafer alerts us in any attempt to make facile correlations between the short story and the lyric poem,[4] these brief narratives do need to be examined by the word as well as by the sentence or the paragraph, indeed, one of Chopin's pieces, 'The Night Came Slowly' I intend to discuss as a lyric. So, even the use of the word, 'fable', indeed, the only use of the word 'fable' amongst Chopin's titles, in 'Emancipation, A Life Fable', is subject to the interrogation of the course taken by the narrative. According to Emily Toth in her biography, *Kate Chopin*,[5] this piece was written much earlier than the other short stories I want to consider here, around 1869–70, and not published in her lifetime. It does, however, provide an appropriate starting point for my discussion for the following reasons: the story plays with its self-declared genre, that of 'fable', Chopin's use of language responds to a close and detailed reading and, additionally, the narrative can be placed in the context of the external reality of the political situation in the Southern states in the late 1860s to productive effect.

It is my intention throughout this chapter to focus on Chopin's short short stories – those which cover less than two pages or one thousand words – not because I am a reader addicted to counting words, but because these stories can give a firm direction to a thematic and structural analysis of Chopin's fiction as a whole. Reading in detail stories which have not, in general, been treated seriously by critics can perhaps provide an enhanced awareness of the complications of Chopin's authorial voice. My discussion of 'Emancipation, A Life Fable' will lead into consideration of three of the short short stories which have race at the heart of their fictional concern. I will then continue to look at questions of individual freedom in narratives which have a concern with the position of women in society at their core and from there move onto those stories which are most usually described as vignettes in order to consider some of the issues about what constitutes story rather than sketch or anecdote.

Chopin's only self-declared fable opens Per Seyersted's edition of *The Complete Works of Kate Chopin*[6] and, since the beast fable is the most common form of this genre, from Aesop onwards, the use of the genre definition in the title signals the fact that the story will be woven around an animal. From the moment of reading the title we expect to receive a version of a universally acknowledged truth about the human condition as revealed through an example of animal behaviour, a strategy used frequently by Charlotte Perkins Gilman in her beast fables, where the error of human ways is exposed by the comparison and the moral is always clear. Whilst the connotations of 'fable' allow the reader to anticipate an animal story which will reveal truths about the human condition, the word 'emancipation' counterbalances the movement toward a too narrowly genre-bound reading as its primary connotations are human. The word itself derives from Roman law and is generally used to signify manumission, release from bondage, rather than the condition of being free. We are thus directed toward the very question of what it means to be either distinct from or represented by the animal in the deep South of the United States in the late 1860s.[7] In featuring the predictable exemplary animal here Chopin does more than demonstrate the properties of a genre. The use of the fable in itself forces attention back to the question of the granting of human dignity – the right to self-determination – at the heart of the question of emancipation; those who would deny the status of human to the enslaved were not unused to equating slaves with beasts.

Chopin's use of the fable goes beyond the illustration of the human condition with an example from the animal kingdom, it forces its readers back to examine the terms of its understanding of words like emancipation and even fable. The genre itself is implicated in a too casual assignment of human and animal, sentient and insentient, reasonable and unreasonable and, crucially, free and not-free. The beast in the story – caged at first and then allowed to taste the uncertainties of liberty – represents both acceptance and denial of the force of fable; it shows what happens when you allow figurative language to harden into a truth but also what potential is released when you allow figurative language to illustrate a truth but also convey a sense of its limitations.

The animal, Chopin tells us, 'throve in strength and beauty under care of an invisible protecting hand' but this apparent health and well-being, once acknowledged, is overwhelmed as a consideration by the narrative impetus toward freedom. The weight of the prose is against confinement and for the celebration of the random, the uncertain, and, above all else, of the 'Unknown', thus dignified in the fable with all the importance of the proper noun. The argument of the pro-slavery lobby that 'the peculiar institution' provided a benign and caring system which removed the onerous pressures of responsibility for oneself and others from those enslaved is refuted by the momentum of the narrative. The animal is kept in ignorance of the wider world, lying 'in the sun beam that he thought existed but to lighten his home', afraid of change and unskilled: 'for such a task his limbs were purposeless'.

This briefest of narratives manages to contain within it the limitations of the past, the hazards of the present and the possibilities of the future through a skilful use of tense. The parabolic or fabular opening: 'There was once...' moves into a description of the situation in the past and from there into the present, with a shift of tense to the immediate: 'again and again he goes to the open door'. As the animal is affected by the lure of the outside, unknown world so the pace of change, of risk and self-exposure is communicated by the 'mad flight' in which he is 'heedless that he is wounding and tearing his sleek sides – seeing, smelling, touching of all things'.

Chopin's representation of the contingencies of dependency drives the narrative forward as it often does in her longer fictions. The pain of freedom is not minimised, even the benefits of drinking from 'the noxious pool'[8] are insisted upon by the didacticism of the definite article, the pool becoming thus symbolic of all negative but formative experience. The fable, and often the short story in general, is predicated on the idea of change, a turning point, a necessity. This fable is imperative in its demands upon both writer and reader; nothing less than 'Life' is the subject and the connection must be made between the basic level of the experiences which are being charted by the animal's progress through the world and the beginnings of the new world experience for those so recently existing as slaves in the land of the free. The fable is also a version of the paradox of the fortunate fall; free will and self-determination lie outside the cage of pre-lapsarian innocence and ignorance. In this piece Chopin refutes the argument of those who insist that slavery is a benign institution as well as those who under-estimate the fearfulness of freedom. Chopin's oft-quoted diary entry for 22 May 1894, written after a visit to see a school-friend who had become a nun 20 years before and whom Chopin had not seen during that time, expresses straightforwardly and brutally her opinion of any life which is conducted in isolation: 'When we came away, my friend who had gone with me said: "Would you not give anything to have her vocation and happy life!" There was a long beaten path spreading before us; the grass grew along its edges and the branches of trees in their thick rich May garb hung over the path like an arbor, making a long vista that ended in a green blur. An old man – a plain old man leaning on a cane was walking down the path holding a small child by the hand and a little dog was trotting beside them. "I would rather be that dog" I answered her. I know she was disgusted and took it for irreverence and I did not take the trouble to explain that this was a little picture of life and that what we had left was a phantas-magoria.'[9]

Freedom is also at the heart of the narrative in 'The Bênitous' Slave', 'Old Aunt Peggy' and 'A Little Free-Mulatto', all short short stories of 1892 and all concerned with troubled individual identity within the society of post-bellum Louisiana. The title character of 'The Bênitous' Slave', Old Uncle Oswald, has no recognisable autonomy. His loyalty to the family who owned him 'fifty years since' is his only authenticating idea of self. Their loyalty, however, has not been commensurate with his – 'He had belonged to others since' – and withal he has failed to adjust his sense of identity to the economic realities which proscribe the terms of his existence in the post-war world. His fate is held in common with the land that once belonged to the Bênitous: 'The family had dispersed, and almost vanished, and the plantation as well had lost its identity.' The self-image of the slave is the only constituent of the ante-bellum social structure to endure, the individual human legacy of slavery is not so easily 'dispersed', the identity of the slave is not so easy to lose.

The relationship between Old Uncle Oswald and those who find themselves responsible for him is articulated by Chopin through a variety of euphemisms. 'Monsieur', a man identified by his hon-orific not his name, 'kept' the old man; he and the doctor decide to ' "do something" ' with him; the institution for which he is destined is a place where he will be 'cared for'. The ultimate disposal of Old Uncle Oswald's services – 'gratuitous services' – also falls to Monsieur. The restless anxiety at the heart of Old Uncle Oswald's being is to be appeased and inner peace restored by such a disposal, by the return of the slave into bondage, albeit of the mildest kind. Chopin does not allow the narrative to rest at the point of disposal, however. She ends: ' "My name's Oswal', Madam; Oswal' – dat's my name. I b'longs to de Bênitous," ' and someone told me his story then'. His story, such as it is, has never belonged to him; his story is the story of the South. Single-minded adherence to one idea has ruined the South, sapped its initiative, restricted its progress, caused it to run away from the realities of the modern world, and left it with nothing but nostalgia. Well-mannered, dignified, loyal beyond reason, fit only for a few tightly circumscribed tasks, Old Uncle Oswald is a perfect representative of the peculiar institution; the 'venerable servitor'[10] expresses the South in all its desolation of purpose and intent.

Old Uncle Oswald awaits orders from a Bênitou; 'Old Aunt Peggy', however, will answer only to her maker. On the make herself she understands the power of words to profess loyalty and the power of things to convey emotions; she eulogises the artefacts which are synecdochic of the sentient life of the slaveholders:

> "Mist'ess, I's come to take a las' look at you all. Le' me look at you good. Le' me look at de chillun, – de big chillun an' de li'le chillun. Le' me look at de picters an' de photygraphts an' de

pianny, an' eve'ything 'fo' it's too late. One eye is done gone, an' de udder's a-gwine fas'. Any mo'nin' yo' po' ole Aunt Peggy gwine wake up an' fin' hers'f stone-bline.''

After such a visit Aunt Peggy invariably returns to her cabin with a generously filled apron.

Without the opportunity or the means by which to accumulate her own memorabilia, the possessions which speak of a leisure class, Old Aunt Peggy nevertheless knows the significance of the things she itemises in the life of the white family; she also knows the negative value of the slave too old to work. Only the slave-owners can lay claim of ownership to things which speak of a refined, aesthetically aware culture – the piano, photographs, pictures, but also, and the connotations are clearly tragic rather than comic here, the retention and ownership of its own children, big and little. Possessor of neither things nor known descendants of her own to look after her in her old age, the only value Old Aunt Peggy has is in mystification of that age and in flattery of the appurtenances which distinguish the master-race from her own. Her own mistress-stroke, however, is in recognising that she is an equivalent to the photograph, the picture or the piano in speaking of a past unchanged by the war: 'In the general reconstruction of the plantation which immediately followed the surrender, a nice cabin, pleasantly appointed, was set apart for the old woman.' Old Aunt Peggy herself is an ornament, a curiosity; her presence reminds the white family of their former status as slave-holders, it reminds them of the loyalty they once commanded and, crucially for Aunt Peggy's purposes, it allows them the luxury of continuing to keep one person at least 'in idleness'.[11] Chopin's fiction in general is not concerned with things, with material possessions; her fiction is uncluttered with the sort of physical detail that in lesser writers might be used to indicate character, scene or age. If things are important in post-war Louisiana it is because the state is full of broken things, of derelict shacks and plantations gone to ruin; where things are whole they are at the heart of conflict in the narrative – as in 'A Dresden Lady in Dixie', 'A Very Fine Fiddle' or, as discussed, in 'Old Aunt Peggy' where the possession of certain artefacts, lined up beside the possession of children, is an indicator of the value system of a whole culture.

The last of the short short stories I consider to be centrally concerned with the question of race and individual freedom is 'A

Little Free-Mulatto'. Caught between the black and the white, too 'proud' to be either, the Jean-Ba' family are bound by their colour, by their position in between 'the big house' of the whites and the 'cabin doors' of the blacks. They are forced into isolation by the fear of what it might mean to cross boundaries, to relax one's sense of difference from both white and black. The real victim of this 'unyielding pride' is Aurélia, the child, the future of the South. It is only when the family move to 'paradise', 'L'Isle des Mulâtres', that Aurélia is allowed to conduct relationships with people outside her family. Paradise here then is the place where difference is eradicated or never existed, paradise is monochrome; in paradise pride need not exist but unfortunately paradise here is predicated on removal and isolation.

In this story of four hundred words Chopin manages to give a picture of the South which speaks vastly beyond itself. The first thing we learn about M'sié Jean-Ba' is that his appearance is painstakingly 'fine and imposing', that it is constructed upon the fact that he could, if he so wished, travel 'in the car "For Whites"'. As Aurélia sits with her mother 'There seemed to be nothing for her to do in the world but to have her shiny hair plaited', and whilst the shininess of her hair is a representative detail of her physical type, she nevertheless shines alone. There is 'nothing' for her in the 'world' outside but isolation which is self-imposed but reinforced by the colour-coded structure of society, a structure kept in place by the maintenance of difference. Race here, as in 'The Bênitous' Slave' and 'Old Aunt Peggy', is everything, it is the determining and determinant factor in a Louisiana life. In all three instances, in order to free themselves from the limitations of race, the protagonists have to embed themselves more firmly into their colour, to become more narrowly defined by their assigned social and ethnic rôles. As Chopin says in 'Old Aunt Peggy', at regular intervals the old woman 'delivers the stereotyped address',[12] she must act the part she was once assigned and has now made work for her benefit. Old Uncle Oswald can only rest when his physical location matches his doggedly maintained sense of identity and Aurélia's family need to eradicate difference from their lives in order to 'breathe an atmosphere which is native to them.'[13]

The whole history and legacy of Louisiana slavery is contained within these brief tales; each fable, sketch or yarn is a palimpsest upon the primary story of racial division and inequality that is the story of the South. As I have already indicated, Chopin's short

short stories are most properly read with the sort of attention which we might give to the lyric poem and nothing better illustrates this imperative than the stories which deal with race. The individual word demands attention, its range of inference is the means by which the reader can attain some sort of sense of the rôle of character and event, type and typology within a larger frame of reference than the few hundred words on the page would seem to promise at first glance. The fact of slavery is the prior event which determines the course of any action reported in the story; without the cultural referents of slavery and emancipation the tales would be simple homilies on the subjects of freedom, loyalty, cunning or pride; with those referents, however, there is a whole culture to be surveyed.

The same can be said of stories which do not deal with questions of ethnicity but with other forms of inequality and oppression. One of Chopin's most economically eloquent short stories is 'Doctor Chevalier's Lie' written in 1891 and published in *Vogue* in 1893.[14] A great deal of its cogency inheres in Chopin's limpid deployment of the strategy which also effects the realisation and subsequent dismantling of the stereotypical in the short short stories which are principally concerned with race. The predictable course of action, the enactment of expected social rôle or fulfilment of stereotype – all these are undermined and interrogated by the embedding in the narrative of dissonances which take the form of both indeterminacy of meaning and also authorial insistence upon uniqueness or individuality. The whole of 'Doctor Chevalier's Lie' is organised so as to question the cliché upon which the story depends. Chopin sets the reader up to expect sameness: 'The quick report of a pistol rang through the quiet Autumn night. It was no unusual sound in the unsavory quarter where Dr Chevalier had his office. Screams commonly went with it. This time there had been none', but quickly establishes difference. The story is predicated on absolute predictability and yet contains within it the capacity to acknowledge what is distinct or even unique. As the shot is heard so 'The doctor closed the book over which he had lingered so late, and awaited the summons that was almost sure to come' – the contiguity of 'almost' and 'sure' providing that moment of hesitation for the reader to be prepared to resist the movement toward closure – the closure of possibility, of interpretation and of story. Is the doctor expecting this particular death? Is this why he has 'lingered so late'? If we read this story with a total susceptibility to inference then there is barely a sentence, barely a word which is without ambiguity. Whilst Chopin uses a descriptive language which seems not to admit any possibility but the inevitable – the 'sameness of detail', 'The same scurrying', 'oft-recurring events', 'same groups of tawdry, frightened women', leading up to 'a dead girl stretched somewhere' – the precipitate qualities of the syntax prepare the reader for the divergences from the stereotypical which are both imminent and immanent. The generic nature of the case is forced to yield to the specific as the doctor looks at a body which he expects to be semiotically as well as physically dead, but finds that it has signification as an individual life speaking as it does of another social context. Chopin moves into the open, using straight-forward denial: 'and yet it was not the same.... Yet it was different.... This one was not' to refute the reader's expectations.

The girl's family, recollected by the Doctor, are the archetypal homesteaders, representative, even mythic American figures, articulated through the indefinite article and cliché: 'A little sister or two; a father and mother – coarse and bent with toil'. Chopin paces her explanation of the girl's background so that the claim that 'their handsome girl...was too clever to stay in an Arkansas cabin', seems in many ways the most predictable part of the family saga of log-cabin to big city. The recognition on the part of Dr Chevalier that the inevitable narrative which takes a girl from the country to the whore-house is, however, changed by his personal knowledge of this girl's previous life, changed by the presence of the prior event behind and within the text which places the destruction and death of the woman in the context of her family's great expectations of life in the city. He thus alters the outcome of the tale; he wrenches the predictable story of the fallen woman away from its usual ending and gives it the closure which rightfully belongs to another story. He engages in the rituals associated with another kind of death: the death that celebrates the untimely end of another fictional construct – the dutiful daughter, the pure woman – so as to allow the Arkansas family to mourn the live girl they knew, not the dead girl the hard facts of life in the city made her: 'The following day he wrote a letter. One, doubtless to carry sorrow, but no shame to the cabin down there in the forest. It told that the girl had sickened and died. A lock of hair was sent and other trifles with it. Tender last words were even invented.'

The story in this way becomes the Doctor's and his rewriting of it shifts attention to the effect that the events of the night have or may have on his reputation. The chief focus of the local audience for the girl's story is not the number of deaths in this quarter of the city, not the particular death of this girl, but the extent of the Doctor's involvement in the death. However, it transpires that any sign of concern from Dr Chevalier, any evidence of a compassionate response to an individual case is sufficient to discredit him in the public eye but not enough to disgrace him.

The shocking event here is not the fact of death, that is too predictable to be worthy of notice from writer or audience, but the fact that the Doctor treated a death in this quarter as a unique event, not as an unremarkable and inevitable part of his night's work. The Doctor, the professional man, is the object of interest, not the serial production of corpses in the 'unsavory quarter'. Women like this girl, with her origination in the Arkansas cabin, are not usually allowed to have the dignity of a story, the story belongs to the doctor whose reputation may be affected. The extent of the cynicism and corruption in society at large is revealed by the general apathy over the dead girl and the irony that the doctor may indeed have had something to do with her death, may indeed have been responsible for ruining her – he says 'I knew her well', and may not be telling an untruth. No-one is willing to investigate the rumours in order to confirm or deny, however: 'Shoulders were shrugged. Society thought of cutting him. Society did not, for some reason or other, so the affair blew over.'[15] The tidying up of the girl's ending for the audience in the Arkansas cabin only serves to vex and discomfit the audience in the city and indeed, the reader. It only takes one girl to be distinguished from the crowd, one corpse to have a number of different stories attached to it, to prove that all girls, all tales of coming to the city, are capable of individual interpretation.

The story of old Uncle Oswald seems to prove that he is one among many: 'No-one took the slightest notice of the old negro drowsing over the cane that he held between his knees. The sight was common in Natchitoches',[16] but the telling of the tale of his life gives him an individuality as well as a representative function, it shifts his generic status from being one among many to being the one among many whose story speaks most forcefully of the disempowering of individual identity in Southern society. 'Dr Chevalier's Lie', with a luminous brevity, illustrates one of the central hypocrisies of Chopin's age, that sex had never been more widely available and yet had never been less discussed or even acknowledged in polite society. It may be the case that the girl was known to Dr Chevalier in the city as well as the country, that he facilitated her instalment in the brothel, that he knew of her suicidal feelings and therefore awaited the call on that night; he would not be alone in using the services of prostitutes but one of many professional men who frequented the whore-house.[17] Conversely, he may not have seen her between the hunting trip and the night of her death, in which case he is a man capable of putting his own reputation at risk for the sake of bringing comfort to those in rural Arkansas who still believe in some American dream of freedom, opportunity and success, even for women. Chopin does not privilege or preclude either explanation.

Whilst not concerned with the matters of life and death which absorb Dr Chevalier, the story 'A Harbinger', published in the *St Louis Magazine* in 1891[18] does treat, through the story of a summer infatuation, the distortions and impositions which a single point of view can have on a subject and the subject is again a woman who has no voice in the narrative. Chopin end stops the story at the outset, delimiting our responses: 'Bruno did very nice work in black and white; sometimes in green and yellow and red. But he never did anything quite so clever as during that summer he spent in the hills.' From the beginning he is quantifiable and the story seems to be closed; he will 'never' do anything so 'clever' or 'nice' again as he once did in a particular summer. This paragraph is the opening parenthesis around the story before Bruno becomes the centre of consciousness: remembering what it was like for him that summer, recollecting the influence that his time in the hills had upon him but not upon others. There is no room for Chopin's overview in the middle portion of the story, the perspective we are offered on past events is entirely Bruno's. He thinks about Diantha exclusively in terms of his feelings for her and effect upon her. He dwells in the world of means whereby his part in her awakening is somehow without end; she will never, it seems to Bruno, move beyond that significant moment without him being there to witness and guide her development.

This short short story contains within it a very good example of Chopin's ability to derive the maximum possibility from the placing of quite simple words in positions which vex straightforward readings. She says: 'The big city seemed too desolate for endurance often' when describing Bruno's winter mood, the placing of 'often' at the end of the sentence rather than after 'The big city' drawing attention to the specific and numerous occasions upon which he felt 'desolate' rather than the general condition of desolation being felt by all who live in the city. The adverbial phrase is distinguished by its placing at the end, it arrests attention and draws inferences rather than resting unobtrusively in a sentence which would read 'The big city often seemed too desolate for endurance.' Chopin's prose is brilliantly compressed here, taking us to the end of Bruno's summer with Diantha at the same time as it addresses its beginning and duration. Diantha is endlessly available for him: she 'posed for him when he wanted', and like the artist and creator of effect that he is, or once was, he expects to find the picture as he left it, waiting for him to put the finishing touches. Diantha, the wild flower of his imagination, however, appears at the centre of another type of painting, the village wedding; she has been 'gathered' and transformed into 'a white-robed lily'.

Chopin closes her parentheses: 'Foolish Bruno! to have been only love's harbinger after all! He turned away. With hurried strides he descended the hill again, to wait by the big water-tank for a train to come along.' The closure of the story is inherent in the structure that encases Bruno's version of events; Chopin has a point to make in her visible containment of the tale but the point, as usual, is slippery. Does the story advocate *carpe diem*, does it demonstrate the fickleness of women, does it mimic the summer itself in its description of an infatuation that must end with the season? It is perhaps in the parentheses around the story that the most linguistic clues can be found – at the margins of narrative. At the beginning Chopin patronises Bruno: his work is 'very nice', it is 'clever'; at the end she makes her contempt more visible: 'Foolish Bruno!'. He has indulged himself that his own perspective, that of the artist, is the only one of importance; Chopin offers us a distance on his view of the hills, it is not all picturesque – it has the prosaic 'big water-tank' as well as its 'delicate-leafed maples',[19] and, above all else, it is not static.

The aesthetic that would freeze Diantha in time would probably disdain to treat the subject of another of Chopin's short short stories as fit to feature as the heroine of a romance. In the case of 'Juanita' the brevity of the form allows Chopin to take this unlikely heroine and make of her the centre of many different tales. This story was published in the Philadelphia journal, *Moods*, in 1895[20] with the reflective piece, 'The Night Came Slowly', which I intend to discuss alongside 'Juanita' as they were written as well as published together. Juanita is a character who would be at home in an urban myth: everybody knows someone who claims to know what her life is like and how she manages to attract so many and varied suitors – the 'wealthy South Missouri farmer', the 'Texan millionaire who possessed a hundred white horses', in despite of 'her five-feet-ten, and more than two hundred pounds of substantial flesh...clad in a soiled "Mother Hubbard"'. There are more people willing to tell tales about Juanita than can be counted, and it is these chattering classes that Chopin is rebuking in 'The Night Came Slowly' with her railing against both books and men. Juanita, with inscrutable if not invisible intent has disdained the attentions of the high and mighty and has, instead, fixed her affections on a 'one-legged man' who, by all accounts, seems to combine both physical and financial undesirability. Juanita's preference for 'the one-legged man' over and above her more prestigious suitors is almost the stuff of faery as 'They go off into the woods together where they may love each other away from all prying eyes save those of the birds and the squirrels. But what do the squirrels care!'.

The reasons for Juanita's choice are not a part of the story and thus are removed from any consideration except to consign them to the realms of the mythic – urban or otherwise – through the description of the ridiculous picture which the vast Juanita and her incomplete and withered spouse present. What does concern Chopin centrally in the story is the rôle of audience in making and pursuing narrative, a procedure followed with energy but without success in attaining a sense of the truth about the disposal of Juanita's affections. The whole town of Rock Springs has witnessed the efforts of those who court Juanita unsuccessfully. These proceedings, conducted largely in public, it seems, are reported by any number of people, the general proliferation of voices ready to speak on the subject being effectively communicated by Chopin's use of the passive voice – 'It was ...said', 'she was said', 'it was learned', 'as was proven' – the movement toward 'proven' parallelling the movement from conjecture to fact. The fact of the 'baby', however, is tempered by the enduring mystery of the 'wandering preacher', the 'secret marriage' and the 'lost certificate'. But the narrator seems willing to let them go and as Juanita and her husband move out of range of the 'prying eyes'[21] and into the natural world they follow the path that Chopin tries to pursue in

'The Night Came Slowly', away from the world of moral judgements into the natural world of physical sensation.

This piece is constructed, like 'A Harbinger', inside a frame, here
a frame of social reference, whilst the inner text constitutes what
amounts to a guided sexual fantasy through the night-time world
of nature. The parenthesis serves as a dismissal of mankind and its
clumsy attempts to understand both human and Mother nature but
the interior monologue which follows – descriptive and sentient
though it is – cannot quite eliminate the social world as it intrudes
as both reference point and physical presence. Here is the whole
story:

> I am losing my interest in human beings; in the significance of
> their lives and their actions. Some one has said it is better to
> study one man than ten books. I want neither books nor men;
> they make me suffer. Can one of them talk to me like the night –
> the Summer night? Like the stars or the caressing wind?
>
> The night came slowly, softly, as I lay out there under the
> maple tree. It came creeping, creeping stealthily out of the valley,
> thinking I did not notice. And the outlines of trees and foliage
> nearby blended in one black mass and the night came stealing
> out from them, too, and from the east and west, until the only
> light was in the sky, filtering through the maple leaves and a star
> looking down through every cranny.
>
> The night is solemn and it means mystery.
>
> Human shapes flitted by like intangible things. Some stole up
> like little mice to peep at me. I did not mind. My whole being
> was abandoned to the soothing and penetrating charm of the
> night.
>
> The katydids began their slumber song: they are at it yet. How
> wise they are. They do not chatter like people. They tell me only:
> "sleep, sleep, sleep." The wind rippled the maple leaves like
> little warm love thrills.
>
> Why do fools cumber the earth! It was a man's voice that broke
> the necromancer's spell. A man came today with his "Bible
> Class." He is detestable with his red cheeks and bold eyes and
> coarse manner and speech. What does he know of Christ? Shall I
> ask a young fool who was born yesterday and will die tomorrow
> to tell me things of Christ? I would rather ask the stars: they have
> seen him.[22]

The lyrical interior text is a Whitmanesque, erotically charged account of communion with the natural world. Syntactically the second paragraph of the story works just as a poem by Whitman works, with the mass of observed detail taking the reader into the night scene, adding and expanding until the terrestrial, 'the maple tree' gives way to the cosmic, 'the star' but never without losing a sense of the 'I' speaker, the seeing and sentient eye. From the 'caressing wind', through the narcotic injunctions of the katydids to the 'little warm love thrills', the speaker is abandoned to an ecstasy of sensation which is powerful enough to resist the intrusion of the voyeurs who 'peep' at the prone figure enjoying the amorous attentions of the night.

So, where is story or plot in all this? Does this piece contain either character or action? What seems to be the most powerful plot is prior – 'they make me suffer' – and the railing against the intruder with his ' "Bible Class" ' and his ignorance builds on this picture of world-weariness and even anger against the works of man and humankind's unceasing attempts to account for the ways of the natural as well as human world. The only action in the story is in the sensations experienced by the monologuist whilst lying beneath the tree. Chopin's version of transcendentalism, like Whitman's,[23] is expressed in the expansion of the individual consciousness into the natural world, but it is not an unequivocal celebration of all constituents of the cosmos; the plots which are hinted at – the events of both today and yesterday – serve to exclude 'human beings' from the eulogy addressed to the night. The character which is developed is that of the narrator; world-weary, cynical toward organised religion, unafraid to take bold action yet oppressed by social mores. Like Juanita at the end of her story, riding off into the woods, the narrator attempts to lose self-consciousness through immersion in nature, but whilst Juanita has the advantage of silence, the narrator here has the responsibility of language. Chopin could have written a poem about the night – she wrote poetry throughout her life – but she did not, she wrote a story and thus the frame around the pæan to nature is as important as the celebration of the sensual effects of the natural world in darkness. Any encounter with the natural world is inevitably affected by the contingencies of the social world; the monologue is not only framed by the narrator's disenchantment with humanity, it is intruded upon by voyeurs; the lyrical tribute to the 'Summer night' cannot be sustained beyond brevity, the plottings and interpretation of the human world will always be present and always intrude.

Chopin's 1893 piece 'An Idle Fellow' is in many ways from the same mould as 'The Night Came Slowly'. This monologue, rejected by seven magazines before she gave up trying to have it published,[24] places the experience of the scholar up against that of the people watcher, locating the secret of 'the language of God' in the man who communes with his fellow men rather than with the scholarly wisdom of ages. The 'idle fellow'[25] resists instruction from the scholar, he is endlessly distracted by the variety of the natural world and whilst this is first presented as a sign of mental weakness, of a superficial intelligence, by the end the narrator has come around to the idea that there might be alternative forms of wisdom, that Paul's knowledge is as profound and as important as any which could be garnered from dedicated scholarship.

The narrative impetus is very much the same as in 'The Night Came Slowly' only it is the social world which is here celebrated, the insights which one human being has into the heart of another. It is a different constituent of Chopin's larger portrayal of the dangers and intemperances which arise from the pursuit of a single point of view. The relentless devotion to a fixed idea, like that of white supremacy for Armand in 'Désirée's Baby' or an obsession, like that which develops in the widower in the story 'Her Letters', is always ruinous. Chopin's stories and sketches have, with an overwhelming consistency, structural and linguistic adherences to multiplicity of perspective. The genre of the short story in her hands becomes not only the vehicle for the tale but the means by which the form itself is critiqued, its limitations tested and its margins stretched.

The tale of 'Boulôt and Boulotte' is a good illustration of what Chopin could do with the limits of a story which has been most usually described as a vignette of Louisiana life. Published in *Harper's Young People* in 1891[26] and singled out for special praise by W.D. Howells,[27] this piece has been read straightforwardly as a sketch which exposes the foolishness of the children in not wearing the new shoes that the narrator tells us they are ready for: 'When Boulôt and Boulotte, the little piny-wood twins, had reached the dignified age of twelve, it was decided in family council that the time had come for them to put their little naked feet into shoes.' It is, of course, a good joke that the children do not wear their shoes but there is a larger significance to the story which tells of their reluctance to begin wearing them. Once they put them on they are no longer those equal and indistinguishable beings, 'the piny-wood twins', they are man and woman. Boulôt with his 'fine stout brogans' and Boulotte, whose shoes 'are of the glossiest, with the highest of heels and brightest of buttons' can never be the same again once they cross the gender divide marked by their footwear. The shoes are synechdochic of all that is gendered in the adult life which is about to be embarked upon. The equality of the activities through which they raised the money to buy the shoes, the indistinguishability of the appearance of one from the other – 'two brown-skinned, black-eyed 'Cadian roly-polies' – even their solidarity, their ability to tell the same story, will now disappear as one will wear shoes to carry him through the dust whilst the other will wear shoes she will be afraid to 'ruin in de dus'.[28]

Chopin prepares us for the coming differentiation of the twins by the first glimpse that their assembled siblings have of them as they come through the trees; as 'Boulotte's blue sun-bonnet appeared, and Boulôt's straw-hat' so we are alerted to the differences which already exist in their appearances when facing the outside world. An even more significant division will be the result of the final assignment of one of them to the realm of the functional and one to the decorative. Both hat and shoe are at once symbolic of their sex and their destiny. Boulotte, 'mistress of the situation', can think of every reason why her shoes, made to be pretty not practical, should not be worn in the dust, Boulôt, on the other hand, can only look 'sheepishly down at his bare feet'. There is, of course, no reason why the walk home from town through the woods could not be carried out in his 'fine stout brogans'[29] but once Boulotte puts on her shoes the walk will never again be as free from restraint as it was on that day. The profound implications of the apparently simple act of buying the twins' first shoes, for this reader at least, moves 'Boulôt and Boulotte' out of the category of sketch or vignette, and into story. With the purchase of the shoes things have irrevocably changed, the rites of passage into adulthood have begun.

The month before 'Boulôt and Boulotte' appeared, the same magazine, *Harper's Young People*, published Chopin's story 'A Very Fine Fiddle'.[30] Richard Fusco, in *Maupassant and the American Short Story: The Influence of Form at the Turn of the Century*, links this story to Maupassant's 'Les Bijoux' in terms of its 'contrast technique' and in so doing he distinguishes it from other stories written by her at roughly the same time. Whilst I dissent from Fusco's view that short short stories like 'Boulôt and Boulotte' and 'The Bênitous' Slave' have 'plots so unadorned that they verge on retreating from fiction back to the expository essay' and his other assertion that 'In these simple stories Chopin does not employ structure to attack manners, behavior, or customs',[31] his observations on Chopin's use and development of Maupassantian techniques in 'A Very Fine Fiddle' do open up interpretative possibilities. Fusco categorises 'Les Bijoux' as a 'contrast text', by which he means that instead of concentrating upon the moment in the narrative when some sort of change is effected, 'a contrast story shifts our focus away from the change itself to the consequences of that change.'[32] In this way the story thus encompasses a before and after structure for interpretation – as does, I would argue, 'Boulôt and Boulotte' – but in 'A Very Fine Fiddle' the contrast structure is more transparent, with the turning point being the sale of the violin. This sale forces the reader back to scrutinise the issues which are raised in the first part of the story in the light of the second. What price art or the aesthetic if children are cold and hungry? What kind of symbol is the violin in this community? In belonging to a European past, as witnessed by its quality, its age and its rarity, what relevance has it in the log cabin which is predicated as a very separate space even from 'the big plantation'?

Like Mr Shimerda in Willa Cather's 1917 novel, *My Antonia*, old Cléophas is not good for much in the New World except to play the violin in order to forget present misery and remember a past in which different values had potency. The story opens: 'When the half dozen little ones were hungry' a regular occurrence then, and one which is not followed by 'their father took up his gun and went hunting' or anything which addresses physical need, but with 'old Cléophas would take the fiddle from its flannel bag and play a tune upon it'. From the outset Chopin weighs practical necessity against the aesthetic, old Cléophas's sufficiency as a provider against the fact of his children's hunger: 'Perhaps it was to drown their cries, or their hunger, or his conscience, or all three.' The reading position of the audience is thus controlled by a symmetry in the writing which constantly weighs necessity against art. Old Cléophas is clearly an inadequate parent; Fifine has to take responsibility for the welfare of her siblings, and she identifies the fiddle with the taking of avoiding action by her father, as a thing which is out of context and thus useless to the family in their situation of need. The 'flannel bag' which Chopin is careful to mention twice, even in so brief a tale, marks it out as special, as protected and privileged in the protection it is given in contrast to the children who, we later learn, have 'bare feet' as well as 'hungry mouths', and their home, which needs a new roof. Like the father in the story 'A Rude Awakening', also published in 1891, who is brought to a sense of his responsibilities for his family by the shock of losing his daughter, albeit temporarily, old Cléophas is forced into re-arranging his priorities but the nature of the change is of the soul rather than the conscience here. The loss of the fiddle and its history is not underestimated by Chopin; she allows old Cléophas the last word: ' "I b'lieve, me, I ain' goin' play de fiddle no mo' " ' – his aesthetic life will be impoverished by the change but the quality of life for five children will be enriched.

The finely maintained balance in the writing here is such that where Richard Fusco sees Fifine as 'aggressive and tone-deaf' I read her as desperate and rightly outraged at her father's sense of priorities; there is room for both interpretations here. Where Fusco sees the story as centrally concerned with 'the survivability of artistic sensibilities in a hostile environment'[33] I see it as a more tentative text which treats the impossibility of making the choice between the pursuit of art and the quotidien demands of everyday life. When Paula von Stoltz in Chopin's early story 'Wiser Than A God' chooses the musician's career over that of wife, she has only herself to consider. She is not responsible for anyone else and so can be free to be the artist who 'dares and defies' as Mademoiselle Reisz would have it in *The Awakening*.[34] The story of 'A Very Fine Fiddle' is necessarily more equivocal, balancing as it does the claims of 'hungry mouths' against a 'lustreless instrument'[35] in the precarious lives of old Cléophas's children. Chopin makes no judgements, presents no moral and leaves us to weigh art against necessity.

Written at the same time as 'The Bênitous' Slave' and 'Old Aunt Peggy', indeed, all, according to Emily Toth, written in two days in a burst of creativity in January 1892,[36] 'A Turkey Hunt' is another anecdotal story which relies upon the outside perspective of the narrator to eschew vignette and endow complexity upon the narrative. Like the tale of 'Juanita', the story here centres on a local character, Artemise, a notoriously work-shy member of a plantation household. The members of this household, all of whom are deployed in the turkey hunt which forms the main action of the story, are strictly divided by the way in which they are identified. The I speaker is never named, Monsieur and Madame are known simply by these titles, sufficient as they are to denote their status and separate them from the rest of the household who are all known by their first names. Artemise, again like Juanita, an unpromising subject for the limelight, is placed at the centre of the narrative. The matter of the turkey hunt begins and ends the story, reported in the past tense, but the introductory description of Artemise and her ways is conducted in the present, in a compelling tone which offers a real mystery to be solved: 'Artemise is in some respects an extraordinary person. In age she is anywhere between ten and fifteen, with a head not unlike in shape and appearance to a dark chocolate-colored Easter-egg. She talks almost wholly in monosyllables, and has big, round glassy eyes, which she fixes upon one with the placid gaze of an Egyptian sphinx.'

What is 'extraordinary' about Artemise is the paucity of facts known about her and offered by her; sphinxlike indeed, she never volunteers information but only responds to questions and instructions in the most literal and minimal way. She is apparently the least important member of the household: she is the only one of those referred to by her first name without a household designation to follow it: 'Alice, the housemaid', 'Polisson, the yard-boy', 'Aunt Florindy, the cook'. She evades categorisation just as she evades the carrying out of instructions and is possibly the smartest or the stupidest person on the plantation – no-one knows. The turkey hunt itself is barely of interest; even Chopin concedes at the beginning that if Christmas were not imminent, it would be of no interest. What is of interest here, however, are the dynamics of the plantation household: the way in which its members are named, the silence surrounding certain types of knowledge – Artemise's age for instance – and the terms of her existence. She is seemingly functionless and at random within its structure, sleeping '"In uh hole"' – 'the hall'[37] – and endlessly in search of a private space in which to tuck herself away. She sleeps in the area which everyone walks through and where the family assembles, and is sent from there to do the bidding of whoever happens to be passing; she is without a fixed meaning, unlabelled, unlocalised and always enigmatic.

Two other stories written in the early part of 1892 are also concerned with the way in which tales are told and then immediately changed by the apprehensions of both internal and external audiences. 'The Turkey Hunt' becomes Artemise's story because of narratorial bias but 'Croque-Mitaine' and 'Ripe Figs' use the tension between those designated as tellers and those who are told to tease out the difference which arises between narrative intention and actual reception. The brief 'Ripe Figs' eventually published in *Vogue*[38] in August 1893, is a very simple tale which uses the rhythm of country life and particularly seasonal change, to mark out times of significance in the social world. Whilst the figs ripen all too quickly for the adult, Maman-Nainaine, they take what seems to be an age to Babette, eager as she is to make the visit to her cousins. This gentle, lyrical story sets in opposition the perspectives of youth and age upon the passage of time, the processes of growth and fruition are the focus for their antithetical comprehensions of time. In attaching the condition of change to the natural world Maman-Nainaine has chosen something visible and local which is also capable of registering two dramatically different temporal positions. In the story 'Croque-Mitaine', however, the Parisian governess makes a number of obvious mistakes with her choice of story, chief amongst which is its lack of local authenticity.

In order to verify the tale of 'Croque-Mitaine' P'tit Paul goes naturally to those who know both the landscape and its indigenous stories and thus the location of all supernatural beings – 'The darkies'. Their denial of the existence of any such 'hideous ogre' emboldens P'tit Paul sufficiently to check the truth of the tale for himself and he is rewarded by its enactment and subsequent deconstruction: 'Then a most singular thing happened. Croque-Mitaine stood still in the road, rested his pitch-fork, and removing his hideous face, began to mop his head with the flag of truce!'. The removal of the head and the revelation of 'Monsieur Alcée going to a masked ball'[39] is sufficient to put P'tit Paul and his siblings in charge of the governess and her power as a storyteller. They will not be frightened again because they now know that there is a banal and very local explanation for the monster. This story asks its readers to consider the terms and conditions upon which stories are authenticated. Superstition is expected to be the province of the slaves or ex-slaves because real knowledge, education, has always been denied to them. Their technique for dealing with a fear that could become all-consuming, that is, the total lack of control over their own lives, is to delimit the places where the fearful lurks. This attempt at control is also exercised by the child. He takes steps to satisfy himself that this new story does not contain that which will really threaten him and thus his only source of dissatisfaction with the governess is removed. The landscape is susceptible to story and, indeed, a new one is generated by the appearance of Monsieur Alcée, but it is also susceptible to individual interpretation. What we think we understand as a given, a specific, like the revelation to P'tit Paul that 'Croque-Mitaine' is Monsieur Alcée, is just another fiction and as such, as precarious a foundation for certainty as any other.

The imminence of the end in Kate Chopin's short short stories makes us alert to the connotations of every word but also to the transactions which must take place between writer and reader. There is a responsibility to read carefully, to look for the reasons why the storyteller might wish to choose this brief form over other more fully developed narrative genres and, as I mentioned at the outset, a careful attention paid to structure and language in these brief tales is good preparation for reading in detail in the longer works. The pieces discussed here, without exception, deserve the dignity of the title of story in their power both to reveal and develop our apprehensions about character and event. They reverberate byond their local significance; the buying of the shoes becomes the act of growing up into pre-ordained gendered rôles, the death of a whore provokes a look at the moral values of a whole society, the fable of a caged beast speaks of the terms in which a society chooses to describe the crucial difference between confinement and self-determination.

The power of the signifying detail should not be underestimated in Kate Chopin; she never fails to give us the tools with which to interpret her fictional world. She did purvey Louisiana whimsy to a Northern American audience but embedded within her texts is a far from whimsical frame of reference which speaks of a society which codifies discrimination and oppression, which rushes to judgement and which refutes the necessity for interpretation which might accommodate individual variation. Her stories are dense with meaning, but not one of those meanings is fixed or immutable. Local colour could, at first glance, seem to be at its most black and white in the short short stories but, as we saw in the story, 'A Little Free-Mulatto', only in paradise is the world so easily defined as one or the other. Everywhere else we are as semiotically confused as M'sie Jean-Ba' – not dignified by the full honorific of Monsieur but also not referred to by his unadorned first name – poised on the line between black and white and too 'proud' to yield to either interpretation. Chopin, as ever, leaves it up to us to choose – but only if we must.

Notes

1. See Kate Chopin's disclaimer of responsibility for the eventual fate of Edna Pontellier in *Book News* of May 28 1890 as reprinted in Seyersted, Per and Emily Toth (eds). *A Kate Chopin Miscellany* (Natchitoches: Northwestern State University Press, 1979), p. 137: 'Having a group of people at my disposal, I thought it might be entertaining (to myself) to throw them together and see what would happen. I never dreamed of Mrs. Pontellier making such a mess of things and working out her own damnation as she did. If I had had the slightest intimation of such a thing I would have excluded her from the company. But when I found out what she was up to, the play was half over and it was then too late.'
2. *A Kate Chopin Miscellany*, p. 119.
3. Lohafer, Susan *Coming to Terms with the Short Story* (Baton Rouge: Louisiana State University Press, 1983), p. 94.
4. *Coming to Terms with the Short Story*, pp. 18–24.
5. Emily Toth, *Kate Chopin*, p. 97.
6. *Complete Works*, p. 37.
7. Emily Toth dates this piece as having been written in late 1869 or 1870. *Kate Chopin* p. 414.
8. 'Emancipation. A Life Fable', *Complete Works*, pp. 37–8.
9. *A Kate Chopin Miscellany*, p. 92.
10. 'The Bênitous' Slave', *Complete Works*, pp. 189–90.
11. 'Old Aunt Peggy', *Complete Works*, p. 193.
12. *Complete Works*, p. 193.
13. 'A Little Free-Mulatto', *Complete Works*, pp. 202–3.
14. *Kate Chopin*, p. 415.
15. 'Dr Chevalier's Lie', *Complete Works*, pp. 147–8.
16. *Complete Works*, p. 190.
17. In her book *Divided Lives: American Women in the Twentieth Century* (London: Penguin Books Ltd., 1993), Rosalind Rosenberg says that at the turn of the century 'an estimated 70 percent of all white men' visited prostitutes 'at some point in their lives' (p. 13). In Ruth Rosen's book, *The Lost Sisterhood: Prostitution in America, 1900–1918*, Baltimore and London: Johns Hopkins University Press, 1982, there is a full account of the scale of prostitution in New Orleans, pp. 77–79.
18. *Kate Chopin*, p. 415.
19. 'A Harbinger', *Complete Works*, pp. 145–46.
20. *Kate Chopin*, p. 232.
21. 'Juanita', *Complete Works*, pp. 367–68.
22. 'The Night Came Slowly', *Complete Works*, p. 366.

23.   Much critical attention has been paid to the relationship between Chopin's work and the poetry of Walt Whitman, particularly the theme of awakening into a new, spiritual life as expressed, primarily, in *The Awakening*. See Leary, Lewis, *Southern Excursions: Essays on Mark Twain and Others* (Baton Rouge: Louisiana State University Press, 1971) and Ringe, Donald, 'Romantic Imagery in Kate Chopin's *The Awakening*', *American Literature* 43 (1972), pp. 580–8.

24.   *Kate Chopin*, p. 215.

25.   'An Idle Fellow', *Complete Works*, pp. 280–1.

26.   *Kate Chopin*, p. 193.

27.   *Kate Chopin*, p. 192.

28.   I am indebted to my colleague, Kevin McCarron, for ideas generated in a lively team-taught session on this and others of Chopin's short stories.

29.   'Boulôt and Boulotte', *Complete Works*, pp. 151–2.

30.   *Kate Chopin*, p. 415.

31.   Fusco, Richard *Maupassant and the American Short Story: The Influence of Form at the Turn of the Century* (University Park: The Pennsylvania State University Press, 1994), pp. 146–7.

32.   *Maupassant and the American Short Story: The Influence of Form at the Turn of the Century*, p. 64.

33.   *Maupassant and the American Short Story: The Influence of Form at the Turn of the Century*, p. 149.

34.   *Complete Works*, p. 946.

35.   'A Very Fine Fiddle', *Complete Works*, pp. 149–50.

36.   *Kate Chopin*, p. 206.

37.   'A Turkey Hunt', *Complete Works*, pp. 191–2.

38.   *Kate Chopin*, p. 207.

39.   'Croque-Mitaine', *Complete Works*, pp. 200–1.

5

Edith Wharton and the Coherence of the Novella: From Initiation to Disillusion

The three novellas I want to discuss here, *The Touchstone*, *Sanctuary* and *Madame de Treymes*, all date from the early part of Edith Wharton's career, between 1900 and 1907, when she was making the transition from short story to novel writing. The intermediate length and scope of the novella form allowed her to attain a coherence of design, language and content which is perhaps unparalleled in her other fiction. Wharton was, at this time, mapping out her fictional territory in both thematic and structural terms and whilst these novellas do not, perhaps, contain her most compelling narratives they have other claims to dynamism and distinctness. Amongst other significant features, the novellas share a central concern with problem solving, where the problem is articulated both as plot and structure; in other words, technical questions absorb Wharton in the construction of these texts and the solutions she comes up with deserve close attention.

The novella is, by its very nature, a compromise of a genre but in so being is also an enabling form and Wharton's use of it in these narratives and also in her later, linked novellas, *Old New York*, published in 1924, puts on display her ability to achieve a consonance of form and content. There are all sorts of intermediate features discernible in these novellas: they are middling sorts of narratives in terms of length and they are middling sorts of narratives in terms of tragic import; the characters are pretty mediocre representatives of the human race and are testamentary evidence to endurance rather than to excitement or fulfilment. Disappointment is clearly the keynote in all three stories and their very median nature reflects this, indicating something significant about the issue of structure and style in relation to content. They do, however, also contain within themselves indicators to the narrative organisation of much of Wharton's fiction, long and short, which centres on an achieved coherence of language and subject, of pace and narrative impetus. Whilst much of the narrative drive in these three texts is fuelled by a movement between initiation and disillusion, the writing itself moves between initiation and accomplishment, between the writing of the first and the last Wharton assumes control of her medium and her message. The problem she solves in these narratives is the one of how to order and consolidate subject, language and structure.

These three stories are all in some way concerned with failures of communication between people, a theme which haunted Edith Wharton throughout her writing career. She returned repeatedly in her fiction to the tragic consequences of the misunderstandings which arise between lovers and friends as easily as between strangers. In these novellas Wharton pays meticulous attention to her own language in order to foreground the inescapable imprecision of words which communicate emotion, using acts of speech and writing as indices of failure, not success, in making contact. Constant misunderstandings of words, signs and feelings distinguish her characters' dealings with each other. In *The Touchstone* Stephen Glennard can feel only 'inarticulate misery'[1] when remembering his relationship with the writer Margaret Aubyn. In *Sanctuary*, Kate Orme passes from co-habitation with one man to another – from father to husband to son – but can never say the things she means and be understood. Only as the story closes can she feel at last the response of a sympathetic intelligence but even then the understanding between her and her son is accomplished wordlessly by some sort of telepathic communion of a shared morality. In the tale of cross-cultural confusions, *Madame de Treymes*, the failure to understand the different uses to which two nations put their means of communication, whether words or signs, has the endlessly expansive American, John Durham, filling all the empty spaces of his native land with talk and the French family of Malrive reserving their few words as a means of maintaining, unbroken, their ancestral line and age-old practices of mystification.

The novellas have many common areas of interest, but they are given different treatments and different degrees of prominence in the telling of the individual tales. All focus centrally on moral dilemmas and the guilt and shame which accompany the choices we make. They all treat the secondary rôle that women invariably play in society, regardless of capability, the conflicts between private and public spheres and, most poignantly, the inevitable failure of romantic love in a world full of competing individual appetites and ambitions. In each instance the title of the novella is absolutely crucial in communicating a sense of the theme which comes to dominate the story; the titles resonate beyond the particular situation into a larger field of connotation and meaning. *The Touchstone* is a metaphor for a test of superlative quality or worth which can, by its very nature, exist only in the abstract. So Margaret Aubyn's love – exposed to public view in the publication of her letters – reveals an emotional as well as an artistic sensibility which has reached a pitch of perfection, but, both her self and her writing are wasted on a lover who cannot respond and an audience which can similarly never come up to her standards or expectations. The whole narrative is advanced on the proffering of oppositions to what Margaret Aubyn may or may not have been as played out in the central consciousness of the man who failed to love her. *Sanctuary* deals, quite literally, with places of safety, in both actual and figurative terms, as Kate Orme seeks to find a moral refuge for herself in the mission she undertakes. *Madame de Treymes* herself comes to embody all that is inexplicable in the organisation of upper-class French society, particularly as it affects women. From the very beginning of the novella Wharton sets in opposition the way in which the French and American nations communicate, making their differences, not merely of language but of intent, meaning, and signification, the central point of both mystery and conflict; Madame de Treymes is the person who, to tragic purpose, most nearly embodies the strengths and weaknesses of the 'common principle of authority'[2] to which all subscribe.

   The Touchstone has always received a good deal of attention from critics who are concerned with Wharton's biography as well as her fiction.[3] My reading of the novella does not ignore the resonances of the story of Margaret Aubyn in relation to Wharton's own history but takes some of the issues with which Wharton, as beginning novelist, was grappling, both in her professional and private life, and examines them as they feature as aesthetic considerations. *The Touchstone* is, above all else, predicated on tension, upon oppositions; Margaret Aubyn and Alexa Glennard are set up as antithetical and from this all other polarities flow. The use of counteraction is not only thematic, however, but structural, allowing Wharton a clear and progressive series of contrasts through which to develop the narrative: literariness and non-literariness, plainness and beauty, 'intellectual audacity'[4] and 'smiling receptivity',[5] material and spiritual, public and private, unloved and beloved, the wealthy and the financially precarious and, centrally, the contested area of what constitutes the masculine and what the feminine.

In the opening section of the novella Wharton sets up the rivalries that will determine the course of events. Glennard, as the only reflector of the action, external and internal, is principally a generator of *bon mots* which remain undelivered, they are smugly retained as private epigrams and judgements which ensure his detachment and bolster his confidence and security in his private resolutions: 'There are times when the constancy of the woman one cannot marry is almost as trying as that of the woman one does not want to'.[6]

Stephen Glennard is the textual authority on the question of what women are, and his essentialist pronouncements on the nature of the female of the species are used to shore up the failing sense of both emotional and intellectual certainty in his own life. His financial incapacity to marry Alexa Trent is expressed by negative and negating definition against Margaret Aubyn; without the consent of either woman he sets them up in competition for his favours, talking of 'rival' and 'foil',[7] constructing a relationship between them which does not exist except in his own internal dialectic. Thus, his refusal to love one of the pre-eminent women of the age actually becomes the means by which he can maintain the myth of his own proactivity, the illusion of having the ability to make choices which sustains his idea of masculine superiority in a world which is populated by men who are more successful and wealthy than he is.

The Touchstone is full of references to what women are, are supposed to be, and, most significantly in terms of the use of such generalisations in the text, to their weaknesses, weaknesses that are gender-specific. We hear early on about an 'intuitive feminine justness that is so much rarer than a reasoned impartiality';[8] this is followed by 'if man is at times indirectly flattered by the moral superiority of woman, her mental ascendancy is extenuated by no such oblique tribute to her powers... brains, in a woman, should be merely the obverse of beauty'.[9] In larger gatherings we are introduced to 'the flitting inconsequences of the women' and Mrs Armiger, Mrs Touchett and Mrs Dresham are sneeringly dismissed: 'As to the other ladies of the party, they were simply the wives of some of the men – the kind of women who expect to be talked to collectively and to have their questions left un-answered'.[10] Alexa is not spared her husband's patronising reflections; she gives 'the feminine answer',[11] 'She had said the proper thing as she would have put on the appropriate gown or written the correct form of dinner invitation. Glennard had small faith in the abstract judgements of the other sex: he knew that half the women who were horrified by the publication of Mrs Aubyn's letters would have betrayed her secrets without a scruple',[12] and, most rancorously, 'What woman ever retained her abstract sense of justice where another woman was concerned? Possibly the thought that he had profited by Mrs Aubyn's tenderness was not wholly disagreeable to his wife'.[13] Wharton makes the generalisations incremental in order to chart the inescapable nature of the internal logic of Glennard's movement from the generic, through the species, to the individual – his wife – as his disdain, and his desperation, progresses. But the woman who is really at issue in all his judgements is Margaret Aubyn, all his opinions are expressed as contrapuntal to the woman who, until irretrievably *wronged* by the man – here through the publication of private letters – is positioned as unfeminine, as unattractive in her arrogation of the masculine prerogatives of superior cleverness and articulacy and is therefore not subject to the generalisations with which Glennard keeps the female world at a distance. Margaret Aubyn must become a helpless victim before she can be, in Glennard's terms, a proper woman: 'All that was feminine in her, the quality he had always missed, stole toward him from her unreproachful gaze.'[14]

The majority of Glennard's declarations, crucially, pertain to speech or felt responses; where women are concerned, unless they are uttering platitudes or sending their words out into a void from which they expect no reply, he is uncomfortable with them and the disdain he feels for that which he constructs as their predictability is a part of the machinery by which he sustains his own difference and distinction. It therefore becomes structurally inevitable that Wharton will position Glennard's personal crisis, the change on which this novella is suspended as fundamentally as any shorter story, around the question of what a woman may or may not say or write or even be. He comes to recognise, by the end, that he has used Margaret Aubyn as the touchstone for every judgement he delivers but that he has made her a negative touchstone. What is feminine, and crucially, what is desirable, has been articulated in contradistinction to Margaret and the only way to salvation, to the retrieval of his sense of 'self-esteem', is to recognise and act upon the achieved 'immense redistribution of meanings'[15] that makes her an individual, not the piece of 'public property'[16] that he has colluded in establishing.

Glennard has always proceeded, until the crisis brought on by the decision to publish Margaret Aubyn's letters, on the basis of total confidence in his own grounds for judgement. These grounds can be explicitly stated, as indeed they are, repeatedly, in the text, as represented by the unequal combat between 'looks and brains'[17] or pure intellect versus 'pure profile',[18] where reasoned argument and originality lose every round to the 'gift of silence'.[19] The most compelling part of the contest arranged here between intelligence and appearance is Wharton's aligning of the clever woman with the text, providing a metaphoric depth which complicates Glennard's attempts to define the woman as intuitive, reactive and decorative rather than intelligent and innovative. The fact that Margaret Aubyn, 'the poor woman of genius'[20] in Glennard's description, is an author, a creator in her own right, ensures her defeat on the terms he sets out with, because it is, in his value system, the province of the man to read, edit and interpret. It is only as the end result of a series of tragic misreadings of both himself and others that Glennard can give Margaret Aubyn authority as a far-seeing and effective creator and reader of men, one, after all, who finally achieves her ambition to form the spine of Glennard's sentient existence.

Central to the achieved structural, symbolic and thematic consonance of the novella is Barton Flamel's explanation of the relationship he has with his books: ' "Some men", Flamel irresistably added, "think of books merely as tools, others as tooling. I'm between the two; there are days when I use them as scenery, other days when I want them as society; so that, as you see, my library represents a makeshift compromise between looks and brains, and the collectors look down on me almost as much as the students" '.[21] By posing the question, what are books for? the text also asks what women are for. They are not, as the narrative sequence of *The Touchstone* demonstrates, to be set up as one thing or the other, as binary oppositions; they are not reducible to a single dimension because the formula will not hold. Margaret Aubyn is, by the end, established as a woman to love and be loved, not as a 'personage'

but a 'person'[22] with multiple meanings, not a single interpretation.
Where books are susceptible to misreading or even to treatment as
furniture or decoration rather than use, how much more vulnerable
are women, constantly articulated by Glennard as ornamental and
desirable only so long as they keep silence? He turns metafictioneer
in order to belittle Margaret Aubyn, as when he describes her
attempts to make herself into the woman of fashion: '. . . no woman
who does not dress well intuitively will ever do so by the light of
reason, and Mrs. Aubyn's plagiarisms, to borrow a metaphor of her
trade, somehow never seemed to be incorporated within the text.
Genius is of small use to a woman who does not know how to do
her hair'.[23] His obsession with looks and preference for surfaces
that betray no hint of what they might conceal is figured forth in
the text in language and imagery which signifies only wilful misunderstanding and misuse of the writer's vocabulary. He pillages
her lexis, jeering at the tropes of her 'trade' as he, safe in the self-
definition as 'not a man who concerned himself with literature',
rests assured in the confidence of his 'rational perspective'.[24]
Margaret Aubyn's letters are wrenched out of their private significance into the public arena: 'The little broken phrases fled across
the page like wounded animals in the open . . . helpless things
driven savagely out of shelter'[25] where they form a literal representation of thwarted communication but also the inescapable fact
that words, texts and even human lives mean different things to
different audiences and different times. Glennard rails against 'the
general futility of words',[26] language itself becoming the scapegoat
for his inadequacy to rise to Margaret Aubyn's expectations of him
until he acquires the humility necessary to learn 'the rudiments of a
new language'.[27]

In a further augmentation of the structural and thematic
exploration of estrangement and confusion much of the figurative
language which charts the breakdown of certainty in the second
half of the novella derives from landscape and the topographic, a
metaphoric feature which *The Touchstone* shares with *Sanctuary*
and, to a lesser extent, *Madame de Treymes*. Wharton offers the
human soul as 'an unmapped region, a few acres of which we have
cleared for our habitation; while of the nature of those nearest us
we know but the boundaries that march with ours';[28] not only are
people described in terms of their alien and alienating geographies
but they have unexplored regions even within themselves. The
exterior landscape, as the action progresses through a series of

public and semi-public spaces, acts chiefly to re-inforce the idea of
the irremediability of individual isolation as the most compelling
topographic tropes and images use the connotative power of the
public space to express the interior: 'He felt like an offender taken
down from the pillory and thrust into the soothing darkness of a
cell.'[29]

The novella chronicles a series of re-positionings and
adjustments brought about by a moral crisis which ends with the
re-locating of a once-perfect relationship on a lower level of fulfilment, a scenario familiar to readers of Wharton's later novels,
where the charting of such a process of disillusionment becomes
one of her most powerful and enduring themes. The oppositions
which seem so starkly delineated at the outset are unlearned by the
events following Glennard's decision to publish. He must convert
what was once ungratefully received, the 'gift of her imagination'[30]
into a channel of communication by which he can essay some
understanding of the complexities which underlie ' "The happiness
of giving" '.[31] The place where Glennard and his wife re-locate
their relationship, however, gives space to both parties to come to
an understanding of the compromises necessary to sustain a life
together. Partially freed from the imprisoning certainty and
smugness of his relentless reflex to judge and discriminate,
Glennard has to re-orientate himself in a world where things are
not as predictable as if they were oppositions; the edges are
blurred, divisions are indistinct and above all else, the 'distorting'
power of the single gender-biased point of view is recognised, even
if not relinquished: 'the woman's instinctive subjectiveness',[32] with
which he credits his wife, proves to be his final piece of essen-
tialism. This, as with all his dubious generalisations about women,
is refuted through the progressive revelation of the inadequacy of
his estimation of Margaret Aubyn, the touchstone again. As other
people read and interpret the letters so, ironically enough, their
private nature is revealed to him. His version of her has been that
she is a woman who falls short of the requirements for intimacy
because of the inescapably public nature of her utterances; what is
actually revealed through the process of real publicity is that she
can only be approached and known through the effect that she has
upon others.

There are no unqualified successes or happy endings in the three
novellas here discussed, unless the moral triumph at the close of
Sanctuary can be considered grounds for celebration of the human

capacity to be scrupulous and decent. This text has never received much praise from critics and Wharton's biographer, R.W.B.Lewis, reports that during its composition she referred to it as 'Sank' and, uncharacteristically, had very little to say about it once written and published.[33] I, however, have more than a few good words to say about *Sanctuary* which has a number of interesting and provocative features, not least of which is its innovative treatment of the question of the moral work of women in the culture. The premise upon which the plot is predicated is in many ways extraordinary and represents one of Wharton's boldest experiments, opening as it does with the purposeful exclusion of romantic love from consideration in the marriage plot. Additionally, in general terms, the novella treats a number of what would become Wharton's most recurrent themes, and also makes effective use of the satiric mode which would come to fruition in her 1913 novel, *The Custom of the Country*. The chief target of and vehicle for Wharton's satire in *Sanctuary* is Mrs Peyton Senior, with her self-serving delicacies and scruples, who also serves an important structural function not only as a point of moral contrast to Kate but also as an awful warning of what Kate might have become if she had not been awakened, before marriage, to the sordid contingencies of what is involved in the maintenance of the 'social health'.[34]

Another structural principle, used repeatedly in Wharton's later work, is also established in the novella where she draws powerful contrasts and imagery from language usually found in other contexts, for example in the law, commerce, science, anthropology or the church, but which has a particular relevance to the tale she is telling. In *Sanctuary* the languages of the law and the church predominate, Wharton incorporates them into the everyday speech of those involved in the working out of the central dramatic situation and is particularly insistent in her use of the full extent and range of words which denote places of safety, refuges both literal and metaphorical. This language not only extends and develops the central idea of sanctuary but helps to define what we attempt when we seek clarification of essential moral questions – those which are at the heart of our legal and religious systems – so as to make them of practical use in our own lives.

There are two time zones in the novella, the period before Kate Orme's marriage to Denis Peyton, and a period about twenty-six or -seven years later during her son's young manhood, and these have a number of organisational and thematic correlations which are entirely dependant upon moral issues for their existence. Wharton isolates Kate Orme at the heart of both halves of the novella; she is the centre of consciousness throughout, and it is through her vivid and particular morality, marked from first to last as in sharp contrast to those around her, that the heights and depths of the drama are realised. Time passes in the space between the two halves of the novella according to the plan conceived by Kate Orme at the end of Part One; there have been no challenges to her idea of her purpose and therefore nothing to occupy the reader in terms of the narrow definition of narrative interest we have been given. The plot is resumed at the moment of challenge to Kate's solo crusade to save her son from moral turpitude, the huge gap of time being a plot as well as structural device, indicating as it does to the reader that with the important decision taken, the principle thus enacted sets the agenda for all the intervening years until the action is resumed with the moral test of Dick Peyton, a test which will also deliver the final judgement upon Kate's sacrifice of self and whether it has been worthwhile. The unnarrated years give a further point of emphasis to the story's concentration upon moments of moral crisis, both halves of the narrative structure are suspended on the contingencies of a moment of reckoning.

The novella was serialised in *Scribner's Magazine* in July 1903 and published in book form in October of that year and, at the beginning of the story, Kate Orme is delineated as very much the type of girl at whom magazine fiction was targeted, protected as she has been from any 'open discussion of life'. So, within the confines of the narrative, Kate can be positioned as both subject and audience. The existence of other types of woman is not unacknowledged in the text but they are strictly defined as outside Kate's moral purview, the 'woman who was of course "dreadful"'[35] whom Arthur married, the platitudinous Mrs Peyton, whose morality is dependant upon the principle of trying 'to ignore the existence of ... horrors'[36] and, in the second half, Clemence Verney, who is constructed as having 'a pagan freshness in her opportunism'.[37] Thus, the only other women who feature here are positioned outside the ethical sphere drawn around Kate Orme and the practice of her rigorous morality.

Whilst the explanation and the reason for her moral isolation from all those around her is that she has been carefully maintained in a state of ignorance, as the story progresses her isolation becomes increasingly self-willed as well as culturally enforced. The opening pages of the novella give us a young woman, recently engaged, whose emotional well-being is actually dependant upon the knowledge that her fiance cannot penetrate to her most intimate spaces: 'She found herself in a new country, wherein he who had led her there was least able to be her guide'. Kate Orme is a woman who 'could not imagine sharing her deepest moods with anyone',[38] and indeed, relies upon Denis Peyton's obtuseness to keep him from coming too close to her imaginative or moral centre. She is, apparently, grateful that he cannot follow the complexities of her response to the tragic story of Arthur Peyton: 'Would she never learn to remember that Denis was incapable of mounting such hypothetical pyres? He might be as alive as herself to the direct demands of duty, but of its imaginative claims he was robustly unconscious. The thought brought a wholesome reaction of thankfulness.'[39] There is a peculiar inversion of innocence and experience in process here; Denis, who 'knew about these things!' is less capable of understanding the worst human terrors because his failures of imagination protect him from comprehension of 'moral darkness'.[40] So, the young woman who has been carefully safeguarded from too much knowledge of the world: '- such things are kept from girls'–[41] is the one capable of plumbing the depths of the 'abyss' because she has been nurtured to reverberate to every nuance of the moral 'labyrinths'[42] that lead away from the points at which she encounters, in her imagination, the complexities of the outside world. It is in her imagination, in fact, that most of Kate's encounters with the business of living take place. For the majority of the novella, in the second as well as in the first part, she is an observer, excluded from the action that is going on elsewhere. Kate Orme, later Peyton, spends her own narrative space in moral debate with dilemmas and questions that are being enacted in the lives of others, her marriage and her motherhood always seeming to position her outside the possibility of direct action and in a secondary rôle. As a wife, we are told at the beginning of the second part of the novella, she had briefly aspired to fill the paradigmatic supporting rôle, that of the politician's wife, but, 'the experiment ending in failure, as Denis Peyton's experiments were apt to end',[43] she withdraws from engagement with the outside world. In marrying Denis Peyton, Kate Orme takes on, with total, almost fanatical, seriousness, the woman's place and function as it has been communicated to her by her own and her husband's family. Faced with the truth of her own inconsequence in the

continuing story of 'the private disposal of family scandals'[44] she
carries that essentialist prescription – 'the sacrificial instinct of her
sex'[45] – to its limit as an answer to those who would exclude her
from participation in the 'larger issue' of the guardianship of the
'social health'.[46]

Kate, as we see her on the threshold of the narrative, knows no
constraint on her intellectual and emotional freedom; at one with
her world she gives rein to a transcendentalist overflow of harmonious and expansive feeling: 'Then, as her eye adapted itself, as
the lines flowed into each other, opening deep vistas upon new
horizons, she began to enter into possession of her kingdom, to
entertain the actual sense of its belonging to her. But she had never
before felt that she also belonged to it; and this was the feeling
which now came to complete her happiness, to give it the hal-
lowing sense of permanence.'[47] This apparently limitless expansion
of the individual consciousness into the current of the world comes
about because she is about to be married, and, as already noted, in
despite of, not because of, the person who is responsible for the
change in her status and capacity. It is in marriage that Kate Orme
believes she is to be fulfilled by taking possession of her birthright
as a grown woman. However, at the crucial moment of fulfilment
or consummation the events surrounding the death of Arthur's
widow and child all combine to change dramatically the version
of marriage which she is about to embrace, shifting the subject of
her attention from herself and Denis to the child they might have
together. One of the central events leading to the change is a
conversation she has with her father about a scandal which has
been hushed up within her own family and the way in which his
account of the matter is revelatory of whole-cultural attitudes to the
business of marriage for women:

> It was a bad business; he was sorry Kate should have been mixed
> up with it; but she would be married soon now, and then she
> would see that life wasn't such a Sunday-school story. Every-
> body was exposed to such disagreeable accidents: he remem-
> bered a case in their own family – oh, a distant cousin whom
> Kate wouldn't have heard of – a poor fellow who had got
> entangled with just such a woman, and having (most properly)
> been sent packing by his father, had justified the latter's course
> by promptly forging his name – a very nasty affair altogether;
> but luckily the scandal had been hushed up, the woman bought

off, and the prodigal, after a season of probation, safely married to a nice girl with a good income, who was told by the family that the doctors recommended his settling in California. *Luckily the scandal was hushed up*: the phrase blazed out against the dark background of Kate's misery. That was doubtless what most people felt – the words represented the consensus of respectable opinion. The best way of repairing a fault was to hide it: to tear up the floor and bury the victim at night. Above all, no coroner and no autopsy!

She began to feel a strange interest in her distant cousin. "And his wife – did she know what he had done?"

Mr Orme stared. His moral pointed, he had returned to the contemplation of his own affairs.

"His wife? Oh, of course not. The secret has been most admirably kept; but her property was put in trust, so she's quite safe with him."

Her property! Kate wondered if her faith in her husband had also been put in trust, if her sensibilities had been protected from his possible inroads.[48]

There are a number of moral and value systems being contested here, both the predominant ethical systems of the culture are invoked through legal and religious language which is, however, compromised by the distorted manner of its use. Mr Orme's language derives from the school of sanctimony and providence to which Mrs Peyton, Denis's mother, subscribes, and his use of the words that make up the received system of ethics are put to deviant purposes, to denote, in most instances, expedience rather than principle. The word 'moral' refers not to a code but to the lesson he requires her to learn from the retelling of the sad and sordid fable of the distant cousin, 'in trust' and 'safe' refer not to loyalty and confidence and the safety of the individual (female) person, but to her property and the depredations that might be made upon it by the 'prodigal'. The marriage of convenience here is at the convenience of the good name of 'the family', the person least to be considered in any of the proceedings is the 'nice girl' brought up like Kate – 'These were not things about which young girls were told'.[49]

It is at this point that Kate realises that marriage, as the culmination of her training as a girl identical in all respects to the unwitting victim of the 'secret' so 'admirably kept', is not the means of entry to the 'garden enclosed'[50] but to 'a vast system of moral sewage'. This is her true destination and the only virtue in continuing with her plans to marry Denis is that she already knows where she is going. There is also a revision, a heightening or intensification of the narrative point that attaches to the use of the language of landscape and territory between the writing of *The Touchstone* and *Sanctuary*. Kate is, in topographical terms, constructed in the colonial relationship to her father: 'His daughter, as part of himself, came within the normal range of his solicitude; but she was an outlying region, a subject province; and Mr Orme's was a highly centralized polity.'[51] Governed, as she is, her welfare is irremediably adjunct to the well-being of the centre, in this instance the centre of self-satisfaction and selfishness that is her father. She is, like territory, to be disposed and maintained in the most economically expedient and profitable manner and unless she is compliant then the 'social health' which relies on the ignorance and gullibility of young women like her will be threatened.

Marriage is the point at which the civil and the religious law coincide and although both the law and the church are publically accountable institutions they have dimensions which are intensely personal, as demonstrated in the marriage contract. Not only is marriage the point of intersection for the sacred and the secular, however, but it is the culmination of the procedure by which 'girls brought up in ignorance of life'[52] receive their disillusionment, as Mr Orme advises when he warns Kate about the leaving behind of the 'Sunday-school story'. In being disabused of the belief that marriage is 'simply the exquisite prolongation of wooing'[53] before instead of after marriage, however, Kate is able to convert the use of the woman's body – the central focus, after all, of courtship and consummation and of the processes of mystification and subsequent defilement – to a different use, changing the meaning of 'sanctuary' in the process. In order to achieve this she must literally become the place of safety herself: in a 'vision of protecting maternity' she offers herself up as a physical sanctuary so that the sin can be expiated through her personal 'climax of effacement'.[54] She uses the female body as the place wherein the seed of the sinner will be rehabilitated and transformed into a new life in whom the struggle between good and evil can be enacted; in her struggle to find a means of 'expiation'[55] she makes herself the 'refuge' which alone can reconcile the imperatives of the public and the private resonances of 'sanctuary' itself. She makes 'old names... serve for such new meanings' and in so doing she not only exposes the unspoken truth at the heart of the 'system' – that the struggle is enacted in and through the body of the woman – but also that the woman can be made to transcend the boundaries of her 'ignorance' in order to feel 'a surge of liberating faith in life, the old *credo quia absurdam* which is the secret cry of all supreme endeavour'.

The climacteric is Kate's surrender of the self, directed as it has been towards the exclusive contemplation and pursuit of romantic love, in favour of a wider embrace, the 'passion of charity for [the] race'. Kate's abandonment of self-gratification is expressed in the language of religious ecstasy. The secular equivalent to Wharton's formulation of Kate's 'sacrificial instinct',[56] however, is to be found in Charlotte Perkins Gilman's *Women and Economics*, published five years before *Sanctuary* in 1898, where Gilman positions the traditional system of courtship as she sees it: the 'primitive restrictions of a purely sexual relation' as firmly in opposition to a strategy 'based on a spirit of inter-human love, not merely the inter-sexual'.[57] The whole of *Sanctuary* is a testament to the inextricable links between love, marriage and money; every story within the story, from Arthur's involvement with the kind of woman 'who prey on such men',[58] through Kate's distant cousin's entanglement with the same stereotype, to her own marriage, all confirm the intimacy of the relationship between the three. It is only in Dick's refusal to use Darrow's architectural plans and the contingent refusal of him as husband by the woman who believes in 'marriage by capture'[59] and success at any cost, that the tradition is refuted. Gilman's exegesis of 'The Menace of Present Conditions' in 1898 has the same moral imperative as that which underlies *Sanctuary*:

> The method of action of our particular cat's-paw combination of the sexes – the mother-father doing the work of the helpless creature he carries on his back; the parasite mate devouring even where she should most feed – has been this, as repeatedly shown: because of sex-desire the male subjugates the female. Lest he lose her, he feeds her, and, perforce, her young. She obtaining food through the sex-relation, becomes over-sexed, and acts with constantly increasing stimulus on his sex-activities; and as these activities are made economic by their relation, she so stimulates industry and all progress. But, – and here is the natural end of an unnatural position, a position that serves its

purpose for a time, but holds in itself the seeds of its own destruction, – through the unchecked sex-energy, accumulated under the abnormal pressure of the economic side of the relation, such excess is developed as tends to destroy both individual and race; and such psychic qualities are developed as tend also to our injury and extinction.[60]

The unnatural ignorance and dependance of women, critiqued by Gilman and exemplified in *Sanctuary* with all the moral clarity of the allegory, is shown to produce terrible results. The blind sanctimony of such as Mrs Peyton, the helpless ignorance of Arthur's wife who is wronged by Denis's superior knowledge of the law, the woman who must resort to forgery after having her means of survival removed, the 'nice girl' married to the prodigal in ignorance, but with her money, if not her person, protected, and finally, and most terribly, the ruthless 'parasite' produced by the system, Clemence Verney and her valorisation of going 'straight to the thing one is after';[61] all these women and their 'mates' are victims of the system. It is in Kate's decision to break the 'sex-relation', substituting the 'vision of protecting maternity', that the progress toward the 'larger social uses'[62] of the relationship between men and women, as Gilman has it, can be realised. The entanglement of Dick Peyton and Clemence Verney is a setback on the road to the achievement of a higher purpose and meaning to both social and economic relations between the sexes, providing, as it does, a regression to the old ways where 'the parasite mate' ensnares the 'the male'. Kate's new vision of the processes and possibilities of maternity is triumphant, however, as she is ulti-mately rewarded by the restoration of her son, purified and freed from the toils of the sophisticated and sophistical arguments of his lover, and ready, as he says, not to regard her morality as 'an obstacle any longer, but a refuge'.[63]

Sanctuary, once examined with its morality as a dynamic means by which Wharton can, like Gilman, express the age, rather than as an embarrassment to readers whose aesthetic sensibilities are offended by the obvious, provides a rich surface with a complex patterning of the points where the individual and the communal intersect. It is later, in Wharton's novel of 1920, *The Age of Innocence*, that the combination of Christian ethics, natural science and sociology reaches its artistic apogee in her work, but in this novella the technique which both uses and interrogates the sacred and the secular in their changing relation within the lives of men and women is laid down to good effect. In *Sanctuary*, the novella form, not underestimating its usefulness as an intermediate, experimental medium at this stage of Wharton's career, allows for a consistency and cogency of argument, a compression of external event alongside an expansion of internal reflection, and, as in *The Touchstone*, a consonance of figurative and operative language.

In *Sanctuary*, the drama is constructed around the transfer of attention and devotion from husband to son, from romance to maternity. In *Madame de Treymes* an equivalent shift is at the heart of the action but its structural rôle is as distinct from anything on offer in *Sanctuary* as its cultural rôle. This difference can be plainly seen in the manner in which the Malrive family deal with the breakdown of the Marquis' marriage: 'we simply transferred our allegiance to the child – we constituted *him* the family.'[64] Where one decision speaks of an individual's resolve to act up against and in despite of the 'collective sense of justice'[65] – such as it is – the other is the very voice of society acting in concert to 'give him back to his race, his religion, his true place in the order of things'.[66] Both *The Touchstone* and *Sanctuary* speak of misunderstandings and misinterpretations of the public and private dimensions of language, the implications of such misprisions being enacted, in the main, within the confines of the individual life; high drama here is chiefly interior drama.

Whilst personal crisis is expressed through a variety of metaphoric resources in the first two novellas, *Madame de Treymes* is more monolithic in its troping: language itself and the society it expresses is the source of the majority of surface and subterranean meaning, and the drama involves nothing less than the clash of cultures between two nations. The lexical resources of the law and the church are variously applied and misapplied by those actors in the moral theatre of *Sanctuary* but in the story of *Madame de Treymes* there is no room for individual use or for interpretation, the law and the church represent the two areas where there is no possibility of translation or even of understanding. As John Durham says to Madame de Treymes ' "Your French justice takes a grammar and a dictionary to understand" '[67] and such works of reference are not on sale at the charity bazaars which tantalize the Americans by giving them access to but no intimacy with the Faubourg.

In many ways the most urbane and sophisticated of these novellas, *Madame de Treymes*, was Wharton's first extended venture into the 'International theme' and its opening pages in particular are among the most resonant and seductive in her work. She offers us a delicate series of advances and withdrawals, the implications and interpretations of the tiniest details of social conduct, in all its cross-cultural reverberations, entice the reader on as John Durham thrills to the nuances of Madame de Malrive's behaviour. The French scene in *Madame de Treymes* is always described in shades of darkness within and dazzling light and open spaces without. The interior lives of her Parisians are hinted at in terms of half-tones and shadows whilst the Americans exist in the full glare of literal and metaphorical sunlight. As Fanny comments after a visit to Mrs Durham: 'She took me back into that clear American air where there are no obscurities, no mysteries'.[68] The Faubourg where the old French families make themselves rare is always described as grey, as 'unmapped';[69] it is not on the tourist route except when one of its inhabitants provides a meagre guide to the vicinity in order to get something from a visiting American. Otherwise the blinds are always drawn and the shutters closed.

As in the case of the other two novellas discussed here the coherence of the subject, language and structure in this text is sustained by a high degree of aesthetic resolution or finish. However, where *The Touchstone* and *Sanctuary* are in possession of a morality which is in dispute as a part of the plot, but which receives some form of affirmation at the end, there is no clear morality on display in *Madame de Treymes*. The obfuscation of intent and meaning practised by the Faubourg is depicted without authorial arbitration, Wharton does not privilege any of the moralities made visible here unless it is the moral aesthetic; that which finally defeats Durham is the Hôtel de Malrive:

> Durham that afternoon presented himself at the proud old house beyond the Seine. More than ever, in the semi-abandonment of the *morte saison*, with reduced service, and shutters closed to the silence of the high-walled court, did it strike the American as the incorruptible custodian of old prejudices and strange social survivals. The thought of what he must represent to the almost human consciousness which such old houses seemed to possess, made him feel like a barbarian desecrating the silence of a temple of an earlier faith. Not that there was anything venerable in the attestations of the Hôtel de Malrive, except in so far as, to a sensitive imagination, every concrete embodiment of a past order

of things testifies to real convictions once suffered for. Durham, at any rate, always alive in practical issues to the view of the other side, had enough sympathy left over to spend it sometimes, whimsically, on such perceptions of difference.[70]

The beautiful conflict of manners and mores enacted between John Durham and the whole of the Faubourg, is conducted with due regard to the aesthetic considerations, both sides see the advantages, the reasons and the grace which underlie the conduct of the other side. The real human suffering which lurks just beneath the surface of the spoken word is subordinated to the maintenance of the 'organized and inherited system'[71] of French society; there is never any question of the individual being given priority over the collective. Whilst Madame de Treymes is in desperate personal trouble and is also, eventually, moved to sympathy for John Durham, she does not waver in her adherence to her class; the social order which is represented by the Hôtel de Malrive is too powerful an institution, too effective a means of social control to be betrayed. The tragedy of *Madame de Treymes* is that having once recognised the superior complications of the older civilisation Durham is left with only his adherence to an 'abstract standard of truth'[72] in return for renouncing his love.

Wharton makes it plain that it is Durham's attraction to the complexities of French society which is being enacted in his courtship of Fanny de Malrive. Although the woman from whom Durham awaits an answer to his proposal of marriage was once Fanny Frisbee of New York, it is in the change between Miss Frisbee and Madame de Malrive that her attraction lies: 'And it was the mystery, the sense of unprobed depths of initiation, which drew him to her as her freshness had never drawn him'.[73] It is in his proposal, however, that John Durham feels most the inadequacy of his own culture, the paucity of his own offer of nation as well as self as he reads only the 'derision of what he had to offer in the splendour of the great avenues tapering upwards to the sunset glories of the Arch'.[74] American cultural mores, the behaviour of the American girl, indeed of the American courting couple, lie behind Durham's heightened sense of pleasure in the simplest of Parisian encounters, and Fanny's 'exotic enjoyment of Americanism'[75] confirms him in a condition of cultural dislocation which is both wonderful and terrible to him. Her acquired foreignness is intrinsic to the sustenance of his ardour: he 'even felt a pang of disappointment, a momentary fear least she should have stooped a little from the high place where his passion had preferred to leave her'[76] when she seems to return his attentions too quickly.

There is a strong sense that the attractions of a Fanny de Malrive, so different to those of Fanny Frisbee, can be aligned in some respects with the mature and 'ordered beauty'[77] of Paris itself. The words that Wharton repeatedly uses to describe the city are to do with its having been planned, informed by a larger spirit of both use and beauty but answering ultimately to the human need for continuity and support. The emphasis and use of repetition in her prose here suggests that the grandeur of Paris supplies much of the grandeur in its inhabitants' lives. However, it is in use, and Fanny de Malrive has surely been used, that people and their cities acquire dignity and grace. One of the first principles of Wharton's art is that it should reflect a wider aesthetic which, whilst looking with a fresh eye – and that surely belongs overwhelmingly to the American – also attempts to understand the enduring meaning of the work of centuries, work which reflects both artistic and practical considerations and work which is still active in the culture. Fanny Frisbee has been made over by her European experience:

> Yes, it was the finish, the modelling, which Madame de Malrive's experience had given her that set her apart from the fresh uncomplicated personalities of which she had once been simply the most charming type. The influences that had lowered her voice, regulated her gestures, toned her down to harmony with the warm dim background of a long social past – these influences had lent to her natural fineness of perception a command of expression adapted to complex conditions.[78]

What John Durham sees before him is a woman who has been, on the European plan, matured and made more complicated and interesting by marriage rather than, as in America, 'cut off from men's society in all but the most formal and intermittent ways' on her wedding day as Wharton laments in her 1919 study of *French Ways and Their Meaning*.[79] Fanny's natural talents have been made articulate by her exposure to the intricacies of French society and Durham can see only benefit in this process; she attracts him with her experience as she could never do with her innocence.

Wharton's figurative language here draws attention to the coherence of the achieved effect in terms of the way in which expression is controlled. Durham is reduced to silence by the 'possibilities' opened up not only by Fanny's behaviour but by the the full prospect of the Tuileries, with its cultivated and 'complicated beauty' in contradistinction to the uninspiring 'uncomplicated personalities' of his native land. It is in Fanny's conduct in the face of his speechlessness that Durham becomes aware of the essential difference in her: 'There was apparently nothing embarrassing to her in his silence: it was a part of her long European discipline that she had learned to manage pauses with ease. In her Frisbee days she might have packed this one with a random fluency; now she was content to let it widen slowly before them like the spacious prospect opening at their feet'; her urbanity sharpens his awareness of the American tendency to fill all empty spaces with words. In France he is made aware of a civilisation where things are left unspoken, where place and time and ritual take the place of verbal communication or the inevitable 'national interrogation'[80] as Wharton has it.

Whilst Fanny has learned silence and to speak wordlessly with her body, however, she has also learned the uses to which her French in-laws put their reticence in its most sinister aspects. Her induction into the ways and means of the Faubourg has enhanced her own 'significance', her connotations are endlessly, as Durham reflects, 'unspecified', 'throbbing', 'thrilling', 'charged',[81] and the erotic stimulus he receives from her sophistication blinds him to the negative aspect of such 'mystery'.[82] Fanny herself, however, puts the other side of the case, outlining the cultural imperative of the unspoken as it affects her son:

> There is nothing in your experience – in any American experience – to correspond with that far-reaching family organization, which is itself a part of the larger system, and which encloses a young man of my son's position in a network of accepted prejudices and opinions. Everything is prepared in advance – his political and religious convictions, his judgements of people, his sense of honour, his ideas of women, his whole view of life. He is taught to see vileness and corruption in everyone not of his own way of thinking, and in every idea that does not directly serve the religious and political purposes of his class.[83]

However negatively Fanny presents the ideological inheritance of her son, there is a coherent world-view behind the cultural certainty, one which privileges tradition, excludes change and is beyond the reach of discussion or alteration. The 'complicated beauty' of Paris is a mirror image of the attitudes and convictions of a whole nation, fuelled by 'solidarity' and composed of people who, as Durham comes to realise, 'hung together in a visible closeness of tradition, dress, attitude and manner, as different as possible from the loose aggregation of a roomful of his own countrymen'.[84] The silence which surrounds this solidarity, however, moves, for John Durham, from the alluring, through the alienating to the threatening. His dealings with Madame de Treymes as the apparent mediator between him and the 'labyrinth of "foreign" intrigue.'[85] are marked by a spurious frankness which Wharton aligns with the 'fluency in self-revelation which centuries of the confessional have given to the Latin races'.[86] But confession, as Durham, neophyte as he is, has to learn, concerns only individual transgressions against the establishment, whether of church or state, not enlightenment or change; repentance here is not dynamic but retrograde. Clarity is always suspect and, as Fanny de Malrive knows to her cost, the only safe procedure is to look 'for the truth always in what they *don't* say'.[87] There is nothing left at the end of *Madame de Treymes* except adherence to a principle of truth which finds expression in renunciation; Durham must abjure the way of silence he has learned in Paris, go to Fanny de Malrive and 'tell her everything'.[88] For Durham, as for Kate Orme, Stephen and Alexa Glennard, between initiation and disillusion there is no space for the individual to flourish, for intentions or desires to be realised or for an understanding to be reached which might ameliorate the 'great moral loneliness'[89] which is unashamedly at the heart of Wharton's work in the novella.[90]

Notes

1. Wharton, Edith *Madame de Treymes: Four Short Novels* (London: Virago Press, 1995), p. 5.
2. *Madame de Treymes*, p. 216.
3. One of the most thought-provoking and thorough readings of the novella is conducted by Lev Raphael at the beginning of his book, *Edith Wharton's Prisoners of Shame: A New Perspective on her Neglected*

Fiction (New York: St. Martins Press, 1991). Raphael makes *The Touchstone* central to his thesis and conducts an interpretation of the text which encompasses the critical and the biographical.

4. *Madame de Treymes*, p. 10.
5. *Madame de Treymes*, p. 34.
6. *Madame de Treymes*, p. 9.
7. *Madame de Treymes*, p. 16.
8. *Madame de Treymes*, p. 8.
9. *Madame de Treymes*, pp. 11–12.
10. *Madame de Treymes*, pp. 34–5.
11. *Madame de Treymes*, p. 30.
12. *Madame de Treymes*, p. 47.
13. *Madame de Treymes*, p. 59.
14. *Madame de Treymes*, p. 61.
15. *Madame de Treymes*, pp. 77–8.
16. *Madame de Treymes*, p. 27.
17. *Madame de Treymes*, p. 23.
18. *Madame de Treymes*, p. 31.
19. *Madame de Treymes*, p. 36.
20. *Madame de Treymes*, p. 4.
21. *Madame de Treymes*, p. 23.
22. *Madame de Treymes*, p. 14.
23. *Madame de Treymes*, p. 12.
24. *Madame de Treymes*, pp. 15–16.
25. *Madame de Treymes*, p. 41.
26. *Madame de Treymes*, p. 36.
27. *Madame de Treymes*, p. 78.
28. *Madame de Treymes*, p. 44.
29. *Madame de Treymes*, p. 60.
30. *Madame de Treymes*, p. 15.
31. *Madame de Treymes*, p. 82.
32. *Madame de Treymes*, p. 79.
33. Lewis, R.W.B. *Edith Wharton: A Biography* (London, Constable & Co. Ltd., 1975), p. 123. More recently, Gloria Erlich discusses the novella alongside *The Touchstone* as 'paired stories written out of childhood experience that was revived by the death of the author's mother' in her essay: 'The Female Conscience in Edith Wharton's Shorter Fiction: Domestic Angel or Inner Demon?'. Bell, Millicent (ed.) *The Cambridge Companion to Edith Wharton* (New York, Cambridge University Press, 1995), p. 114.
34. *Madame de Treymes*, p. 110.
35. *Madame de Treymes*, p. 88.
36. *Madame de Treymes*, p. 104.
37. *Madame de Treymes*, p. 143.
38. *Madame de Treymes*, pp. 85–6.
39. *Madame de Treymes*, p. 95.
40. *Madame de Treymes*, p. 94.
41. *Madame de Treymes*, p. 91.
42. *Madame de Treymes*, pp. 94–5.

43. *Madame de Treymes*, p. 116.
44. *Madame de Treymes*, p. 110.
45. *Madame de Treymes*, p. 113.
46. *Madame de Treymes*, p. 110.
47. *Madame de Treymes*, p. 86.
48. *Madame de Treymes*, pp. 109–10.
49. *Madame de Treymes*, p. 90.
50. *Madame de Treymes*, p. 111.
51. *Madame de Treymes*, pp. 108–9.
52. *Madame de Treymes*, p. 112.
53. *Madame de Treymes*, p. 112.
54. *Madame de Treymes*, pp. 112–13.
55. *Madame de Treymes*, p. 101.
56. *Madame de Treymes*, pp. 112–13.
57. Gilman, Charlotte Perkins *Women and Economics*, 1898, re-printed. Carl N Degler. (New York, Harper Torchbooks, 1966), pp. 140–142.
58. *Madame de Treymes*, p. 98.
59. *Madame de Treymes*, p. 124.
60. Gilman, Charlotte Perkins *Women and Economics*, pp. 140–141.
61. *Madame de Treymes*, p. 124.
62. Gilman, Charlotte Perkins *Women and Economics*, p. 142.
63. *Madame de Treymes*, p. 162.
64. *Madame de Treymes*, p. 217.
65. *Madame de Treymes*, p. 111.
66. *Madame de Treymes*, p. 218.
67. *Madame de Treymes*, p. 217.
68. *Madame de Treymes*, p. 174.
69. *Madame de Treymes*, p. 179.
70. *Madame de Treymes*, p. 212.
71. *Madame de Treymes*, p. 188.
72. *Madame de Treymes*, p. 221.
73. *Madame de Treymes*, p. 178.
74. *Madame de Treymes*, p. 167.
75. *Madame de Treymes*, p. 179.
76. *Madame de Treymes*, p. 201.
77. *Madame de Treymes*, p. 178.
78. *Madame de Treymes*, p. 179.
79. Wharton, Edith. *French Ways and Their Meaning* (New York, D. Appleton and Co., 1919), p. 115.
80. *Madame de Treymes*, p. 167.
81. *Madame de Treymes*, pp. 165–7.
82. *Madame de Treymes*, p. 178.
83. *Madame de Treymes*, p. 172.
84. *Madame de Treymes*, p. 188.
85. *Madame de Treymes*, p. 189.
86. *Madame de Treymes*, p. 197.
87. *Madame de Treymes*, p. 201.
88. *Madame de Treymes*, p. 222.

89. *Madame de Treymes*, p. 111.
90. See my discussion of *Madame de Treymes* in relation to the work of Henry James and in the context of Wharton's *The Reef, The Custom of the Country* and *French Ways and their Meaning* in Chapter 2 of my book *Edith Wharton: Traveller in the Land of Letters* (Basingstoke: Macmillan, 1990).

6

Edith Wharton, Literary Ghosts and the Writing of New England

In this chapter I intend to look at the regional in Edith Wharton's short fiction, at her different intentions and strategies when writing about New England but also the continuities between all the stories here selected, from the earliest, 'Friends', published in *The Youth's Companion* in 1900,[1] to the last, 'All Souls', published posthumously in *Ghosts* in 1937. Whilst the short novels, *Ethan Frome* and *Summer*, published in 1911 and 1917 respectively, are Wharton's best known works of regional fiction, they will be used only as reference points throughout the discussion as they relate to the thematic variations within 'The Angel at the Grave' which featured in the collection *Crucial Instances*, published in 1901, 'The Young Gentlemen' and 'Bewitched', both of which appeared in *Here and Beyond*, published in 1926, as well as the two stories already mentioned.

There are a number of ways in which these particular stories can be ascribed to different genres; all respond to readings which take into account the traditions of local colour and of the gothic, generic categories which can be said to have, in general terms, the epistemology of women's lives as a common concern or rationale. The designation of writers as local colourists has often, as in the case of Kate Chopin's regional writings, been a way to categorise and contain certain authors within the constraints of a particular narrative topography. Writers like Chopin, however, as I have discussed, can be seen to employ all kinds of strategies to maximise the potential of the particular genre, converting limitations into opportunities for exploration beyond the constraints which determine both life and art in order to test the limits of expression and expressibility. Indeed, a variation on the gothic and one of Wharton's familiar modes, the ghost story, can be used, as Chopin used local colour, to incorporate otherwise controversial subject matter in the tale. Wharton, in fact, does this in the story

116

'Bewitched' where the extra-marital sex indulged in by Saul Rutledge at first glance seems to make him a necrophile and at second a plain adulterer. For Saul Rutledge, as well as his creator, the supernatural could be a cover for sexual adventure.

Like Kate Chopin, Edith Wharton has been subject to critical pigeon-holing since the very beginning of her publishing career. Amy Kaplan, in her book *The Social Construction of Literary Realism*, notes the repeating pattern within critical approaches to Edith Wharton of seeking to contain her within a single tradition – whether it be as novelist of manners, as anti-modernist, as a member of the school of James, or even as woman writer – but goes on to relocate her as 'a professional author who wrote at the intersection of the mass market of popular fiction, the tradition of women's literature, and a realistic movement which developed in an uneasy dialogue with twentieth-century modernism.'[2] The positioning of Wharton in the literary marketplace at the beginning of a discussion in which I want to consider her work as regional writer is crucial to avoid any misunderstanding about why I want to embark upon such a reading. Like Chopin and Gilman, Wharton was writing as a professional but also as an artist who was heir to a complicated set of regional and aesthetic precedents and was seeking the best means of assimilation as well as innovation.[3] To consider Wharton as a writer of New England tales, even as a local colourist, will, I hope, throw open new possibilities of interpretation rather than close them down and complicate rather than simplify the way in which we read her work.

I want to focus here on the stories where Wharton immersed herself in the regional in order both to exploit its potential and expand its aesthetic possibilities. My approach is not biographical – 'All Souls' in particular has attracted numerous critics who are concerned with Wharton's biography as well as with her fiction[4] – neither is it psychological. It is genre-specific in so far as it groups a selection of stories together in order to examine both what form local colour or the genre of regional writing might take in Wharton's fiction and how that might be complicated by her strategic deployment of the characteristics of other types of fiction. The tales here considered are all part of the gothic core of Wharton's work as identified by Kathy Fedorko in her illuminating study of *Gender and the Gothic in the Fiction of Edith Wharton*,[5] but the way in which I intend to use the gothic is as another means of establishing links with other cultures, other traditions and human instincts deeper than reason. In this way, the ghost story, in particular, becomes yet another means of forging links with a common human history as well as a demonstration of the supernatural as made manifest in the texture of New England life.

Wharton's fiction, whether in transaction with the supernatural or not, exposes the complex web of personal and whole-cultural relationships which lie behind the paintless wooden houses of the region and the means by which to make sense of this world. My strategy in reading the New England tales is broadly similar to Martha Banta's approach in her essay, 'The Ghostly Gothic of Wharton's Everyday World', whereby she identifies Wharton's 'ghostly gothic... within the cultural context of the flourishing science of ethnography, just then being touted as one of the best new ways to study cultural contexts'. By extending the remit of Banta's scrutiny of the ghostly to incorporate the stories which can be categorised as regional, it is possible to see local colour – as it expresses, through fiction, the essential characteristics of a region or ethnic group – having powerful parallels with the imperatives of ethnography in the scrutiny of the customs, habits and distinctive features of a particular human geography. As Banta says: 'Ethnography analyzes the ways societies form around nuclei of "sacred" manners and mores whose function continues into the present from the past, with the power to dictate the relation of individual conduct to values instituted by the community.'[6] Both as an empiricist – writer of travel books and guides to foreign cultures – and as the weaver of ghostly tales, Wharton specialised in the construction of narratives which incorporate and yet also contrast different cultures, different ages, and even different worlds – of nature and supernature.

Reading a coherence into Wharton's New England short fiction – taking as representative these five short stories, written between 1900 and 1937, her beginning and her end as a published writer, can also force a rethink of the ways in which we contextualise her work. It is never possible to read Wharton's fiction as bound to a single genre or to a particular space; she always worked to imbue the thematics of her tale into the fabric and structure of her writing and these were as various as the genres she used. To return to Amy Kaplan's explication of Wharton's position as artist at the turn of the century, Kaplan borrows Wharton's own language from her 1897 treatise *The Decoration of Houses* to communicate the means by which she marked out a fictional territory which lay between the private and the public: she posits the view that Wharton had 'the goal of appropriating a traditional male discourse of architecture to transform a traditional female discourse of interior space. "Interior architecture" turns domestic space inside out, to project a borderline area at the intersection of the private home and the streets of the public marketplace'.[7] Wharton's regional stories are all concerned with borderlines, with the territory between private and public space, between culture and anarchy, and she figures forth the intermediacy of the turn of the century lives of her characters through the exterior and interior architecture of New England.

The New England tales are concerned with lives seemingly conducted on the edge of civilisation and yet these lives are affected by the contiguity of the existence of fragments of other distinct but still overlapping cultures. The landscape in 'Bewitched' for instance, bears traces of both Native-American and Colonial prior settlement, the complex inheritance of the region being mediated through the spiritual and social confusions of the thinly scattered inhabitants who remain. As Nancy Bentley notes in discussion of *Ethan Frome* and *Summer* in her essay ' "Hunting for the Real": Wharton and the Science of Manners', these novellas contain 'a dialectical movement between social forms and the volatile social energies that animate and sometimes alter them . . . the rural culture of Wharton's New England is structured by the same "tense equilibrium" between custom and crisis that Malinowski discovered among the Trobrianders'.[8] Wharton's New England is as much a society in transition as the New York of *The House of Mirth* or *The Age of Innocence*. In contrast with the highly regulated and elaborately ritualised lives led by the American aristocrats in these novels, the inhabitants of the New England tales may seem to be merely subsisting, both physically and intellectually. This does not mean, however, that their stories are not concerned with history, with aesthetics and with tradition. The starkness of the landscape in fact highlights the extremity of both need and choice for the denizens of a New England caught, now as ever, between the sacred and the profane, the past and the present, Europe and America, God and the Devil.

It is not, therefore, an act of re-marginalisation to place even a small part of the work of Edith Wharton in the context of the tradition of local colour but an opening up of a combination of different possibilities. Decades after her rescue from the outskirts of American literature and firm repositioning in the centre, to read some of her short novels and stories in the light of the conditions of the regional is not the result of a perverse wish to force her into the company of those from whom she so desperately wanted to distinguish herself, but to re-examine the terms and conditions of her claims for distinction, made here in the pages of her autobiography, *A Backward Glance*:

But the book to which I brought the greatest joy and the fullest ease was *Ethan Frome*. For years I had wanted to draw life as it really was in the derelict mountain villages of New England, a life even in my time, and a thousandfold more a generation earlier, utterly unlike that seen through the rose-coloured spectacles of my predecessors, Mary Wilkins and Sarah Orne Jewett. In those days the snow-bound villages of Western Massachusetts were still grim places, morally and physically: insanity, incest and slow mental and moral starvation were hidden away behind the paintless wooden house-fronts of the long village street, or in the isolated farm-houses on the neighbouring hills; and Emily Brontë would have found as savage tragedies in our remoter valleys as on her Yorkshire moors. In this connection, I may mention that every detail about the colony of drunken mountain outlaws described in *Summer* was given to me by the rector of the church at Lenox (near which we lived), and that the lonely peak I have called 'the Mountain' was in reality Bear Mountain, an isolated summit not more than twelve miles from our own home. The rector had been fetched there by one of the mountain outlaws to read the Burial Service over a woman of evil reputation; and when he arrived every one in the house of mourning was drunk, and the service was performed as I have related it.... Needless to say, when *Summer* appeared, this chapter was received with indignant denial by many reviewers and readers; and not the least vociferous were the New Englanders who had for years sought the reflection of local life in the rose-and-lavender pages of their favourite authoresses – and had forgotten to look into Hawthorne's.'[9]

As an assessment of the two named American women writers – and in the light of her 'rose-and-lavender' comment it seems impossible to imagine that Wharton knew Wilkins Freeman's *Pembroke*[10] or 'Old Woman Magoun'[11] - this has more to do with rhetorical effect than critical judgement. As Candace Waid says:

'Wharton's claim that the local color writings of Jewett and Wilkins covered over the grim realities of New England village life are not consistent with either the texts themselves or her contemporaries' reading of them.'[12] Wharton's selective rationale for writing New England does actually provide a means, however, by which to extend the terms in which we describe the genre of local colour as practised by women writers at the turn of the century as well as to look at the terms on which Wharton was willing to be considered a regionalist.[13] In other words, to take Wharton on her own terms and to explain why she wanted to be in the genre but didn't want to be considered as a purveyor of the picturesque, why she didn't want to be compared with Jewett and Freeman but she did with Hawthorne.

Edith Wharton did not so much write about New England in the nation but New England in the world; she placed her stories of the ghostly in New England, for instance, alongside ghostly tales of seventeenth century Italy or France, just as Hawthorne did. Eight of the eleven stories she brought together in the collection of ghost stories published in 1937[14] have rural settings, two in France, one in England and the others either in New England or the Hudson valley. The location, for Wharton, was often the structural principle on which her story was predicated; the landscape – both natural and humanised – is as important as the people who inhabit it, and, as its condition and its limits unfold, so the narrative takes shape. The equalisation of the territory of the tale of the supernatural on both sides of the Atlantic sustains the connection that Wharton wanted to make with Hawthorne as the writer who delivered a complicated New England to the world as well as to his own country. Carol Singley in her *Edith Wharton: Matters of Mind and Spirit* also makes the connection between Wharton and Hawthorne central to her discussion of New England, especially in the context of *Ethan Frome*: 'Both writers saw in the New England landscape a fundamental and irreconcilable duality, a Manichean opposition between good and evil, spirit and flesh, that is indigenous to American Calvinism.'[15] The tensions thus generated in the work of both writers have a particular potency in the stories which invoke the occult, the occult thus becoming one of the means by which the region could be most effectively mediated to its audience.

In many of the stories inflected with the characteristics of local colour, ghostly and otherwise, Wharton was writing a fiction about the intellectual heritage of America – most transparently in 'The Angel at the Grave' – but she was also looking for an effective way to communicate her vision of the everyday lives of the inhabitants of some of the oldest settlements in the United States. Central to this vision is the question of social class and its manifestation in the structure of New England society. In the stories she writes which have rural locations yet are entirely concerned with the lives of the wealthy, vacationing New Yorkers or Bostonians who seek a retreat in the country, as in 'The Triumph of Night' (1914), there is very little that relies on the specific topography of the region except, of course, the murderous winter cold. In 'Bewitched', and certainly *Ethan Frome* and *Summer*, however, the lives of the poorest citizens are intricately bound up with the legacy of the past, they are influenced by that which makes a landscape more historically resonant and the class issue might thus be read as an equalising, not divisive, means of establishing the community of the culture. All Wharton's true New Englanders are struggling with the inheritance of a complex civilisation as well as the strains of life in the 20th century and social class is one of the areas of con-testation. In 'All Souls' Sara Clayburn is absolutely dependent upon her servants for the sustenance of life and even sanity; their betrayal of her present needs in their adherence to an atavistic call of supernature is proof that the past is not the property of those who occupy the biggest houses; the landscape is host to a wealth of superstition and tradition apart from that which is visible in Whitegates, 'built... about 1780' and its mistress, 'of good Colonial stock'.[16]

Local colour in Edith Wharton's work pays tribute to the com-plexity of the inheritance of the past and the struggle to bring it into the 20th century. It is primarily concerned with the loss of cer-tainty, with secularisation and, as in all regional fiction, with med-iating a way of life to an audience unfamiliar with the conditions of existence for those who inhabit what might be considered remote regions. This remoteness is thus not simply geographical it is also cultural and historical. The stories I have chosen to discuss all begin with an allusion to fallen grandeur or to the refusal of the narrator or his or her subject to return to the location of the story: failure in or rejection of New England is the keynote established at the outset. The signifying details of the small New England town – whether successful in its commercial life, as with Sailport in the story 'Friends', or derelict, as in 'Bewitched' – indicate faded splendour, memorials to disappointments which echo down the years from previous inhabitants of a hostile landscape.

Edith Wharton's New England is usually a deadening, even dead, location. Her regional writing does not celebrate the remote or the picturesque or even the intellectual traditions which have dominated American culture since its inception: it views them with an eye as clear as Ellen Olenska's after having looked at the Gorgon: ' "She doesn't blind one; but she dries up one's tears" '.[17] New England is, for Wharton, a place of failure or, at best, of retrieval of some consolation from the ruins. The story which at first sight is her most Jewettesque, 'Friends', begins as it means to go on: 'Sailport is an ugly town'[18] but concerns the leaving of New England rather than continuation of the life that might be led therein. It does not require any act of critical excavation to read this story as we often read the work of Wharton's bugbears, Jewett and Freeman; it is, without doubt, centrally concerned with female friends, with communities of women, and women carers. The poverty of opportunity for women is the subject of the tale and its structure reinforces this theme. So far, so Jewett. The story could not, at first sight, be more straightforwardly about acts of friendship between women, emphasising their enduring solidarity even in the face of financial desperation, composing their mutual loyalty and love against a hastily assembled backdrop of betrayal by the unreliable and largely stereotypical male, 'away down in Texas' and married to 'another woman'.[19]

This story is untypical of Wharton in all sorts of ways although there are some thematic and stylistic trailers to her later fiction here. Susan Goodman productively identifies the plot of 'Friends' as one of two standard storylines within Wharton's fiction in that it 'outlines the novelist's concern with analysing where the temptations and the benefits reside in relationships between women, and as the ending illustrates, the chief benefit is to oneself'.[20] In addition to the early working through of a narrative line which thus becomes, in some respects, paradigmatic in Wharton's fiction, what is also characteristic of the writer in this early work is the aesthetic distance she establishes between the authorial voice and the inhabitants of 'Sailport'. This manner of narratorial control is particularly a feature of her historical novel, *The Valley of Decision*, on which she was working in 1900 when 'Friends' was published in *The Youth's Companion*. The opening three paragraphs of the short story relay unmediated the narrator's critical disdain for the streets and harbour, the fourth takes account of the views of the town's inhabitants – which are acknowledged as divergent from the narrator's – but from there onwards the town features only as it can supply an exterior commentary on the life of Penelope Bent. In a structure which is repeated in all five stories Wharton establishes the place before the persons but then interweaves topography and character type to illuminate and extend the picure of both. As Penelope Bent attempts to reassume her place in the town so its landmarks: 'a large brick building with brownstone angles and a massive porch. It stood by itself at the end of the street, with an air of moral superiority that at once proclaimed it to be one of the public schools of Sailport',[21] at first connote safety and security but soon reflect only the 'way to a profounder estrangement'.[22] This movement enacts in some measure the distance which is plotted for Penelope by the narrator in the manner in which the story opens. The signifying details of the townscape tell a tale of private complacency and civic neglect; the streets 'are full of snow and mud in winter, of dust and garbage in summer'. It is however, in the description of the architecture of the town that Wharton communicates her profoundest sense of the state of New England affairs:

> The streets, too narrow for the present needs of the town, run between buildings of discordant character; the new brick warehouse, like a factory chimney with windows in it, looking down from its lean eminence on the low wooden 'store' of a past generation, and the ambitious office building, with its astrologer's tower and rustications of sham granite, turning a contemptuous side wall on the recessed door and balustraded roof of the old dwelling house which had been adapted to commercial uses with the least possible outlay.[23]

This paragraph of description is but a single sentence. It expands and explains the terseness of the opening: 'Sailport is an ugly town' by demonstrating in one long breath the particular combination of both practical and aesthetic negligence that leads to such ugliness. The streets are not spacious enough even to service the commercial needs of the port; the buildings have been erected without attention to the style or purpose of existing structures; no effort has been made with the external appearance of the 'warehouse' and, finally, the attempt at the decorative by the architects of the 'ambitious office building', is exposed as 'sham' and 'contemptuous' of the shabbily treated 'old dwelling house'. The only approbative words here are bare notes of stylistic detail: 'recessed door and balustraded roof', a descriptive manoeuvre that becomes very familiar in Wharton's New England writing, and particularly in *Summer*,[24] where the details of the decorative fragments that still adhere to the ruined houses in and around North Dormer signify simultaneously both the presence and absence of an aesthetically sophisticated populace.

The public face of Sailport thus prepares us to see the private lives of its inhabitants chiefly through the buildings and streets that they inhabit. The squalor of the lives of Vexilla Thurber and her family is anticipated by the external appearance of the house 'divided from the sidewalk by a strip of down-trodden earth enclosed with broken palings'[25] and reinforced by the grimy, disordered interior with its variously physically or morally impaired inhabitants. The confined space occupied by Penelope Bent and her mother is one where the cramped living quarters are matched by an equivalent constriction of emotional and intellectual freedom: 'The two women lived in that involuntary familiarity from which neither speech nor silence can give sanctuary.'[26] The pinched lives of the women are compounded by the starkness of their choice of life whilst they remain subject to the ties of Sailport: the very existence of their dependent relatives forces them to a decision as between marriage and teaching. In a town reliant for its commercial success on the sea, the only connection they have with the economic reality of their place of residence is metaphoric: Penelope has been reduced to a state where she has 'a look of shipwrecked terror'[27] and Vexilla has an 'oscillating walk that suggested a ship with her steering gear out of order'.[28] The woman who has been left high and dry by the failure of her marriage plans and the woman whose face, and body, does not quite fit with the notion of 'smart'-ness adhered to by the school board can be illuminated by the dominant tropes of this sea-faring town but they remain firmly outside its commercial or (un)aesthetic boundaries.

It is the action of the rather meagrely villainous Mr Dayton which highlights the true condition of her existence for Penelope as the disruption in her plans is sufficient to precipitate a personal crisis of enormous proportions. In language which anticipates that which Wharton employs in her 1905 novel, *The House of Mirth*, when expressing the sentient response that Lily Bart makes to the vision of community she receives in Nettie Struther's kitchen,

Penelope Bent is retrieved from 'the brink' by a vision of community:

> The experiences of the last weeks had flung her out of her orbit, whirling her through dread spaces of moral darkness and bewilderment. She seemed to have lost her connection with the general scheme of things, to have no further part in the fulfilment of the laws that made life comprehensible and duty a joyful impulse. Now the old sense of security had returned. There still loomed before her, in tragic amplitude, the wreck of her individual hope; but she had escaped from the falling ruins and stood safe, outside of herself, in touch once more with the common troubles of her kind, enfranchised forever from the bondage of a lonely grief.[29]

She is given the opportunity to commit herself to the wider world and to a sense of 'common' purpose which is credited with the power to redeem her from isolation. The evidence of civic neglect which opened the story gives way at the end to a vision of expansion and renewal in the public as well as private sphere.

The fiction here colonises that 'borderline' which Amy Kaplan marked out as Wharton's particular territory, bringing the lives of women out into the streets of the big city, and, crucially, allowing recovery from her own encounter with the rocks, 'the wreck of her individual hope'. Her failure to marry will not be permitted to be the single defining moment in Penelope's life. The humiliation of being jilted by her fiancé for another woman which drives 'Poor Joanna' to Shell-heap Island in Jewett's *The Country of the Pointed Firs*,[30] such a denial of both self and community is not an option offered to Wharton's New England women. Penelope Bent refuses to be determined by the failure of her marriage plans but also by the alternative job for a woman, that is, schoolmistress. She will plunge, albeit tentatively, into the multiplicity of possibilities offered by the city; in 'moving with decision toward a definitely chosen goal'[31] she is seizing a hitherto masculine prerogative, leaving the small town behind her, as the 'smart ones'[32] do in *Ethan Frome*.

Not all of Edith Wharton's women get away. In a story which is concerned with a very different version of New England, the woman who is 'The Angel at the Grave' mounts a vigil over a tomb which fast becomes her own. She is in thrall, not to economic necessity, but to the intellectual hegemony of the generic type dominant in this landscape, Concord male. Wharton's consistent note in this story is of ironic distance; from the outset it is plain that the shrine, the repository of outmoded pieties, which Paulina sustains with her devotions, is to be treated sardonically. The narratorial voice which expressed aesthetic disdain, or even despair, whilst controlling the view of Sailport shown to the visitor, modulates into that of the cultural connoisseur, with a broad sweep of opinions encompassing past, present and future prospects for New England in relation to 'an admiring nation' and, indeed, to 'all the capitals of Europe'.[33]

There are three competing lexicons within this story: the language of transcendentalism, with its distinctive mixture of the plain and the semi-mystical, the language of the natural scientists and the language of the established church. All the interior and exterior furnishings of New England's intellectual traditions are on display here, as is the rapidity with which one set of dogmas or dogmatists can give way to the next. This is first made visible in the contending discourses which have give shape and expression to Paulina's life, but the language of the three are ultimately inter-changeable: 'I do like a congruous background – don't you?',[34] comments Paulina's final visitor. Paulina's aunts have adapted themselves as a species to the demands of their situation: 'there are spines to which the immobility of worship is not a strain'[35] but Paulina's transformation is shown to be as a result of a particular coincidence of cultural influences, not least amongst which is deprivation. The intellectually hungry child, reared in the far West, and desperate for mental nourishment is brought together with the confluence of New England and European religious philosophies in the work of Orestes Anson. Like Wharton's Vance Weston, to whom the architecture of the Hudson River in the novel which bears its name was 'the very emblem of man's long effort, was Chartres, the Parthenon, the Pyramids',[36] Paulina finds the key to an intellectual existence in the milieu of the Anson House but uses it only to lock herself inside the 'tomb' that she has colluded in building:

The House, by the time Paulina came to live in it, had already acquired the publicity of a place of worship; not the perfumed chapel of a romantic idolatry but the cold clean empty meeting-house of ethical enthusiasms. The ladies lived on its outskirts, as it were, in cells that left the central fane undisturbed. The very position of the furniture had come to have a ritual significance: the sparse ornaments were the offerings of kindred intellects, the steel engravings by Raphael Morghen marked the Via Sacra of a European tour, and the black-walnut desk with its bronze ink-stand modelled on the Pantheon was the altar of this bleak temple of thought.

To a child compact of enthusiasms, and accustomed to pasture them on the scanty herbage of a new social soil, the atmosphere of the old house was full of floating nourishment. In the compressed perspective of Paulina's outlook it stood for a monument of ruined civilizations, and its white portico opened on legendary distances.[37]

Whilst the unadorned idea can reverberate unchecked in the 'empty meeting-house' which is free from the clutter of generations of ritual, the hierophants of the temple occupy 'cells' which are as hierarchically bound as those of any members of an older religious order; their subservient, supporting rôle is firmly identified with past practice. The syncretism between ancient religions, alluded to in the incorporation of references to 'the Pantheon', Catholicism and the Quakerish faith of New England is both a mark of continuity as well as change, of natural selection in action as well as the enduring power of tradition. The inhabitants of this version of New England are simultaneously heirs to the whole of Western European civilisation – symbolised by the engravings of the 'Via Sacra of a European tour' – as well as to the work of the new 'Olympians' of Brook Farm; the language of religions old and new is ultimately interchangeable. In such a climate of 'promiscuity' of faith and expression the superannuation of Anson's philosophy is, Paulina comes to realise, inevitable: 'The change had taken place as slowly and imperceptibly as a natural process. She could not say that any ruthless hand had stripped the leaves from the tree: it was simply that, among the evergreen glories of his group, her grandfather's had proved deciduous.'[38]

Up against this cycle of replacement and renewal of faith – of religious or philosophical writings – Wharton places the empiricism of evolutionary processes, ironically locating the only certainty in the inevitability of change and development. Real originality is located in the language of science. The 'cloudy rhetoric' of Anson's writings and the terms in which his acolytes express their devotions are the 'dust' in the 'tomb hung about with dead ideas', whilst the 'decisive summons from the outer world'[39] is not a supernatural event, it speaks of the only 'sure' thing – scientific discourse, or 'scientific jargon'[40] as it appears to Paulina. The fire is re-lit in the temple of Orestes Anson as his work once more becomes a cause worth celebrating. The movement from the beginning to the end of the story is one which shows Paulina's act of memorialisation to have been validated. She is saved from the specimen status she is given at the outset: 'She had been born, as it were, into a museum, and cradled in a glass case with a label'[41] by the arrival of George Corby; he is the person who can now explain what Paulina has lived for, he can save both her and Orestes Anson from the fate of being labelled 'Use Unknown'[42] like the exhibits Newland Archer and Ellen Olenska mourn for in the Metropolitan Museum in *The Age of Innocence*.

Richard Brodhead, in his study of *Cultures of Letters: Scenes of Reading and Writing in Nineteenth-Century America*, talks about the range of offerings that might be found in the literary magazines, and particularly in the three most successful: the *Atlantic Monthly*, *The Century Magazine* and *Harper's Monthly Magazine*. He says: 'The great staple of these journals, the virtually mandatory item in their program of offerings, is the short piece of touristic or vacationistic prose, the piece that undertakes to locate some little-known place far away and make it visitable in print.'[43] In 'The Angel at the Grave', Wharton did just that, but instead of taking her readers to a remote geography, she conducted them to a New England that offered not only a specific topography but a history – the history of America in the western world – which could be mediated through the New England landscape and its inhabitants. Corby talks about the Anson house as if it were a reconstruction with the 'seclusion, the remoteness, the philosophic atmosphere' as much a product of a carefully staged re-enactment of the past as the 'jolly portraits', the 'books' and the 'elms'.[44] The story asks its readership to move beyond the picturesque, however, beyond the small talk of the tourist to the hard business of research and possible revelation. The resurrection of Orestes Anson as publicly noteworthy is concomitantly the redemption of Paulina; she asks Corby: ' "Then you believe in him?" '[45] and the reason why he might do so is not as important to her as the act of faith itself. Anson may have been translated from philosophy to science but this transformation is immaterial beside the notion of greatness, of worth, which must adhere to Anson if Paulina's life is not to have been lived in vain.

As subsequent generations revalue and reorientate understanding of what has been achieved in the past, so that past, in dialogue with the present, is altered; heritage is in the eye of the beholder. Wharton's regional fiction is as much concerned with ideas of history as with location, that which Brodhead identifies as the fashion for making the unvisitable accessible in prose has a parallel in Wharton's explanation of her motivation for writing *The Age of Innocence*;[46] that the only means of access to the 19th century for a post-1914-18 war generation was through the historical novel, a genre which foregrounds difference not continuity. My reading of Wharton as local colourist is designed to place her work in the broad context of developments in turn of the century American art and culture but also at the intersection between old and new Americas as expressed through the decline of small town New England as an ideology as well as a topography.

Wharton's story 'The Young Gentlemen', written in 1923 and published in 1926 is, in more ways than one, also about the national heritage but it is, additionally, profoundly concerned with the condition of privacy in the culture. These issues find expression in the narrative through an account of the contingencies of the development of tourism as a leisure-class pursuit. The bantering tone with which Wharton opens 'The Angel at the Grave': 'The House stood a few yards back from the elm-shaded village street, in that semi-publicity sometimes cited as a democratic protest against old-world standards of domestic exclusiveness',[47] and which is sustained throughout in the structure of the narrative as it follows the fall and rise of 'the House' as a place of pilgrimage, has no place in the later story. Waldo Cranch is an old New Englander, an authentic native in a little town otherwise dominated by incomers from the city who describe themselves as 'the tribe of summer visitors'. This nomadic group, made mobile by money, leisure and a claim to artistic stature, are the self-proclaimed curators of Harpledon, the guarantors of its situation as site of special cultural interest. The whole of the opening section of the story is devoted to the establishment of Harpledon as a place of particular interest to the tourist, and it begins as it means to go on: 'The uniform newness of a new country gives particular relief to its few relics of antiquity – a term which, in America, may fairly enough be applied to any building above ground when the colony became a republic.' Wharton establishes the situation of the town as being once more upwardly mobile, having been early settled as 'a thriving sea-port', abandoned during a more utilitarian age 'unmenaced by industry' as it was, and finally, taken over by those who 'nearly all professed to have "discovered" Harpledon'.[48]

This story, whilst it clearly treats the legacy of the past, is also a story of transition, marking, in as certain a manner as Henry James's 1886 novel, *The Bostonians*, the movement into the glare of publicity brought about by the expansion in the mass media. The exposure of Cranch's secret in the 'illustrated magazine' marks the passing of an age of trust and discretion, signalled by the failure of loyalty in the servant who betrays Cranch first to the press and then to the police, but also in the narrative retrospective on a time when 'front doors at Harpledon were always open'[49] unless, like Waldo Cranch, your house concealed a secret. The 30 years since Cranch, his faithful retainer and 'The Young Gentlemen' came to Harpledon are decades of massive social change, from a time when the place was actually a refuge from the threat of the indecent exposure of the children in Europe in the shape of the approach from the 'circus man'.

The resumption of his Americanness for Waldo Cranch is also the resumption of a privacy which he considers a part of his native entitlement. As Catherine says: 'It was a lonely lost place at that time...but it was a solitary life for so young a man as Mr Cranch was then, and when the summer folk began to settle here I was glad of it.'[50] It is interesting in terms of the complex series of private and public demarcations of territory that take place within the tale that Cranch's desire for privacy is attributed by all his friends to his Spanish blood. The accusation is, of course, in the light of the heavier responsibility attributed to the Spanish heiress by Cranch and Catherine, more accurate than its perpetrators can know, but the fact remains that Cranch has actually returned to America in order to preserve his secret, a secret which becomes synonymous with his pride. He expects to be able to operate as a much more private citizen in America than in Europe. When the narrator and Mrs Durant are considering Cranch's angry reaction to the duplicity of the architect their dialogue takes a familiar Harpledon turn when the peculiarities of their 'most brilliant man'[51] are at issue: '...Mr Cranch resents such liberties intensely. He's so punctilious." "Well, we Americans are not punctilious, and being one himself, he ought to know it by this time." She pondered again. "It's his Spanish blood, I suppose...he's frightfully proud."' (Wharton's ellipses).[52]

The nature of Americanness is under discussion in this story. There is a pointed reference to a recently learned lesson at the beginning: 'And now that civic pride has taught Americans to preserve and adorn their modest monuments, setting them in smooth stretches of turf and nursing the elms of the village green',[53] and the story does not let the question of what constitutes a national heritage rest. Wharton problematises the attention paid to appearances by looking behind or underneath the 'quaintness' of the town, even making special mention of the fact that 'the Cranch house was not quaint'.[54] Indeed, there is nothing picturesque about 40-year-old children, revealing as they do the impossibility of changing or ignoring the past. Harpledon itself becomes symbolic of a facile and sterile attitude to history; it is a town now inhabited by 'artists and writers' not 'India merchants'[55] and its heritage becomes an occasion for display not use. Blame for what is 'bad' is shown to be too easily placed upon such as the 'swart virago',[56] a conjuration of so much that is dark, dangerous and unknowable in the demonology of New England.

Wharton however, complicates the simple attribution of good or bad by offering alternative versions of the past. When Catherine describes Waldo Cranch's wife as 'the loveliest, soundest young creature you ever set eyes on' she is colluding in the demonisation of the 'old Spanish she-devil';[57] the inference is that no blame could attach to one so beautiful and therefore 'sound'. But the narrator's Aunt Lucilla, proved by the turn of events in the story to be wise not foolish, is an alternative teller of the tale of Harpledon; her residence pre-dating even Cranch's return, she knows about the rocking-horse, and she also re-tells the story of the Spanish heiress in a: 'tone of elegy. "Ah, poor thing, they say she never forgot the sunshine and the orange blossoms, and pined off early, when her queer son Calvert was hardly out of petticoats"'.[58] There are different ways of telling the story of the past and Wharton leaves her readers in no doubt that it is in the eyes of his audience that Cranch cannot bear to have his secret acknowledged. His suicide is the last act of a selfish pride; Catherine's explanation for his death: 'He rushed out and died sooner than have them seen, the poor lambs; him that was their father',[59] cannot do other than acknowledge that it is the exhibition of his sons before the world that he cannot live through; his own expectation of pain, not theirs, drives him to his death in the full knowledge that they will be seen. The boy-men are left to the tender mercies of the narrator as well as to Mrs Durant, but the self-confessed inadequacy of the narrator even to look upon this particular legacy of the past both opens and closes the narrative.

The young gentlemen are embodiments of the indissolubility of the ties of history that link America and Europe, and the fatal admixture of pride and stubbornness that kills Waldo Cranch testifies to the folly of seeking to deny the past by concealment or wilfulness. There is no place for secrecy in the brightly illustrated world of the magazines because a very particular version of the past is for sale; the Boston millionaire 'who came down on purpose to buy the picture' and the 'clever sketches'[60] sold to the illustrated magazine by the Boston architect are all evidence of the successful marketing of an American past which once it takes what it wants will exclude the young gentlemen, atavistic remnants as they are. They are exposed for exposure's sake, but once the worst is known then the village green is 'smooth' again and the picturesque predominant once more. Only Mrs Durant, ageing before the narrator's eyes, takes on the responsibility of the twin legacies of blood and money from the European past. The tension which is generated between the audience for the regional and its exponents is achieved through the very use of the form. The public appetite for local colour manifests itself in picture-buying raids from Boston, the artefacts of the region are appropriated and the 'atmosphere' is briefly sampled. Any contestation of the meaning of the past is evaded, however, by the eradication of the reality of the indigenous context, here, the painful sight of 'The Young Gentlemen', who even the narrator, that most self-conscious of local residents, has 'never yet had the courage to go down to Harpledon and see'.[61]

As I have already suggested, Hawthorne is the figure behind much of Wharton's New England writing and his is the precedent she claimed to be following. This is particularly the case in the two stories amongst my selection which can be classified as 'ghost' stories and which feature in the dedicated volume of supernatural tales she published in 1937. These stories are, however, very different in the use they make of the genre and particularly in the way they treat ambiguity within their narrative structures. Ambiguity is productive in both 'Bewitched' and 'All Souls' of thematic complexity and thus complicates any genre-bound reading – of both local colour and the ghost story – with other issues, most notably of class, sexuality and history. The ghost story could hardly function without the possibility of the alternative explanation but Wharton puts the escape-route into realism to completely different uses in her two stories. Tzvetan Todorov explains in his book, *The Fantastic: A Structural Approach to a Literary Genre*, the essence of the fantastic: "'*I nearly reached the point of believing*': that is the formula which sums up the spirit of the fantastic. Either total faith or total incredulity would lead us beyond the fantastic. It is hesitation which sustains its life.'[62] In Wharton's tales it is the moment of hesitation that allows space for the familiar New England issues which are raised in the texts to interrogate the generic securities of the supernatural.

'Bewitched' is Hawthornesque in every detail. Not only does Wharton construct her tale in the manner of Hawthorne, the landscape, for instance, is endowed with tragic, ancient history, native American as well as colonial American, but she makes it impossible for us not to associate her central family – the Brands – with Hawthorne's own Ethan. The ambiguities of the ending are also Hawthornesque as Wharton turns the evidence over to the reader for the attribution of meaning and even the decision about the true course of events. Sylvester Brand in Wharton's story, has been guilty of the same degree of hubris as Ethan Brand; both have sought to intervene in matters properly beyond human control, the secrets of the human heart. The mirthless laughter of these men reverberates throughout the two texts, bitterly accentuating the joylessness of their existences. Brand has separated his daughter Ora from Saul Rutledge and in the working out of the results of this intervention he takes vengeance into his own hands, laying his own family ghosts before his younger daughter, Venny, is exposed as a fraud and a promiscuous fraud at that. He has maintained an unhealthy isolation from his fellow citizens, even to the extent of marrying his cousin and thus turning evermore inward upon his own family and his fiercely maintained pride.

Although Gloria Erlich seems to find it a matter for consternation that Louis Auchincloss's explication of the story has Venny 'masquerading as the ghost of her dead sister',[63] it is surely centrally important in the construction of a tale which is profoundly dependent upon misunderstandings and misreadings of signs and signals not to preclude any interpretation. Wharton's spectre in this story has footprints, it cries out when shot, it bars doors and is susceptible to death by either gunshot wound or from pneumonia after walking barefoot through the snow, but to some of the inhabitants of Hemlock County this constitutes the ghostly. All the empirical evidence is presented to the reader as it is experienced by the centre of consciousness here, Orrin Bosworth, but in true Hawthornian mode, the facts of the case will never be subject to a single reading or to agreement amongst those who are witnesses to the events as they have been told. The evidence of Saul Rutledge's wasted body – having once been a 'straight muscular fellow'[64] – is visible proof that he is being punished for an excess of sexual desire, whether enacted with a living or a dead Brand. It is largely immaterial to Mrs Rutledge, although one version of events would be more productive of common scandal than another, whether his lover is alive or dead, it is his unfitness for work and likely demise that concerns her as one dependant upon his labours. Witchcraft features in the story only in words; the historical precedents of the Brand who was burned as a witch and the story of Lefferts Nash and Hannah Cory – 'They drove a stake through her breast. That's what cured him'[65] – enables Mrs Rutledge to repeat the accusation as appropriate to the final extermination of another Brand.

The existence of the ghost of Ora Brand is deliberately left unproven; supernature here is local language, local lore. Ghosts exist to express history, whether familial or cultural, and Ora and Venny are ultimately inter-changeable because both feature in the story only in someone else's configuration – they are mere ciphers of the otherwise inexpressible in their decaying, embittered and linguistically fixed community. The 'depth of moral isolation' occupied by Ethan Frome[66] is excavated in 'Bewitched' by human hands and hearts and the tragic survivors of such isolation are the real spectres which haunt the landscape. By his actions, here his arrogation of the right to dispose the affections of the human heart and even to take life itself, Sylvester Brand has removed all security and certainty from his life –'' 'Home? What home?'' He said'.[67] The conspiracy of silence which will be maintained between Deacon Hibben, Orrin Bosworth and Sylvester Brand himself will ensure that no-one will ever know the real truth.

When Orrin's sister brings him the news that Venny Brand is dying he pretends that he 'never knew much about her'[68] despite having already persuaded us to the contrary by talking about his own childhood, spent, like Venny's, 'under the icy shadow of Lonetop',[69] by giving the details of Venny's wild and unconstrained life earlier in the narrative and ultimately by turning up as a pallbearer at her funeral. Hemlock County is haunted by an amalgam of cross-cultural superstitions; relics of native Americans and colonial Americans are scattered throughout the landscape of the story but express nothing as powerfully as the awful isolation of the New England settlements:" 'It's a worm in the brain, solitude is' ".[70] The re-application of the same old story to the case of Saul Rutledge is further evidence of the poverty of expression, the deculturation of a landscape that once demonstrated a more complex aesthetic. The Rutledge house, like the decaying mansions visited by Lucius Harney and Charity Royall in *Summer*, holds 'traces of former elegance' in its gateposts and in 'the delicately fluted panels of an old wooden mantel'.[71]

Above all else, the story of 'Bewitched' is concerned with the decline of the culture and civilisation of New England. Its citizens are, in the main, inflexible adherents to an inappropriate text: ' "*Thou shalt not suffer a witch to live*" '.[72] As Kathy Fedorko says, it barely matters in the end which sister: 'was Saul Rutledge's lover, a live woman or a ghost, nor does it matter how either died, since both girls, "the handsomest girls anywhere round", meet the same fate, their sexuality feared and their lives controlled and ultimately ended by patriarchal power'.[73] Whilst not dissenting from Fedorko's reading I would foreground the waste that is signalled by their deaths as representative of the larger desolation of the humanised landscape. The uncontained sexuality of the Brand women in the narrative is constructed as a danger to the whole community – Ora who 'sickened and died' on her return and Venny who 'ran wild'[74] – are marginalised and finally demonised because their energy and inventiveness has no outlet in such a pinched and inflexible community.

Pre-eminent in this tale, as in *Ethan Frome* and *Summer*, its obvious relatives within the Wharton canon, is the landscape as symbolic of its inhabitants; the complexity of their inheritance as New Englanders is always tightly bound by the freezing constraints of the environment. The conflict is not between the electric light used emblematically at the beginning of 'All Souls' and the symbolic presence of the Brand who was burned as a witch in the earlier story. The modern world, for all its 'electricity, central heating and all the modern appliances'[75] is actually more, not less, susceptible to the haunting presence of the past. Wharton's regional fictions are nostalgic projects in the sense that they draw attention to a history inadequately noted, like the legendary 17th-century settlement of Ashmore; but they are stark in their exposure of the harshness of the lives led among the frozen expanses of New England and the confined space that there is for the refinements: '...a black stove planted on a sheet of zinc stuck out from the delicately fluted panels of an old wooden mantel'.[76] As in 'Young Goodman Brown' whether the coven really met or not, in 'Bewitched' whether the dead walked or not, the significant presence is that of Sylvester Brand, frozen not burned into immobility. 'Brand's face was the closed door of a vault, barred with wrinkles like bands of iron' and his counterpart, Mrs Rutledge, with her 'marble eyeballs; the bony hands...bloodless'[77] turned to stone like Hawthorne's 'Man of Adamant';[78] both testify to the petrifying effects of inflexibility, of adherence to a single idea or interpretation.

The eruption of supernature – or not – into these New England lives is the means by which the daily desperation of existence is revealed; on display here are the dire extremities of human need. Wharton's last completed short story, 'All Souls', is a compendium of all the generic tricks with which Wharton wrote New England – local colour, gothic, Hawthorne, heritage, historic – all are brought together in a culture-crossing, gender-ambiguous[79] narration of a tale of solitary terror. We are never told the gender of the narrator and although the fact that Sara Clayburn is undressed and put to bed by her cousin, which would seems to imply that it is a woman, we cannot be certain and there are no real opportunities for further inferences to be drawn. This delicately balanced androgyny is of great interest in the carefully structured tale of class, gender and racial division which is 'All Souls', where the status of every other participant is meticulously drawn and the stepping out from that status the driving force behind the narrative. The absence of gender markers is particularly noticeable because of the specific details that the narrator wants us to absorb about him/her. There is a desperate air of self-justification, a breathlessness, about the opening of 'All Souls'. It is another of Wharton's paragraph-long sentences, with qualifying clause after qualifying clause here excusing, explaining but also rationalising the act of narration. This tone – half of apology and half of vindication – establishes the veracity of the story about to be told, its grounding in established fact and familial relations, and leaves the narrator the space to establish a sympathetic though also self-opinionated voice of her/

his own before embarking upon the business of recounting someone else's story.

The teller of this tale is a literary person who has opinions about both writing and about the supernatural: 'I read the other day in a book by a fashionable essayist that ghosts went out when electric light came in. What nonsense! The writer, though he is fond of dabbling, in a literary way, in the supernatural, hasn't even reached the threshold of his subject'.[80] The knowledgeable literariness of the narrator is drawn in distinction from the matter-of-fact, prosaic character of Sara Clayburn. When told to rest in bed the 'muscular, resolute', 'quick, imperious', Sara looks upon the enforced bed-rest as an opportunity 'for going over her accounts and catching up with her correspondence'; lying awake during the small hours: 'She thought of reciting something to put her to sleep; but she seldom read poetry'.[81] She is thus rendered unfit to tell her own story by her abjuration of literature and her impatience with words. We are concomitantly warned by the manner of introduction of the tale that the person organising the material is someone with literary pretensions who will therefore be structuring and re-ordering the events of All Souls' eve in order to produce a particular effect upon the reader.

The tale is organised so that it is not until the end, the second All Souls' eve, that there is any mention of the supernatural as event within the narrative. Whilst the narrator renders the reader susceptible to the suggestion of occult occurences with the diatribe against modern denials of the ghostly, Sara Clayburn is quickly established as intrinsically in opposition to such superstitiousness. Her resources are predicated on reason, on fact and on established codes of conduct; it is the deviation from the norm of the structure of her household which threatens her personal and social security on the first occasion but on the second it is the deviation from the normal into the paranormal that sends her into exile. Everything about the way in which Whitegates and its denizens operate speaks of the total authority that Sara Clayburn must wield in order to feel secure. The presence of the woman in the vicinity of her house on the second successive All Souls eve is what finally communicates to Sara Clayburn that there are matters beyond her dominion, although she remains uncertain as to their origin: 'My cousin always said that she could not believe that incidents which might fit into the the desolate landscape of the Hebrides could occur in the cheerful and populous Connecticut Valley; but if she did not believe, she at least feared – such moral paradoxes are not uncommon – and though she insisted that there must be some natural explanation of the mystery, she never returned to investigate it'.[82]

Sara Clayburn is offered to the reader by her cousin as the most rational, sensible, authoritative woman imaginable. This sets up the situation whereby there is a hesitation, a suspension of judgement between fixing on the 'natural' as opposed to the supernatural explanation of events. The evidence which Wharton piles up in order to establish the non-appearance of the ghost of Ora Brand in 'Bewitched' is not matched here except by the opposition which is established between the narrator – the controller of events as they are relayed to the reader – and the subject of the story, Sara Clayburn. This is deliberately undermined by the narrator, however, when we are told: 'My cousin, at any rate, always regarded Agnes as the – perhaps unconscious, at any rate irresponsible – channel through which communications from the other side of the veil reached the submissive household at Whitegates'.[83] Ironically enough, it is the rigid demarcation of class boundaries that makes them so susceptible to instruction from either side of 'the veil'. The tension that exists between the real and the fantastic is also a tension between the narrator and her/his subject. The gothic mode reduced to the bare constituents of female fear and imprisonment, both of which are explicit and articulated in the text, is a central, controlling mode but it is also the means by which the text balances its claims between reality and supernature. The threat throughout the main body of the text is entirely natural not supernatural, speaking as it does of abandonment, disloyalty and class insurrection. The tale is only retrospectively fantastic and thus terror is located in actual threat, the effect of the absence of the servants upon a solitary woman with an injured ankle in the middle of a snow-bound, isolated country estate.

The story is centrally concerned with class, as it unites and as it divides, and with the particular appetites of the working class as regards their celebrations of the supernatural. Like the Brand girls, the women who work at Whitegates go off into the wilderness to obtain their sexual gratification. The narrator is quite plain on this subject at the end of the story: 'Anyone who has once felt the faintest curiosity to assist at a Coven apparently soon finds the curiosity increase to desire, the desire to an uncontrollable longing, which, when the opportunity presents itself, breaks down all inhibitions; for those who have once taken part in a Coven will move heaven and earth to take part again'.[84] The call of supernature here is also the call of the erotic, of a sexual experience which, like unmarried sex itself, is beyond the reach of social control, outside the structures which regulate feelings by legal or moral checks. There is no explanation offered by event except the appearance and re-appearance of the strange woman, the interpretation of the day and night spent by Sara Clayburn in an agony of suspense and pain belongs to a narrator who is ready to offer a 'conjectural' explanation of the only force or instinct which could cause such faithful retainers to forget their place.

The text of 'All Souls' is full of references to other lands and modes of existence, other dwelling places, vacation destinations, and other places of origination but at no point is there any differentiation drawn between modes of social organisation; the class structure in this tale is one of the things which is most most firmly embedded in both individual and collective identity. This is a world in which people can talk about having 'inherited' servants as well as houses and furniture and certainty is based upon the maintenance of a class structure which over-rides nationality. Agnes 'the dour old Scottish maid'[85] obeys no other earthly command than that of her mistress, it is only the occult that exercises transcendant power. Both Europe and America are invoked in this tale and the carefully laid details of equivalence between continents in the matter of the carriers of the supernatural are at their most potent here. As is appropriate in a tale which is predicated on class division 'All Souls' is as much about Europe as America. The hemlock into which the woman sent to 'fetch' the servants to the Coven disappears is resonant with multi-cultural signification: in its European plant form it yields a sedative or poison – and a poetic narcotic draught at that – in its North American form it is a larger species, a fir or spruce as opposed to an umbelliferous shrub. The tree can respectively induce altered states or it can conceal; it is the drug which poisoned Socrates, emblematic figure of the Old World, and as a species within the forest in which the Coven will be held it is a part of the wilderness which represents the New. The Hemlock also links 'Bewitched' to 'All Souls' as it is the name given to the County wherein the action takes place in the earlier story.

'All Souls' is the tale most particularly addressed to the 'Celtic sense' Wharton describes in her autobiography as making one susceptible to the ghostly tale, but the dread of anarchy, sexual or political, is the driving force behind the narrative. The story, in some measure, brings to a climax, though not necessarily to any resolution, the competing tensions in the New England stories. What is at issue is the relocation on a different level of understanding of a set of principles which have been the guide for a way of life. When Sara Clayburn limps painfully around her deserted house she finds that her own tightly controlled world has been inverted; her living quarters – the bedroom, the drawing room and the dining room – have been left disordered and unattended, whilst the servants' quarters – the bedrooms, the scullery and the kitchen – have been left with 'an air of scrupulous and undisturbed order'[86] signifying an absence planned for and executed.

The centre of power in the house has shifted from the woman who sits at a properly constituted dinner table: 'In the dining room, the table had been laid for her dinner of the previous evening, and the candelabra, with candles unlit, stood reflected in the dark mahogany. She was not the kind of woman to nibble a poached egg on a tray when she was alone, but always came down to the dining room, and had what she called a civilized meal' to the serving classes who have left a 'carefully scoured table' as evidence of their meticulous consideration in leaving everything in their territory clean before setting off on their All Souls' orgy. The woman who, even with a broken ankle, cannot bring herself to take the quickest route and use the 'back stairs', so powerfully do the staircases of the big house denote the status of their users, faints away when she hears a male voice, and a foreign voice at that, speaking in her kitchen. Just as there is a foreign, unknown, alien presence at the heart of the lure of the Coven so the 'passionately earnest, almost threatening'[87] tone of the male speaker in the kitchen has the power to make her swoon when all other manifestations of silent menace have failed.

Sara quizzes the woman whom she meets in the road about her destination and her purpose because she expects to be in control of her own life, her house, her grounds and the lives of those around her. The strange woman's re-appearance on the following All Souls' eve is proof positive that Sara is as subject to the will of another as her servants. In escaping to the city and the shelter of her cousin's well-serviced 'old-fashioned building'[88] she also, however, puts herself in the power of the narrator's interpretation of events. Logic and common sense lie vanquished in Sara's refusal to return 'to investigate'; the house will now stand empty, 'the power to communicate' which has lain dormant in Agnes until awakened by a 'kindred touch'[89] ironically signals the closing down of Whitegates. Ambiguity in 'All Souls' is circumscribed by the narratorial voice which provides the explanation in retrospect but this is not to say that there are no other options. The genre of the ghost story, carefully managed as it is here, is absolutely dependent upon the difference between doubt and suspicion. In her Preface to *Ghosts*, Wharton said 'when I first began to read, and then to write, ghost stories, I was conscious of a common medium between myself and my readers, of their meeting me halfway among the primeval shadows, and filling in the gaps in my narrative with sensations and divinations akin to my own'.[90] The ability to read one of these stories thus demonstrates the ability to surrender to instinct, to feeling. Sara Clayburn more than any other of Wharton's characters in these stories is precipitate between two worlds, one rational and ordered, one unknown and anarchic.

Every story here is concerned with the conflict between past and present but also between the rational and the emotional. All have been left without an easy rôle; Penelope Bent leaves Sailport for the uncertainty of the city, Paulina Anson must make the best of the ruins of her life in a new belief in Anson the natural scientist, Waldo Cranch chooses to die rather than confess his shame, the Rutledge girls perish in the wastes of their passion and Sara Clayburn refuses, illogically, to expose herself to 'risk' by returning to Whitegates. There are as many dissatisfied and hungry ghosts in exile from New England as there are in dark and gloomy Hemlock County; the past haunts Wharton's landscapes, a past of missed opportunities, of misplaced devotions and misdirected lives. In her discussion of 'Nation, Region, and Empire' in *The Columbia History of the American Novel*, Amy Kaplan writes: 'The regions painted with "local color" are traversed by the forgotten history of racial conflict with prior regional inhabitants, and are ultimately produced and engulfed by the centralized capitalist economy that generates the desire for retreat.'[91] Kaplan's observation is exemplified in Edith Wharton's New England texts; the history of the region, from the pre-Revolutionary massacre by Indians of Colonel Ashmore and his family in 'Bewitched' to the colonisation of Harpledon by artists and writers in 'The Young Gentlemen', is inscribed as a series of violent confrontations between the legacy of the past and the uses which the present makes of it. These stories interrogate preconceptions of the picturesque; through the judicious use of local colour inflected with gothic Wharton substantiates her vision of New England as a place of stark choices and few freedoms, intellectual or physical.

Notes

1. Wharton, Edith *The Collected Short Stories of Edith Wharton*, introduction by R.W.B. Lewis, 2 Vols. (New York: Charles Scribner's Sons, 1968) p. 197.
2. Kaplan, Amy *The Social Construction of American Realism* (Chicago: University of Chicago Press, 1988), pp. 65–66.
3. Donna Campbell in her essay 'Edith Wharton and the "Authoresses": the Critique of Local Color in Wharton's Early Fiction' *Studies in American Fiction*, Vol. 22 (2), Autumn 1994, pp. 169–183, examines to very good effect the 'repudiation' of local colour through 'city landscapes of naturalism' in Wharton's early stories, 'Mrs. Manstey's View' and 'Bunner Sisters'.
4. Susan Goodman in her essay 'Edith Wharton's Inner Circle', in Joslin, Katherine and Alan Price (eds) *Wretched Exotic: Essays on Edith Wharton in Europe* (New York: Lang, 1993), sees 'All Souls' as being essentially concerned with 'the loneliness of being the "extraordinary" woman' (p. 57), drawing a comparison between Wharton's position amongst the friendship group she calls 'the inner circle' and the situation of Sara Clayburn in the story. Gloria Erlich in *The Sexual Education of Edith Wharton* (Los Angeles: University of California Press, 1992) considers 'All Souls' to be an expression of the 'terror of abandonment' (p. 167). Erlich draws a comparison with Hawthorne's 'Young Goodman Brown' but concentrates on an interpretation which has the story mirroring Wharton's own situation as she nears the end of her life in a position of increasing isolation. Candace Waid in *Edith Wharton's Letters from the Underworld* (Chapel Hill: University of North Carolina Press, 1991) also suggests that 'a self-portrait of Wharton at the end of her life' (p. 175) can be discerned in the story.
5. Fedorko, Kathy A. *Gender and the Gothic in the Fiction of Edith Wharton* (Tuscaloosa: University of Alabama Press, 1995).
6. Banta, Martha 'The Ghostly Gothic of Wharton's Everyday World', *American Literary Realism*, Vol. 27 (1), 1994, pp. 1–10.
7. *The Social Construction of American Realism*, p. 80.
8. Bell, Millicent (ed.) *The Cambridge Companion to Edith Wharton* (New York, Cambridge University Press, 1995), p. 60.
9. Wharton, Edith *A Backward Glance* (New York, 1934; rpt. London, Constable & Co., 1972), pp. 293–94.

10. Freeman, Mary E. Wilkins *Pembroke*, 1894 (New Haven: College and University Press, 1971).
11. Freeman, Mary E. Wilkins *The Winning Lady and Others* (New York, Harper and Brothers Publishers, 1909), pp. 243–277.
12. *Edith Wharton's Letters from the Underworld*, p. 94.
13. See Candace Waid's lengthy discussion of Wharton and Wilkins Free man in Chapter 3 of her book, *Edith Wharton's Letters from the Underworld.*
14. Wharton, Edith *The Ghost Stories of Edith Wharton* (New York, Charles Scribners' Sons, 1973), Preface (1937).
15. Singley, Carol *Edith Wharton: Matters of Mind and Spirit* (New York: Cambridge University Press, 1995), p. 112.
16. *The Ghost Stories of Edith Wharton*, pp. 252–53.
17. Wharton, Edith *The Age of Innocence* (New York: D. Appleton & Co., 1920), p. 291.
18. *The Collected Short Stories of Edith Wharton*, p. 197.
19. *The Collected Short Stories of Edith Wharton*, p. 204.
20. Goodman, Susan *Edith Wharton's Women: Friends and Rivals* (Hanover, University Press of New England, 1990), p. 8.
21. *The Collected Short Stories of Edith Wharton*, p. 199.
22. *The Collected Short Stories of Edith Wharton*, p. 205.
23. *The Collected Short Stories of Edith Wharton*, p. 197.
24. See my discussion of the architectural detail of the houses visited by Charity Royall and Lucius Harney in *Summer* in *Edith Wharton: Traveller in the Land of Letters*, (London: Macmillan, 1990), pp. 77–78.
25. *The Collected Short Stories of Edith Wharton*, p. 208.
26. *The Collected Short Stories of Edith Wharton*, p. 205.
27. *The Collected Short Stories of Edith Wharton*, p. 204.
28. *The Collected Short Stories of Edith Wharton*, p. 206.
29. *The Collected Short Stories of Edith Wharton*, p. 214.
30. Jewett, Sarah Orne, *The Country of the Pointed Firs*, (Boston and New York: Houghton Mifflin, 1896).
31. *The Collected Short Stories of Edith Wharton*, p. 213.
32. Wharton, Edith *Ethan Frome* (New York, 1911; rpt. London: Constable, 1976), p. 28.
33. Wharton, Edith *Roman Fever and Other Stories* (New York: Charles Scribner's Sons, 1964), pp. 114–15.
34. *Roman Fever and Other Stories*, p. 128.
35. *Roman Fever and Other Stories*, p. 116.
36. Wharton, Edith *Hudson River Bracketed* (New York, D. Appleton & Co., 1929), p. 354.
37. *Roman Fever and Other Stories*, p. 117.
38. *Roman Fever and Other Stories*, pp. 124–5.
39. *Roman Fever and Other Stories*, p. 126.
40. *Roman Fever and Other Stories*, p. 130.
41. *Roman Fever and Other Stories*, p. 115.
42. Wharton, Edith *The Age of Innocence*, p. 312.
43. Brodhead, Richard *Cultures of Letters: Scenes of Reading and Writing in Nineteenth-Century America* (Chicago, University of Chicago Press, 1993), p. 125.

44. *Roman Fever and Other Stories*, p. 128.
45. *Roman Fever and Other Stories*, p. 129.
46. See my discussion of the historical novel and Wharton's motivation for writing in this genre in Chapters One and Seven of my book *Edith Wharton: Traveller in the Land of Letters*.
47. *Roman Fever and Other Stories*, p. 114.
48. *The Collected Short Stories of Edith Wharton*, pp. 385–6.
49. *The Collected Short Stories of Edith Wharton*, pp. 391–2.
50. *The Collected Short Stories of Edith Wharton*, pp. 401–2.
51. *The Collected Short Stories of Edith Wharton*, p. 391.
52. *The Collected Short Stories of Edith Wharton*, p. 393.
53. *The Collected Short Stories of Edith Wharton*, p. 385.
54. *The Collected Short Stories of Edith Wharton*, p. 387.
55. *The Collected Short Stories of Edith Wharton*, pp. 385–6.
56. *The Collected Short Stories of Edith Wharton*, p. 387.
57. *The Collected Short Stories of Edith Wharton*, pp. 400–1.
58. *The Collected Short Stories of Edith Wharton*, p. 387.
59. *The Collected Short Stories of Edith Wharton*, p. 398.
60. *The Collected Short Stories of Edith Wharton*, pp. 391–2.
61. *The Collected Short Stories of Edith Wharton*, p. 402.
62. Todorov, Tzvetan *The Fantastic: A Structural Approach to a Literary Genre*, Translated by Richard Howard (Ithaca, New York, Cornell University Press, 1975), p. 31.
63. *The Cambridge Companion to Edith Wharton*, p. 115.
64. Wharton, Edith *The Ghost Stories of Edith Wharton* (New York: Charles Scribner's Sons, 1973), p. 151.
65. *The Ghost Stories of Edith Wharton*, p. 156.
66. *Ethan Frome*, p. 62.
67. *The Ghost Stories of Edith Wharton*, p. 166.
68. *The Ghost Stories of Edith Wharton*, p. 164.
69. *The Ghost Stories of Edith Wharton*, p. 157.
70. *The Ghost Stories of Edith Wharton*, p. 161.
71. *The Ghost Stories of Edith Wharton*, pp. 146–8.
72. *The Ghost Stories of Edith Wharton*, p. 156.
73. Fedorko, Kathy A. *Gender and the Gothic in the Fiction of Edith Wharton*, (Tuscaloosa, University of Alabama Press, 1995), p. 112.
74. *The Ghost Stories of Edith Wharton*, p. 158.
75. *The Ghost Stories of Edith Wharton*, p. 252.
76. *The Ghost Stories of Edith Wharton*, p. 148.
77. *The Ghost Stories of Edith Wharton*, p. 166.
78. Kathy Fedorko also draws attention to the likeness between Wharton's descriptions of Mrs Rutledge and Hawthorne's 'Man of Adamant', p. 110.
79. Kathy Fedorko ends her book with a discussion of 'All Souls' which treats productively the indeterminate gender of the narrator, pp. 157–64.
80. *The Ghost Stories of Edith Wharton*, p. 252.
81. *The Ghost Stories of Edith Wharton*, pp. 253–7.
82. *The Ghost Stories of Edith Wharton*, p. 274.

83. *The Ghost Stories of Edith Wharton*, p. 273.
84. *The Ghost Stories of Edith Wharton*, pp. 273–4.
85. *The Ghost Stories of Edith Wharton*, p. 255.
86. *The Ghost Stories of Edith Wharton*, p. 260.
87. *The Ghost Stories of Edith Wharton*, pp. 261–4.
88. *The Ghost Stories of Edith Wharton*, p. 269.
89. *The Ghost Stories of Edith Wharton*, p. 273.
90. *The Ghost Stories of Edith Wharton*, p. 2.
91. Elliott, Emory (ed.) *The Columbia History of the American Novel* (New York, Columbia University Press, 1991). p. 256.

7

The Means and Ends of Genre in the Short Fiction of Charlotte Perkins Gilman

Charlotte Perkins Gilman never wrote anything without having an ideal reader for her text in mind. In an extensive treatise on ethics and society, *His Religion and Hers: A Study of the Faith of Our Fathers and the Work of Our Mothers*, published in 1923, she wrote: 'For women already educated enough to grasp the facts and their relations, and able to make a conviction work, it should require no more than a book or two, a lecture or two, to start swifter social evolution'.[1] With such a faith in the capacity of her readers to bring about change she wrote to a definite purpose and the various and many genres she employed were exploited for all they were worth to serve her didactic intentions. In her monthly magazine, *The Forerunner*, which she published between 1909 and 1916 she worked in a variety of genres as a matter of course. As Ann J. Lane notes in her biography of Gilman, *To Herland and Beyond: The Life and Work of Charlotte Perkins Gilman*, 'She wrote every line of the thirty-two-page magazine herself. Each issue contained editorials, comments and observations, critical essays, book reviews, poetry, and fiction. Each year two full-length books were serialized, ordinarily one fiction and one non-fiction'.[2]

In her autobiography Gilman estimated the readership of the magazine at about 1500 and its circulation 'all over this country, quite widely in Europe, and as far afield as India and Australia'. However, as she makes plain, the ideological and the profitable could never abide together harmoniously in this particular publishing enterprise: 'I have never had a good lecture agent or manager for any length of time. Such a person, to succeed, must have a strong conviction of the value of my work, *and* business ability. These do not coexist...can a press-agent be imagined who would work for a woman who would not allow the least exaggeration or misstatement?.'[3] In the main she relied upon word of

147

mouth and personal letters to those whom she thought would be sympathetic to her causes as her means of publicity, and the limits of the effectiveness of this strategy were reached only halfway to the number of three thousand subscribers that she needed in order to break even.

Gilman expected her readers to move between a multiplicity of genres, especially since the themes and subjects of her work were consistent between fiction and non-fiction and both were educative in intent. Anne Cranny-Francis, in the introduction to her book, *Feminist Fiction*, discusses the manipulation of generic forms by feminist writers, whose intent, like Charlotte Perkins Gilman's, is to expose the workings of the prevailing ideological and aesthetic hegemony. Again in the autobiography, Gilman describes the pitch of desperation to be heard that she reached before embarking upon *The Forerunner* enterprise: 'But as time passed there was less and less market for what I had to say, more and more of my stuff was declined. Think I must and write I must, the manuscripts accumulated far faster than I could sell them, some of the best, almost all – and finally I announced: "If the editors and publishers will not bring out my work, I will!" And I did.'[4] Whilst she refused the title of feminist,[5] there is no doubt that the position she took up was radical and her work issues a ceaseless stream of challenges to the patriarchal status quo. The use of different genres was an intrinsic part of her adversarial stance; in working within the boundaries of convention, both literary and social, she could proclaim her resistance by exposing what constitutes a literary form in rewriting it. As Cranny-Francis says: 'Feminist generic texts are sites of ideological struggle, just as are conservative generic texts – but the feminist texts show the struggle in process.'[6]

The vast majority of the stories I want to discuss here were first published in *The Forerunner* where the only editor Gilman had to please was herself; the effect she was to have upon her audience, not the publisher, was at the forefront of her mind. She was, in many ways, following in the footsteps of her great-aunt, Harriet Beecher Stowe and other women writers whose work was intensely moral, bound up as it was with the advancement of the cause of women's rights alongside the promulgation of the Christian faith. However, where Gilman differs is in the secularisation of her ethical base; she is a sociologist first and a Christian second and the moral imperative of her fiction is often transformative of the spiritual into the temporal. Her reforming vision is to a large extent

Godless, or at least Godless until such time that humanity can be considered worthy of the attention of the God it deserves, meliorism was her creed, not the Calvinism of her Beecher forebears.

In her bitter little piece, 'A Strange Land', published in *The Forerunner* in August 1912,[7] where she ironically outlines the benefits which might accrue to a society which made health and happiness higher goals than profit, Gilman says, in parenthesis: '(Now we were told long since that man was made in the image of God, and some of us believed it, but it did not occur to us to consider if the images were a credit to the original or if we might not improve the copy).' Gilman's own ideological underpinning for all engagement in the public arena is contained within this aside: that humankind can be improved to a point where Godlike stature and status might be attained on earth: the babies here are 'cherubim', the women are 'Graces, walking on real feet'.[8] Similarly, in her fantasy, 'Freed',[9] published in *The Forerunner* five months earlier than 'A Strange Land', once a whole-cultural revolution has taken place, in which most of the fruits of civilisation to date are destroyed 'save for the department of science . . . of biology and chemistry, astronomy and physics, with an anthropology and ethnology that stopped before history began',[10] then, and only then can humanity truly find the Divine: 'And all over the world, the mind of man turned to the thought of God, as it does by nature. And being free from the Load of a Thousand Lies they sought and found, knowing God at work and gladly doing the work of God'.[11]

Nothing happens by faith alone in Gilman's reforming fictions, faith is one of the luxuries of an achieved state of perfection and, in her 1915 Utopian novel, *Herland*, it falls a long way behind other cultural phenomena as a matter worth explaining to the alien visitors. When the national faith is finally broached as a subject between Ellador and the narrator, Vandyck Jennings, then it is predicated as 'a religion which gave to the searching mind a rational basis in life, the concept of an immense Loving Power working steadily out through them, toward good',[12] but the idea of an afterlife is vehemently abjured by the women as a potentially dangerous distraction from the improvement of the living world for future generations of Herlanders. Whilst Harriet Beecher Stowe had only spiritual not secular comfort to offer the enslaved Tom in her enormously influential *Uncle Tom's Cabin*, Gilman dissents from applying this particular doctrinal legacy from the Beecher men and women who were her paternal ancestors. No improvement, for Gilman, can come from those who would seek perfection in Heaven, the only good is, as Ellador says, 'for this life – on earth'.[13]

Gilman's fictions are thus directed and directing of their audience toward the achievement of social improvements; they are intensely moral but they are not Christian in any but the broadest sense. In *His Religion and Hers: A Study of the Faith of Our Fathers and the Work of Our Mothers*, Gilman is clear about first principles: 'Ethics, as we have seen, is a social science'.[14] Indeed, one of the informing contentions behind this book is Gilman's argument with 'death-based religions'; as she says in the chapter, 'Religion and Conduct': 'If we accept the postulate that our main duty here is to improve the human race and the world it makes, then all these static religions are to be condemned in so far as they do not tend to improvement. But if our main postulate is that life here is a necessary evil, a mere stepping stone to life elsewhere, then there is indeed no reason for taking thought for the morrow on earth.'[15] All Gilman's writing, whether fiction or social science, is purposeful, and completely absorbed by 'taking thought for the morrow'; starting from a coherent ethical base, she sought to choose and use the literary genres which would support her pedagogic intentions.

Charlotte Perkins Gilman was not, in her writing of fiction, an artistic innovator in the service of letters; the development of a coherent aesthetic was never her concern. She was, however, a somewhat unwitting innovator in her manipulation of the generic for didactic purposes; 60 years before John Fowles published *The French Lieutenant's Woman*, where the Victorian context is interrogated through alternative endings, Gilman published 'With a Difference (Not Literature)', a story with two endings which provides another option for the daughter, who, discarded by her seducer, is cast out by an angry father. As Carol Farley Kessler comments: 'Gilman provided an "old story" and then continued it beyond the expected ending of a young woman's victimization, to depict a mother standing with her daughter against a punitive and prideful father with sufficient force to change his mind and culminate in an innovative conclusion.... Gilman's closure refuses the death typically meted out to "fallen women" and insists upon this alternative model of finding happiness in working and living independently'.[16] Gilman's radical morality informs and unifies her fiction to the extent that the great iconoclastic ideas which find repeated expression throughout her work in both fiction and non-fiction often have a transformative power over the forms she employs. The genres she uses are picked up and put down as the subject dictates; she moves in and out of fantasy, fable, detective, romance, melodrama, homily, parable and legend with ease and expediency. Above all else she puts to good service any mode which will carry a significance beyond the bare lines of the narrative. In order to bring about her great work, the improvement of the human race, she harnesses any means to her end, and whilst I do not intend to discuss all these genres here, I do want to focus on those which in their formal constituents facilitate the educative enterprise.

It is to do more than to pun on two meanings of generic if we take the variety of uses which Gilman makes of genre and equate it in some way with her all-absorbing interest in theorising the species, the human race. Her fiction is always working with ideas about the generic as opposed to the specific, replete with exempla designed to convert people to the communitarian in preference to individualism, it is inextricably bound up with the process of the modification of traditional practices – literary as well as social – in order to reflect changing needs. Her characters are types but they are so because they function within a society that is dependent on the maintenance of type, particularly gender types. All Gilman's fiction is self-reflective – in the sense that everything refers back to her personal morality – but that morality is predicated on the basis that all and everything must change.[17] Gilman is a writer of great strength and some distinction; her passionate ambition to make the world a better place makes her an original artist as well as a brilliant social scientist[18] and much of that originality stems from the way in which she handles genre.

In this chapter I intend to focus on Gilman's use of the generic in her fiction and to examine particularly the interaction of different genres as they effect and affect the reading position[19] of her audience. Gilman, unsurprisingly, was often at her best as a writer when working within genres which support the didactic enterprise, like fable and romance, but as all of her work is, to a certain extent, social satire – because it is oppositional – the particular use she makes of these educative forms can also achieve transformation of both genre and subject. A rhetorical microcosm of Gilman's manipulation of the generic which goes some way to illustrating my argument can be found in her use of irony, a feature of those of her works which fall into the larger genres of fantasy, legend, fable and romance as well as satire. Gilman's fiction is, in fact, entirely suffused with irony as there is always an opposite state of affairs which acts as an alternative text to every piece she writes. This is represented most straightforwardly in *Herland* where Ourland is the (sub-)standard by which every facet and feature of the womanland is to be measured and applauded. Irony itself, at the most basic level, is an expression which carries an opposite meaning, and any society which is subjected to the ironic is generally offered to the reader as an inferior culture. Satire is by necessity a dialogic medium which forces the audience into a position of dissension from the culture or the people ironised and Gilman's reader, therefore, must identify with the alterity, no matter how radical, rather than take the full force of her contempt for the world order as expressed through the fiction.

In the story or legend 'The Unnatural Mother', published in the November 1916 issue of *The Forerunner*,[20] Gilman's prose is incandescent with irony. The whole rationale behind the telling of a legend is to mark an event as one which has been crucial in shaping the identity of a community. The story of Esther Greenwood as narrated by the Toddsville dames subordinates the truth that Esther saved the lives of 1500 people to the fact that she left her daughter to be a charge upon the town's charity, having sacrificed her own life for the community. That the moral which the women of Toddsville wish to draw – that Esther was a bad and 'unnatural' mother to put the greater good before herself and her child – is so clearly a perverse reading of the legend that the oppositional stance offered to the reader from the opening of the story also precipitates the espousal of other – more contentious – positions advocated by Esther and the father who educated her: "He taught that innocent girl about – the Bad Disease! Actually!" "He did!" said the dressmaker. "It got out, too, all over town. There wasn't a man here would have married her after that." Miss Jacobs insisted on taking up the tale. "I understand that he said it was 'to protect her'! Protect her, indeed! Against matrimony! As if any man on earth would want to marry a young girl who knew all the evil of life! I was brought up differently, I assure you!".[21] As I discuss at length in my chapter on Gilman's use of the analogue, those who teach girls about 'the Bad Disease' would always be, in Gilman's scheme of things, morally sublime, and the unremitting nature of her irony in the telling of this tale pushes the reader into an equivalent, morally radical posture, ultimately forcing complicity in the coercion of the tale away from the ideological position of the townspeople to that once occupied by Esther Greenwood.

Gilman, as already noted, makes effective and dynamic use of the generic where it is consonant with her pedagogic purpose. In 'The Unnatural Mother' she manipulates the properties of legend to her own ends to achieve a high level of coherence between form and theme where the manner of communicating the content – satire – privileges the audience above those who tell the legend to the visiting writer. The genre of legend is one which belongs particularly to the indigenous storyteller; the story relies upon its locality for significance. Here, however, the locality provides evidence only of the perversion of what is contained within the idea of community, the very essence of which should form the substance of a legend. So, in order to reorientate her reader's understanding of what community might mean she wrests the legend away from the point of view of the women of Toddsville and gives it back to Esther Greenwood by introducing the arbitrating voice of the stranger. The use of the outsider to organise the narrative – as in *Herland* and numerous other of Gilman's stories where an incomer, usually a journalist, is sent to investigate the local situation and report back – allows the locals to condemn themselves out of their own mouths and the narrator to organise the information she is given so as to place Esther at the heart of a very different kind of story. Esther's upbringing and young womanhood are narrated in the manner of the fairy tale, without ironic inflection; the 'unnatural mother' thus becomes a heroine whose exploits are raised to the level of the mythic, and the dominant social order is subjected to critical contempt, so that its prejudices and prurience now become the stuff of legend.

The ideological imperative behind 'The Unnatural Mother' is to be found in Gilman's *His Religion and Hers* where she says: 'The woman's conscience runs narrow and deep: she is loyal to her husband even when it means treason to her children, and devoted to her own children with complete indifference to the children of the world. She does not yet recognize that her loyalty is due first to the human race, then to the child of her body, and then to her husband. We cannot expect wide understanding of economics or politics from a so-long subject class.'[22] In the fiction Gilman is able to position her readers so that they espouse the radical, alternative line; the ignorance of those who support the status quo is acknowledged within the text and critiqued at structural level through the tension generated between the narrator and the expressed opinions of those who call Esther an 'unnatural mother'.

As is to be anticipated where a writer is working in as engrossed a manner as Gilman in social satire, genres which in the hands of other writers might be used to comic as well as satiric purposes are incorporated to quite different ends. Her use of the allegoric, for instance, in beast fables like 'Two Storks' and 'Lady Oyster', and in 'Improving on Nature' where animals are used not to represent human traits but to point to an alternative – and better – means of sexual, reproductive and parental organisation, is deadly serious. To elect to use the fable form was in many ways a natural choice for Gilman as she often makes use of comparisons between the human and the animal to reinforce her arguments about the unnatural dependence of women upon men in the established social order. In *Women and Economics: A Study of the Economic Relation Between Men and Women as a Factor in Social Evolution*, published in 1898 and perhaps, more than any other, the book which established Gilman's worldwide reputation as a radical social theorist, she is clear about what we have to learn from other species.

In her first chapter Gilman develops the argument that the human race is 'the only animal species in which the sex-relation is also an economic relation.'[23] and goes on to make specific comparisons with different bird and animal species to prove her point. The comparative strain in Gilman's thesis is an important one in *Women and Economics* and she returns to it over and over again to reinforce her point about the intimate relationship between the economic dependence of women and the 'sale' of the 'sex-relation'.[24] In the fiction the transparency of the fable form serves to make the content more not less cogent in its depiction of the tragic wastefulness of the prevailing social order, especially as regards motherhood. 'Two Storks', originally published in *The Forerunner*, in February 1910,[25] is a fable of birds who are to all intents and purposes human, the stork, after all, is so closely associated with new motherhood that it is, in this context, more or less a dead metaphor and thus must be revitalised in order to carry more complex meaning in Gilman's fable. This is achieved by taking the focus of the story away from the baby-carrier to the species – a movement consonant, after all, with the abiding principle of Gilman's ideas for reforming the organisation of the family.

The language of the fable is anthropomorphic: the male stork is described as 'narrow-minded', as having 'consorted mainly with striplings of his own kind' before marriage, and he is characterised as a ready subscriber to all the standard clichés about women and maternity. The male is the centre of consciousness for the tale, his wife comes to the reader, in his version, mediated first by his pride and then by his outrage, but always as she is constructed through his feelings as a 'Mother' not as an equal. This is not the only version of her the reader receives, however, as constant asides in the narrative allow us to see that her activity and capacity is equal to his. The male stork is strong and young, he takes his share of the responsibility for hatching and feeding the babies, although his participation is ironised by Gilman through his self-consciousness of his great dedication to his task, stimulated as it is by pride of possessorship rather than the 'instincts and processes of motherhood' with which he credits his wife. He is, nevertheless, an instinctive animal, dreaming of what it will be like to fly free again and Gilman soars with him on lyrical heights: 'In his dreams came a sense of vast heights and boundless spaces of the earth streaming away beneath him; black water and white land, grey water and brown land, blue water and green land, all flowing backward from day to day, while the cold lessened and the warmth grew'. He is a beautiful, powerful creature, ambitious to enjoy his freedom, but, Gilman makes plain, so is his wife; her dreams are also of 'days and nights of ceaseless soaring'.

The male stork is content with the way in which his life is structured until it is made clear to him that the physical capacity of his wife and children is equal to his, then his understanding of a world organised for his comfort and satisfaction is threatened. He does not notice his wife's soaring amidst the clouds, he does not recognise his children as grown, their existence is subordinate to his, and 'his highest ideals' – 'shattered' by their aspiration to fly away with him – are in fact dependent upon the fact that he absents and differentiates himself from his family. The urge to migrate is the only instinct given credibility here, however, and it is emphatically a characteristic of species not of gender as is shown in the natural return to the skies by the mother and the 'happiness of the First Flight' of the children. Everything else which the male stork is eager to put down to instinct is revealed by subsequent events to be simply his way of ordering the external world to his own satisfaction. The narrative is structured so that although the male stork is the dominating consciousness we are never without insight into the position of the female; her perspective is phrased almost as a chorus to his: 'They were in her dreams too, but he did not know that.... This was in her dreams too, but he did not know that'. The cumulative effect of the hints and insights into her parallel activity prepares us for the end and for her pre-eminent speed and pleasure: '"But you are a Mother!" he panted, as he caught up with them. "Yes!" she cried, joyously, "but I was a Stork before I was a Mother! and afterward! – and All the Time!"'.

'Two Storks' is one of Gilman's most coherent and lyrical stories and its didactic purpose is a part of its beauty not a distraction from it. All its constituent components work in harmony together to produce a simple yet serious moral which is expressed through language and imagery which both advance the narrative and deepen the meaning. The tendency of the male stork to articulate his feelings in cliché is expressed through his conversion of his social and human relations into proper nouns: 'Her of the Well-built Nest; Her of the Gleaming Treasure of Smooth Eggs; Her of the Patient Brooding Breast, the Warming Wings, the downy wide-mouthed Group of Little Ones' and Gilman demonstrates the inevitable tendency of such pieties to become accepted tenets of the culture when the male's final argument is based on the premise of having translated his own feelings into social rules and norms: 'Your body is for the Wonder of the Gleaming Treasure!...You have forgotten the Order of Nature!'. The female stork, however, like him, has only one instinct – to migrate and so: 'She did not heed him'. She adjusts the chain of proper nouns so that emphasis and importance fall equally on the species, the rôle and the activity; she restores maternity as well as flight to the mundane, ignoring his rhetorical heights and normalising the events of their shared lives: 'Stork...Mother...All the Time...Storks...Flying'. Neither she nor the children allow themselves to be infantilised by language which seems to cherish and protect but actually marginalises and incapacitates, when the 'Precious Little Ones' in their father's definition are seen directly, they flap 'their strong young wings in high derision'.[26]

In 'Two Storks' Gilman allows her woman and children freedom from the ideology espoused by the male and it is the migratory instinct and its overwhelming power which carries the authentication of their independence within the narrative. In 'Lady Oyster', the other beast fable I want to discuss here, all the creatures she depicts as mothers are in thrall to 'the process of maternity' and unable to look beyond it, even so far as the care and control of the resultant children. Published in *The Forerunner* in May 1912,[27] 'Lady Oyster' is a series of dialogues between a variety of new mothers and a series of interested observers of their behaviour. The fable moves up the evolutionary ladder from the Oyster, through the Mud-wasp and the Sheep, to the Human and, as in 'Two Storks', the language is anthropomorphic, all species here having human attributes and representing different types of woman, rather than different types of creature. In his discussion of allegory in *The Fantastic: A Structural Approach to a Literary Genre* Tzvetan Todorov talks about the explicit nature of the existence of two meanings in texts which have allegorical functions and continues: 'Fable is the genre that comes closest to pure allegory, in which the first meaning of the words tends to be completely effaced'.[28] This is certainly the case in this fable where we are not asked to believe, even in the most minimal of ways in the existence of talking oysters or sheep; there is no supernatural activity as there is in other Gilman stories like 'When I Was a Witch'[29] and 'If I Were a Man'.[30] The fable is concerned with morality and is thus a human not an animal matter; the biological processes of reproduction are not being critiqued but the social processes which follow parturition. The creatures which are enumerated quickly become less important for their own species-indicators than their human attributes.

'Lady Oyster' is a complacent being, given definition by what she cannot do rather than what she can and yet, withal, able to feel 'an ineffable, a transcendant satisfaction' with her lot as the generator of 'Three Million Eggs'. The production of such numbers, despite the warning from the 'Captious Crab' that all her eggs will be eaten by predators, is sufficient to reassure the oyster that she has done her 'duty', the word 'duty' resounding throughout this text as an ironic knell. In her turn the 'Lady Mud-wasp' lays eggs and also provides for their nourishment: 'She covered up the neat hole, the elegant eggs, the crippled caterpillar, and pranced in pride and satisfaction, flirting her shining slim body about, quite happy'. Having carried out the minimal 'marvelous processes of nature' the Mud-wasp is 'Merry' and uninterested in the fact that her children will not survive, a bird having eaten their only means of nourishment, 'duty' again is satisfied and she returns to her life of frivolity. The Sheep also is content with having given birth, fed her child and admired its 'superior' beauty. On the subject of the life it will have, even the emotive language of the 'Skeptical Skunk' leaves the Sheep unmoved: 'Presently they will cut his waggle tale off. Continually they will cut his curly wool off. Ultimately they will cut his helpless throat'. The range of duties which the sheep expects to fulfil do not go beyond the basic notion of what it means to be a mother: 'A living lamb, I have nourished it from my own body, a miracle of nature'; the short-term, means not ends are the all-absorbing focus of the mothers herein described.

When Gilman moves onto the human mother matters become more complicated as it is no longer simply life and death but quality of life that is at issue. It is not the fulfilment of a biological imperative that is under discussion as the 'Human Creature' invokes larger social endorsements of the reproductive act as supportive of her complacency: 'With her human intellect, she was able to see and to venerate the long majestic interplay of vital forces which had resulted in this consummate act. With all allied processes, social, civil and domestic, she had fulfilled the law of her being, the process of maternity'. Her interlocutor here, who has a combination of the skills and knowledge consistently valorised by Gilman in her fiction: 'a trained nurse, a skilled kindergartner, and a student of sociology' asks the new mother to think about her child in the context of the whole of society, of 'humanity' at large. It is at this point, however, that the woman and the animals are shown to be equal in their disregard for the long-term and 'the Audacious Aunt' brings us back to the point of departure with her equation of the Human with the Oyster at the close. Her diatribe against unthinking maternity makes explicit the way in which the individual and the species have been forced into opposition and it is this dislocation that is the central concern of the fable. The narrow definition of 'duty' which is subscribed to here is to the self, not to society, and, whilst between the conditions of production of the 'Three Million Eggs'[31] of the Oyster and the single human infant there is no improvement, there is difference. The Oyster cannot move, fixed to its spot it can have no effect on the world, but the human mother can and this is why Gilman contains her message within the fable form. Whilst we can see human limitations and error exposed by comparisons with animals it is only in making a distinct effort to be different from the animal that the world will become a better place. In this way she makes the fable the straightforward bearer of her message of human improvement that is necessarily social improvement.

The animal kingdom is employed to quite different effect in the fable 'Improving on Nature', published in *The Forerunner* of July 1912,[32] where it suits Gilman's purpose to use the animal to point to the distortions and perversions which mankind has perpetrated upon the natural order. As Mother Nature says to man: ' "With all nature behind you for example, and all womanhood around you for illustration, you deliberately chose to evolve this work of art! It shows, my son, how utterly unfit you are to do the choosing" '. The animal kingdom contains evidence of females who are either equal in strength or superior to the male of the species and Gilman also calls up 'a tall, lean savage African woman; a sturdy, straight-backed woman of the hill-tribes of India, bearing great stones upon her head; a vigorous, big-armed German peasant woman; a swift, agile, competent western woman from America; and all of these were big and strong and brave and wise and efficient' to emphasise her point that 'the female of the species' as offered up for scrutiny by the male is both a travesty and a waste. Gilman's emphasis in this fable falls upon the very artificiality of the highly civilised woman; the language she uses to describe the man-made woman is biased toward physical limitation and even enforced impris-onment and disablement. The woman here is 'hobbled, stilted, and profusely decorated,'; she is kept 'shut up in houses and tied up in clothes', a state of affairs perpetuated by the fact that ' "He would only marry the little ones... he only marries the weak ones... he only marries the meek ones... he only marries the decorated ones" '.

'Improving on Nature' is carefully structured to allow both the man and the man-made woman to speak and yet still communicate the sinister aspects of their own behaviour, the woman's complicity with the man's ordering of affairs being crucial to the success of the contravention of the true 'Law of Nature'. In this fable Gilman is able to expose the ideological differences that exist between women as well as between women and men and she lays particular emphasis on the physical consequences of the moral and spiritual imperatives which the man claims as the inspiration for the creation of the female here arraigned before Mother Nature. The clichés invented and applied by the male in 'Two Storks' are as much a part of the armoury of the male here as he tries to justify the qualities of 'small and weak and foolish and timid and inefficient' in the face of all the representative animals Mother Nature puts on display 'as fierce, as clever, as skilful and ravenous as their wild mates', with his recourse to high-sounding abstractions: ' "She is finer and nobler. She is sacred to maternity!" '. As is the case in the two other fables, motherhood is the real subject of the tale and thus the easily demolished claim that the man-made woman is 'sacred to maternity' marks the point at which Gilman's argument gathers speed and energy as the man is forced to admit that she cannot give birth alone, but needs him, as a doctor; she cannot feed the child alone, but needs him as a food manufacturer; she cannot feed, shelter, or defend her child, but relies upon him as a breadwinner; and finally that she cannot educate the child, but relies on him as teacher. It is also at this point that the man is supported in his argument by his 'pet' whose enduring existence depends upon her concurrence and compliance with his social and biological engineering; Gilman is always scrupulous in demonstrating the rôle of the dominated in sustaining the superiority of dominator.

The thrust of Gilman's ideology is, as ever, plain in this tale, but the organisation of the narrative, where the presiding, though dozing, deity is female, and the restoration of the natural order is to a world where women are in the ascendant, is actually uncharacteristically gynocentric in comparision with her other works. Gilman's fictions, like her sociological writings, generally privilege the humanist solution rather than the masculinist or feminist, and, whilst the argument in 'Improving on Nature' is familiar, the solution is not necessarily so. The revolution which is incited here is not only political, it is biological and the examples from the animal kingdom which are offered to the man not only show female equality but demonstrate female superiority, undermining traditional religious precepts along the way. The fable is by way of an awful warning, that once women begin to raise their voices – and those who are 'screaming', thereby causing Mother Nature to wake, never actually appear in the story, they are an invisible but nevertheless tangible threat to male dominance – they will be a powerful force for change whose time has come. Gilman supports her unseen screaming women with the full array of Mother Nature's arguments, dismissing the man's claim for dominance as emphatically as she dismisses his God and therefore the basis for male authority:

"This is an outrage against nature!" he cried. "Is not this the woman that God gave me? Is not this my female?"

"Tut, tut, son!" said Mother Nature, now quite calm again, and even a little sorry for him since he was about to lose his pet. "I can't say about that donation, but I do know that she is not your female – you are her male! Go study your biology!"

And Nature began to pay attention to business again, rather regretting her nap.

The archaic diction of the male, the authority for his claim of pre-eminence is a vague and unsubstantiated 'God' who is brushed aside by Mother Nature as teleologically inauthentic; after all, throughout the fable man has claimed: ' "I made her like this. I prefer her like this. By careful selection and education I have made the kind of woman I like" '. It is thus too late to claim that the inferiority of the woman is anything other than man-made. The real deity here is female, a pragmatic, humorous, powerful female who, in re-establishing the natural order is also re-asserting her predominance over any hastily constructed masculine God. The fable, through the testament of the male to his ability to effect ideological change which results in biological change actually provides the basis for a form of other-directed social engineering which, in concert with the natural world, will reassert normality and improve the whole species. It is motherhood again that is the key; unless the mother of both sexes is made stronger and fitter then there can be no advancement for the human race and it is motherhood that is to make her strong rather than being vaunted as the biological fact that renders her a victim. This tale, like a large number of Gilman's stories, replaces God the (absent) Father with a powerfully present Mother, a substitution that is perhaps at its most radical in the story 'Turned' which does not use allegory, the fantastic or any other device to ameliorate the dramatic effect of Gilman's radical solution to the problem of the wilful abnegation of responsibility by the father, a point to which I will return.

In all three fables Gilman is able to prove her case for change by using the arguments of the other side. In every instance she shows how an expedient arrangement for one sex quickly hardens into an ideological imperative for a whole society; the sophistry of the male, with his easy recourse to the abstract – 'finer...nobler... sacred'[33] – needs to be undone by the practical energy of the wideawake woman – here, emblematically, Mother Nature. The technique whereby the tactics of the ruling class are adopted and adapted by the under class is one which is offered again and again in Gilman's fiction. In stories like 'Making a Change',[34] 'Turned',[35] 'The Widow's Might',[36] 'Mr Peebles' Heart',[37] and 'Joan's Defender',[38] such a strategy in some form or other is the enabling principle of change in the lives which are depicted. However, although these stories, like parables or fables, do clearly point a moral, they also offer the practical ways and means to improve the lot of the individual. This very practicality largely precludes allegorical reading and so, generically, they can be read as exempla, moralised tales, or homilies. They are not theoretic or rich in symbolism, they offer practical solutions to real problems and, apart from the briefest sketching in of individual characteristics, their protagonists are, in the main, stereotypes. So, what is it that makes such pieces worth close attention if there is very little room for interpretative manoeuvre, if the exemplary quality of the narrative is its only reason for being? As Ann J. Lane regularly reminds us in her biography, Gilman was a lecturer, an orator, first; her writing was in many ways a secondary activity to her public speaking and her experience as a speaker taught her the usefulness of the example when making a point. So, perhaps the most productive way to approach the written homilies is to ask the question, are they perhaps as powerful as they are for the very reason that they deny complexity, that they deal in types? In looking at particular aspects of the different stories, I want to tease out why, to put it simply, they are so much better than they should be. Ultimately, and above all else, however, these pieces are deserving of reading in detail because they illustrate brilliantly Gilman's consonance of genre and theme.

These one-dimensional tales are vehicles which communicate the one-dimensional existences that are lived by those trapped within the confines of gender stereotyping. The homily is used to illustrate a preacher's text and these stories illustrate Gilman's sociological texts, but they also do far more than that, they communicate a powerful sense of waste and tragedy, of the misdirection and distortion of human lives, whilst also providing solutions. They are enabling fictions and their very simplicity is their strength as the form foregrounds the boldness of the decision taken by the individual who is forced to break out of convention. The majority of these stories feature women who suffer from having been single-focused and narrowly defined, but Gilman does give the other side of the story, for example, the parasitic helplessness of Emma Peebles in 'Mr Peebles' Heart', is shown to be exploitative of her husband's dedication to his lifelong 'duty... carrying women'.[39] The narratives all posit situations which confine men and woman to single social dimensions but resolution always involves a movement away from convention by one or other of the sexes and the breaking of generic boundaries.

The most complex and in many ways the finest of these pieces is 'Turned', a radical and moving story which structures a variety of contrasts into the course of the narrative which are both explicit and implicit, the most obvious being the differences between Mrs Marroner and Gerta and the most powerful but least evident, the course of events which is conventionally predictable as against what actually happens. The tale carries a thesis but it also communicates a cogent sense of pain and loss; it is not simply the relationship between Mrs Marroner and her husband that is relinquished, it is romantic love itself. Like Gilman's 'Being Reasonable',[40] where two old friends discover they are married to the same man and decide to unite and exclude him from their own lives and the lives of their children, 'Turned' is at its most remarkable in its expression of female solidarity in the face of all the expected turns of plot which are anticipated, partially advanced and then retreated from.

There are three possible endings to the story of betrayal and seduction which is 'Turned'. Mrs Marroner herself speculates upon one possibility unfulfilled in the narrative: 'He had not frankly loved the younger woman, broken with his wife, made a new marriage. That would have been heart-break pure and simple'. Mrs Marroner also sets in motion a sequence of events which seem to presage another, and the most likely, outcome, the dismissal of Gerta: ' "Go and pack your trunk", said Mrs Marroner. "You will leave my house tonight. Here is your money"; a course of action which would lead to the situation anticipated by Mr Marroner. However, the least expected outcome is the one which actually follows when Mrs Marroner refuses to make herself complicit in any process which would blame and punish the victim.

There are two different value systems on display here, the male and the female, and it is clear from Gerta's reaction and Mrs Marroner's initial response that the woman is expected to capitulate and adopt the man's at times of crisis, economically dependant as she usually is upon him. However, Gilman's

Mrs Marroner is a woman of parts; she had a professional life of her own before she married and, it is made plain, it is her intellectual training that gives her the strength to overcome the terrible pain and disillusion inflicted by her husband's action. Gilman's most fiercely held beliefs about the way forward to a better world are on display here and they all concern the place of women in society. Education, paid work, parenting – these are the heart of human life, as Gilman sees it and the narrative lines, fulfilled and unfulfilled, are predicated on the access which the protagonists have or have had to the three. Mrs Marroner has education, she has worked, she is not a parent; Mr Marroner has education, he works, he is not a parent and does not intend to become one; Gerta is not educated, she works but is dependant upon the good will of others to keep her job, she will become a parent whether she wants to or not. The combination of the three essentials held by each determines the course of all their lives but it is only education, possessed by two out of three, which delivers choice in the course of events.

One of the most effective aspects of this tale is Gilman's careful drawing of Mr Marroner; he has inspired the love of a good woman, he, in turn, loves her dearly and seems to understand the value of her esteem and her goodness. However, the seduction of the helpless Gerta, the fact that she is to be the mother of his child, barely registers with him; he feels only anger against his victim: 'Her name aroused in him a sense of rage. She had come between him and his wife. She had taken his wife from him. That was the way he felt.' Her picture of Mr Marroner constitutes one of Gilman's most damning indictments of a society which is predicated on the principle of individualism not communitarianism. Mr Marroner's absorption in his own affairs is such that he does not even acknowledge the extension of his responsibilities into parenthood. It is his wife who takes charge of events and it is in this act that Gilman's most radical revision of the Calvinism of her forebears is realised. Mrs Marroner experiences a 'conversion',[41] the affirmation of faith which will enable her to live amongst the 'elect', but here it is a 'conversion' which is both secularised and feminised. Charlotte Perkins Gilman takes the moral rigour of Calvinist doctrine and transmogrifies it into a practical, humane, womanly creed with which her protagonists can live a decent and honourable life:

Mrs Marroner came of stern New England stock. She was not a Calvinist, hardly even a Unitarian, but the iron of Calvinism was in her soul: of that grim faith which held that most people had to be damned "for the glory of God."

Generations of ancestors who both preached and practiced stood behind her; people whose lives had been sternly moulded to their highest moments of religious conviction. In sweeping bursts of feeling, they achieved "conviction," and afterward they lived and died according to that conviction.

This is the most extraordinary and iconoclastic epiphany in both structural and thematic terms in Gilman's work. In the other stories I discuss as homilies the change, for all are concerned with change, is less dramatically expressed and enacted because the moral imperative is less cataclysmic in its expression and effect. Gilman converts Calvinism and the highest demonstration of evidence of election into an expression of a secular morality sufficient to lift Mrs Marroner above both her own despair and the ending of the tale which would have the backing of the religious and cultural mores of her society. She abjures religion, but she also abjures its central expression in the culture – the conventional home. Refuting husband, Christian doctrines of sin and redemption, wifehood and domesticity, she enters a new world with Gerta at her side and the child before them 'as a bulwark'.[42]

In a simple sense the text or lesson behind 'Turned' is that if given the same degree of education and professional development as men, women can take charge of their own lives and exercise responsible and autonomous moral choices. The disappointment and disillusion resulting from the failure of love and loyalty between the Marroners is not, however, obviated by the ending of the tale; the enduring sense of what has been lost is perhaps more powerful than the final picture of what has been gained. The majority of the other homilies are not so absolute in either their desolation or their remedies although they do not shy away from depicting the extremity of people's needs as in Julia Gordins' suicide attempt in 'Making a Change'. Gilman is always concerned to find a solution; she will resort to murder, as in the case of the violent death of Wade Vaughn in her unpublished detective novel, 'Unpunished', in order to wipe out tyranny or, as in 'Turned', she will provide relationship, job and parenthood in a far from conventional setting, as long as the particular circumstances call for it. But, in most cases, she provides a single, simple yet radical answer to a set of social problems like the return to paid work for both young and old Mrs Gordins in 'Making a Change'. The central thesis of this homily is that all have happier, healthier more well-adjusted lives if they are allowed to carry out congenial work outside the home but there are no casualties, no broken marriages or hearts necessary to this conclusion.

'The Widow's Might' and 'Mr Peebles' Heart' both tell tales of wasted lives – those of the titular characters – and their attempts to rectify the damage done to their individuality by a lifetime of 'duty'. With the death of her tyrannical husband, Mrs McPherson determines upon a choice of life which will gratify no-one but herself, just as Mr Peebles, with the encouragement of his sister-in-law, does what he has always wanted to do, travel. Gilman has Mrs McPherson effect her own radical transformation before the astonished eyes of her children: 'With a firm step, the tall figure moved to the windows and pulled up the lowered shades. The brilliant Colorado sunshine poured into the room. She threw off the long black veil. "That's borrowed," she said. "I didn't want to hurt your feelings at the funeral." She unbuttoned the long black cloak and dropped it at her feet, standing there in the full sunlight, a little flushed and smiling, dressed in a well-made traveling suit of dull mixed colours'.[43] As if by magic she throws off the definition of her that has kept her as secondary to her husband all her life – wife and now widow. The weeds are cast off like an old skin – but in this instance the trappings of widowhood are only a borrowed skin – and a bold, adventurous, financially astute woman is revealed to the children who, only moments before, have been discussing her as a burden to be carried between them. The transformation immediately has an educative effect upon all present as James succumbs to a 'sudden feeling of tenderness' and the daughters see the benefit of receiving a steady income, which they can call their own, from their mother. Similarly Mrs Peebles receives just as much benefit from Mr Peebles' change of life, learning self-sufficiency whilst he is away and benefiting in terms of both intellectual and emotional capacity.

These are simple homilies which illustrate the fact that although lives seem to be over and to have been, to a large extent, wasted and thwarted, it is never too late to seize the opportunity to change, to follow one's own inclination rather then be chained to duty. As Mrs McPherson says: '"Thirty years I've given you – and your father. Now I'll have thirty years of my own."' In both cases Gilman delivers the moment of change to her readers as the central focus of the narrative; plans have been laid in advance of the story's opening, by Mrs McPherson and by Dr Joan Bascomb on behalf of her much-put-upon brother-in-law, but the crucial moment is that of the revelation of the individual revolt against the expectations of those most intimately connected to them.

Gilman rarely gives up on anyone, it is almost never too late to change, but there are a number of instances where people are written off as too far gone in prejudice or custom to be worth the attention of the reforming spirit and such cases are always notable, where they do not depict the straightforwardly villainous, for the manner in which their incorporation in the narrative allows Gilman to critique the social organisation. One such is to be found in 'Joan's Defender' where the agent of change, 'Uncle Arthur', abandons all hope of ever being able to influence his sister away from being 'one of these sofa women'. The story opens with an assault upon Mrs Marsden which makes it immediately clear that there is to be no commutation of her sentence as an inadequate and complaining wife and mother:

> Joan's mother was a poor defense. Her maternal instinct did not present that unbroken front of sterling courage, that measureless reserve of patience, that unfailing wisdom which we are taught to expect of it. Rather a broken reed was Mrs Marsden, broken in spirit even before her health gave way, and her feeble nerves were unable to stand the strain of adjudicating the constant difficulties between Joan and Gerald.

Reduced to invalidity by the cares of her household Mrs Marsden is, it is plain, not much of a mother by anyone's standards. Gilman holds her up, this full-time domestic creature, against the idealised version of maternity as offered by the culture at large and finds her wanting. In contrast to the pre-nuptial Madge who 'used to play tennis, and ... dance all night'[44] the married Madge is exhausted by the responsibility of care for others; patronised and mocked by her husband, defied by her son, alienated from her daughter and given up as a lost cause by her brother, Gilman sacrifices her to the larger purpose of the education of Joan. The story, again, is centrally concerned with parenting and education, with the privileging of boys and men and the enervated women and whining girls that are the by-products of the system.

Gilman protects her homilies from being taken in isolation or as exceptions rather than available-to-all-rules by making connections between her fictions as well as between the sociological writing and the stories. There are often incidental details given in Gilman's tales which do not advance the narrative but are there for the purposes of establishing affinity between tales which, taken together, can be seen to compose an inter-related and mutually supportive narrative network. Cross-referencing, most obvious in the stories which feature Mrs MacAvelly and her friends, has the effect of building Gilman's narratives into a larger multi-purpose structure. She often mentions the *Arabian Nights* in her fictions,[45] and although at first sight it might seem outlandish to suggest that these tales might be – in some measure – a model for Gilman's writing, a number of different features of her work can be usefully compared with those of the *Arabian Nights*, not least of which is the connectedness of people and themes between them. An important part of the homiletic quality of the stories discussed here is their grounding in the quotidian but an equally important part of their appeal is in their precipitation on the verge of the marvellous, a dimension inhabited in many gradations by the *Arabian Nights*.

The homilies are concerned with transformations which, as in the example of Mrs McPherson's shedding of her widow's weeds, are only one step away from the fantastic in the sense that the onlookers of the action find the changes effected astonishing in some degree or other. Mr Marroner is astounded by his wife's actions, the McPherson children are similarly amazed by the appearance of their mother as 'tall, strong' and straight'[46] rather than as a stooping widow, Emma Peebles is 'left gasping',[47] and Mr Gordins 'both angry and hurt'[48] at the conduct of his wife and mother. The stories are all concerned with mundane, domestic arrangements but the will and effort required to bring about change is, in some sense, superhuman, and the effect upon others of such transformations often awe-inspiring. There are instances in which Gilman is explicit in her use of the supernatural; pieces like 'Freed', 'When I was a Witch' and 'If I Were a Man', are all fantasy rather than homiletic tales but they are still so firmly grounded in the problems of everyday life that the fantastic is subdued to Gilman's larger moral and pedagogic purposes.

In the multitude of Gilman fictions which have a Utopian theme the use of the fantastic is closely controlled by the pragmatic nature of both the exegesis and use of what would be, in other circumstances, extraordinary practices or inventions. Gilman's Utopian fictions, where they transact with supernature, do so in order to maintain the hesitation between the real and the fantastic which suspends judgement between what is known and what is possible. As with Todorov's formulation of the ' "instrumental marvelous" ' or the ' "scientific marvelous" ' where 'the supernatural is explained in a rational manner, but according to laws which contemporary science does not acknowledge'[49] improvements which have been made to the social fabric are seen as not so much fantastic as practical. One simple example might be Gilman's idea, repeated endlessly in her Utopian fictions, about food being bought ready prepared rather than cooked in individual houses, anticipating the microwave cookery or take-away restaurants of today. In the stories which depend for some of their effects upon supernature the magical event leads to social or technological developments which have not occurred, yet not only are they imaginable but they are also partly or entirely possible. For example, whilst Mollie Mathewson in the story 'If I Were a Man' will never become a man in a biological sense, she could very easily wear trousers, have pockets, earn money and develop a business sense. The dry, empiric tone of 'When I Was a Witch' contradicts the magical quintessence of the narrative; Gilman's excursus into the economics of the sleeping car swindle perpetrated by the railroad bosses, for example, where she outlines the cost benefit of the present system which charges passengers twice over, provides a good example of the terrestrially bound prose which not only ballasts the fantastic but takes the story briefly into the genre of the economic treatise. 'Freed' posits a 'spell' which wipes out all traces of 'The Past' except certain bodies of scientific knowledge and a limited range of fiction, but it is a spell that could be cast by a nation or even a world determined enough to look only to 'the future'.[50]

So, the fantastic in Gilman's use is a disarming strategy. The necessary business of transformation which is effected by the initial premise in each story, 'that one-sided contract with Satan' in 'When I Was a Witch', the change of sex in 'If I Were a Man' and the events of one night, 'on the mind of humanity was worked a spell',[51] in 'Freed', is sufficient to lift the narrative from the mode of realism and into the realm of the supernatural thereby ameliorating the otherwise damning nature of the cultural critique. The opening gesture toward supernature removes the tale from reception as a realistic picture of everyday life and thus the radical position adopted by Gilman in the stories, yoking the fantastic to questions of the mundane in order to invoke a radical rethinking of the social order, is so propitiating that to dissent from her world view would be as good as to espouse cruelty and venality. From 'The Unnatural Mother' through the fables which, in reinforcing our likeness to the animal also emphasise our ability to be more than instinctive, to be agents of social and even biological change, to the homilies and the fantasies, Gilman's message is plain and the strategies by which she obtains our consent to her radical re-ordering of the world unvarying. She conducts a secularisation of the moral order, she reorientates our view of the processes of reproduction and nurture, so that whilst maternity is at the heart of the majority of the narratives, in one form or other, it becomes the focus for the species rather than for the mother alone.

In 'When I Was a Witch' she says: 'Being a woman, I was naturally interested in them, and could see some things more clearly than men could. I saw their real power, their real dignity, their real responsibility in the world; and then the way they dress and behave used to make me fairly frantic. 'Twas like seeing arch-angels playing jackstraws – or real horses used only as rocking-horses'.[52] The comparisons she makes here reflect the trivialising of women in the culture and the means by which it is effected; the 'archangel' represents the divine potential within, currently demeaned by puerile pursuits, the 'horse' stands for the living, natural creature made into a painted toy, confined to the nursery rather than free and at large in the world. The range of Gilman's fictional enterprise is also contained within these two comparisons: she takes the divine, humanises it in a two-way transaction by showing it as attainable so that it becomes, therefore, earthly as well as heavenly; she takes art and shows it as supportive of, not superior to, nature. She is clear on this matter in 'Freed': 'And of the works of art, some remained, those most true and vital, but many had vanished. Yet there lived the soul of the artist, his love and his power, and the craft of his hand'.[53] Art and life are bound by precedent; conventions, whether social or literary, control and condition our responses to life and literature. For Gilman there could be no literary impulse which was not also a moral impulse and so to rove between genres for the most effective means of communicating the ways and means of change was simply to establish the pre-eminence of the artist over the art and thus to privilege the species at the expense of the individual, destroying the cult of the artist and substituting the application of 'the full strength of the human intellect to the practical problem of life untrammeled by the mistakes of so many dead men'.[54]

Notes

1. Gilman, Charlotte Perkins, *His Religion and Hers: A Study of the Faith of Our Fathers and the Work of Our Mothers*, 1923 (New York: Hyperion reprint, 1976), p. 91.
2. Lane, Ann J. *To Herland and Beyond: The Life and Work of Charlotte Perkins Gilman*, (New York: Meridian, 1991), p. 278.
3. *The Living of Charlotte Perkins Gilman*, pp. 305–6.
4. *The Living of Charlotte Perkins Gilman*, p. 304.
5. Ann J. Lane discusses Gilman's position on feminism, then and now, in the context of *Women and Economics* in her biography of the writer, *To Herland and Beyond: The Life and Work of Charlotte Perkins Gilman*, p. 5.
6. *Feminist Fiction*, p. 19.
7. Kessler, Carol Farley *Charlotte Perkins Gilman: Her Progress Toward Utopia with Selected Writings* (Liverpool: Liverpool University Press, 1995), pp. 182–185.
8. *Charlotte Perkins Gilman: Her Progress Toward Utopia with Selected Writings*, pp. 183–4.
9. Knight, Denise D. (ed.) *'The Yellow Wallpaper' and Selected Stories of Charlotte Perkins Gilman* (London and Toronto: Associated University Presses, 1994), pp. 206–9.
10. *'The Yellow Wallpaper' and Selected Stories of Charlotte Perkins Gilman*, p. 206.
11. *'The Yellow Wallpaper' and Selected Stories of Charlotte Perkins Gilman*, p. 209.
12. Gilman, Charlotte Perkins *Herland and Selected Stories by Charlotte Perkins Gilman*, Barbara H. Solomon (ed.) (New York: Signet Classic, 1992), p. 116.
13. *Herland and Selected Stories by Charlotte Perkins Gilman*, p. 118.
14. *His Religion and Hers: A Study of the Faith of Our Fathers and the Work of Our Mothers*, p. 153.
15. *His Religion and Hers: A Study of the Faith of Our Fathers and the Work of Our Mothers*, p. 194.
16. *Charlotte Perkins Gilman: Her Progress Toward Utopia with Selected Writings*, p. 112.
17. One of Gilman's first magazine pieces, the poem, 'Similar Cases', published in the *Nationalist* in April 1890, was an attack on those who refuse to adapt and change. The poem is included in Ann J. Lane's *To Herland and Beyond: The Life and Work of Charlotte Perkins Gilman*, pp. 363–4.

18. Gilman's contribution to social science has only recently begun to be appreciated in its full range, diversity and originality in recent years. Most influential of her non-fiction texts were *Women and Economics* (1898), *The Man-Made World; or, Our Androcentric Culture* (1911) and *His Religion and Hers: A Study of the Faith of Our Fathers and the Work of Our Mothers* (1923).

19. For an invaluable discussion of the concept of the reading position, especially in relation to generic texts, see Anne Cranny-Francis *Feminist Fiction*, pp. 25–8.

20. Ann J. Lane (ed.) *The Charlotte Perkins Gilman Reader* (London: The Women's Press, 1981), pp. 57–65.

21. *The Charlotte Perkins Gilman Reader*, p. 62.

22. *His Religion and Hers: A Study of the Faith of Our Fathers and the Work of Our Mothers*, p. 55.

23. Gilman, Charlotte Perkins *Women and Economics: A Study of the Economic Relation Between Men and Women as a Factor in Social Evolution*, 1898, reprinted. Carl N. Degler (New York, Harper Torchbooks, 1966), p. 5.

24. *Women and Economics*, p. 95.

25. *'The Yellow Wallpaper' and Selected Stories of Charlotte Perkins Gilman*, p. 205.

26. *'The Yellow Wallpaper' and Selected Stories of Charlotte Perkins Gilman*, pp. 203–4.

27. *'The Yellow Wallpaper' and Selected Stories of Charlotte Perkins Gilman*, p. 212.

28. Todorov, Tzvetan *The Fantastic: A Structural Approach to a Literary Genre* (Ithaca, Cornell U.P., 1975), p. 64.

29. 'When I Was a Witch' was first published in *Forerunner*, in May 1910, and is reprinted in *The Charlotte Perkins Gilman Reader*, pp. 21–31.

30. 'If I Were a Man', first published in *Physical Culture*, in July 1914, and is reprinted in *The Charlotte Perkins Gilman Reader*, pp. 32–8.

31. *'The Yellow Wallpaper' and Selected Stories of Charlotte Perkins Gilman*, pp. 210–12.

32. *'The Yellow Wallpaper' and Selected Stories of Charlotte Perkins Gilman*, p. 217.

33. *'The Yellow Wallpaper' and Selected Stories of Charlotte Perkins Gilman*, pp. 213–17.

34. 'Making a Change' was published in *The Forerunner* in December 1911, and is reprinted in *The Charlotte Perkins Gilman Reader*, pp. 66–74.

35. 'Turned' was published in *The Forerunner* in September 1911, and is reprinted in *The Charlotte Perkins Gilman Reader*, pp. 87–97.

36. 'The Widow's Might' was published in *The Forerunner* in January 1911, and is reprinted in *The Charlotte Perkins Gilman Reader*, pp. 98–106.

37. 'Mr Peebles' Heart' was published in *The Forerunner* in September 1914, and is reprinted in *The Charlotte Perkins Gilman Reader*, pp. 107–15.

38. 'Joan's Defender' was published in *The Forerunner* in June 1916 and is reprinted in *Herland and Selected Stories by Charlotte Perkins Gilman*, pp. 327–335.

39. *The Charlotte Perkins Gilman Reader*, p. 108.
40. 'Being Reasonable' was originally published in *The Forerunner* in August 1915, and is reprinted in *'The Yellow Wallpaper' and Selected Stories of Charlotte Perkins Gilman*, pp. 185–92.
41. Ann J. Lane describes Lyman Beecher, Charlotte Perkins Gilman's great-grandfather and an influential religious thinker, at the beginning of her biography of the writer, *To Herland and Beyond: The Life and Work of Charlotte Perkins Gilman*, pp. 21–4.
42. *The Charlotte Perkins Gilman Reader*, pp. 87–97.
43. *The Charlotte Perkins Gilman Reader*, p. 105.
44. *'The Yellow Wallpaper' and Selected Stories of Charlotte Perkins Gilman'*, p. 97.
45. In 'Joan's Defender' Gilman refers us to the *Arabian Nights* in order to effect a change in narrative pace between describing the existing system and a moment of change: 'Such was the case, as it says so often in the *Arabian Nights*, and then something pleasant happened', *'The Yellow Wallpaper' and Selected Stories of Charlotte Perkins Gilman*, p. 97. Mr Peebles in the story of his 'Heart' is also defined negatively not as the ' "slave of love" of the Arab tale, but the slave of duty', *The Charlotte Perkins Gilman Reader*, p. 108.
46. *The Charlotte Perkins Gilman Reader*, pp. 104–6.
47. *The Charlotte Perkins Gilman Reader*, p. 114.
48. *The Charlotte Perkins Gilman Reader*, p. 73.
49. *The Fantastic: A Structural Approach to a Literary Genre*, p. 56.
50. *'The Yellow Wallpaper' and Selected Stories of Charlotte Perkins Gilman*, pp 206–9.
51. *'The Yellow Wallpaper' and Selected Stories of Charlotte Perkins Gilman*, p. 206.
52. *The Charlotte Perkins Gilman Reader*, p. 31.
53. *'The Yellow Wallpaper' and Selected Stories of Charlotte Perkins Gilman*, p. 207.
54. *'The Yellow Wallpaper' and Selected Stories of Charlotte Perkins Gilman*, p. 208.

8

Charlotte Perkins Gilman's Analogues – Reiterating the Social Health

All readers of Charlotte Perkins Gilman's work know that she tells the same stories over and over again. This feature of her writing I would like to describe as the writing of the analogue – the cognate story – which, in Gilman's work, is recognisable through its intramural narrative affinities. In Gilman's fiction the use of the analogue is more than the mere repetition of particular plots or themes, it is crucial to any understanding of the way in which she organised and expressed both her art and her ideology especially where she is dealing with the relationship between the individual and the social health. In describing her reiteration of stories in this way it is possible to see how she uses particular analogues to place in consistent contradistinction male and female positions on the question of the present, past and future of the constitution of a morally and physically fit society.

In making a schematic division of stories into female and male analogues I am taking Gilman at face value; I am assuming that the gendered oppositions she structures into her fictions are ideological and form the basis for the majority of her work. She herself makes clear divisions such as these in her work, divisions both theoretical and practical, and follows through with straightforward enactments of fictions which elaborate upon and sustain her ideas. I do not intend to interrogate her particular version of social Darwinism here, neither do I intend to scrutinise her views on ethnicity, but to examine her presentation of the gender divide in two of its most extreme positions as it is regularly recapitulated in the fiction. There are many instances in which she does not put her men and women in opposition; in stories discussed in a previous chapter, 'Mr Peebles' Heart' and 'The Unnatural Mother', for instance, Gilman offers her reader decent, intelligent men who are able to sustain intellectual as well as emotional relationships with women. In the stories I term analogues, however, Gilman most usually positions her men and women at odds in the business of social well-being and reform. She takes principles of communitarianism and puts them up against individualism and in doing so encodes women in a particular analogue – one which promotes the social health, and men in another which, often literally, destroys it. Gilman represents idealistic, Utopian stories as female and stories concerned with the most insidious form of social malaise, the sexually transmitted disease, as male.

Gilman actually perpetuates, in despite of the radical position she takes on some issues which would have scandalised many of her women predecessors in the writing of homiletic fictions, the principle that the gender divide is a moral divide. In assigning to women the reforming, truly Christian, nurturing role she is sustaining the conventional position but in adding to the sum parts of her women – making them economically powerful and giving them professions, besides being teachers and kindergartners, they are sanitary engineers, doctors, architects, ministers and reformers – she takes the principle of a distinct female morality into all spheres of life. The female analogues are absorbed by effecting change based on principles of community, education for all and clean living; they are uniformly radical and are structurally and thematically concerned with the finding out and enacting of solutions. It is only, however, when these stories are read in the context of their reiteration that it becomes clear how consistently and in what extremity the divide between what is constructed as female and what male is realised, the male analogues being concerned with the problems arising from selfish individualism and the inflexible maintenance of tradition, with repression and disease.

Stories which are repeated throughout her fiction and involve the setting up of the ideal or Utopian community always have women as active agents although men are not excluded from participation, except, of course, in *Herland*, Gilman's Utopian novel of 1915. The female analogues of communitarian living are concerned with finding solutions through the collective will toward making radical changes to an existing social order which is seen neither to support women's needs nor to provide a decent future for their children. The most straightforward expression of this comes in Gilman's 'Bee Wise' published in the July 1913 issue of *The Forerunner* and set, as are many of her new community analogues, in California, the closest place on earth, for Gilman, to 'Eden'. California, after all, was the state in which, as reported by Ruth Rosen in her book, *The Lost Sisterhood: Prostitution in America, 1900–1918*, 'women successfully lobbied for a mandatory health certificate to ensure that the men women married would be free from venereal disease'.[1] The purpose built 'sample town' of 'Bee Wise', designed to 'set a new example to the world – a place of woman's work and world-work too' – is not exclusive to women but operates such a policy of selection, thereby incorporating reference to the analogue of male disease which is repeated throughout Gilman's fiction: 'But the men were carefully selected. They must prove clean health – for a high grade of motherhood was the continuing ideal of the group'.[2]

The story of sexually transmitted disease is one of the most powerful reiterations in Gilman's body of fiction. In her book, *Sexual Anarchy: Gender and Culture at the Fin de Siècle*, Elaine Showalter describes the gender specific nature of the dissemination of information about venereal disease in the late 19th century: 'While boys and men were lectured, warned, or even terrorized about venereal disease, well-brought-up girls were not supposed to know that such dangers existed'. Showalter also makes the point that the 'literary mythology of syphilis at the *fin de siècle* was very differently expressed by male and female writers'[3] with women like Charlotte Perkins Gilman and the British novelist, Sarah Grand, in her novel of 1893, *The Heavenly Twins*, incorporating information about the disease in their fiction as well as delivering awful warnings about its devastating effects on present and future generations. Gilman's strong views on the subject were straightforwardly enacted in both her fiction and non-fiction: for her, venereal disease was a social problem which must be remedied and a part of that remedy was to disseminate information about its extent and its effects. Her work is not shaped by the aesthetic potential of tropes of sexual infection in either structural or symbolic terms but by the purpose and the language of social reformers like Maude Glasgow, writing in 1910, who highlighted the hypocrisies of efforts to regulate prostitution when no steps were taken to monitor their clients: 'the man who has voluntarily exposed himself to the contagion of a loathsome disease continues even after his infection by the prostitute to have business and social relations as before, with the result that innocent members of society are exposed to a dangerous and contagious disorder to which they have not exposed themselves and from which no effort is made to protect them'.[4]

The defining discourse for Gilman is that of the women reformers who belonged to women's clubs, to organisations like the Women's Christian Temperance Union[5] or the New York Suffragist Association who, in 1912, received a report from the Social Hygiene Association which stated that congenital syphilis 'was estimated as the cause of 30 per cent of all blindness in New York'.[6] Gilman was active in the circles from which calls for reform were being made. The women of the Greenwich Village club, Heterodoxy, of which Gilman was a founding member in 1912, had, as Rosalind Rosenberg says, two dominating concerns: 'their commitment to women's economic independence and their preoccupations with sexuality'.[7] Gilman never espoused the view held by some members of the club, however, that the way forward was to grant greater sexual freedom to women, instead she wrote and lectured in favour of the restriction of the sexual licence of the male. When speaking on the subject of sexually transmitted disease Gilman's language is invariably that of the campaigner, she climbs the rhetorical heights of those who, whether physicians or social reformers, are daily confronted by the devastation wrought by the infected male upon women and children. Ruth Rosen notes that: 'Whereas male reformers typically represented the carriers of venereal infection as women, female reformers typically represented them as men'[8] and Gilman positions her analogues of sexually transmitted disease in conformity to this pattern; the source of infection in her tales is male whilst prevention and cure is female.

Gilman made the stories she wrote about syphilis more than simply indicative of the state of ignorance of women about sexually transmitted diseases. The analogues which deal with such diseases, either centrally or by allusion, are obviously about corruption and infection but by their very nature they are additionally concerned with questions of individualism, tradition and inheritance. The pervasiveness of the story means that tales of infection or contagiousness are also visible presences in the analogues of health, there to represent that which must be eliminated from the world. Whilst the female analogues are driven by the ideological imperative to improve the nation's health, the male analogues are demonstrations of the perpetuation of the evils of the past in the literal form of the passing on of infection. Above all others the analogue of the sexually transmitted disease is the serpent story which haunts Gilman's garden. The communitarian story, always initiated and sustained by the female collective, is the analogue of health and foresight, the sexually transmitted disease story is the analogue of contamination and retrogression and in many forms and guises the two stories thread their way through the whole body of her fiction as well as her sociological writings. In *His Religion and Hers: A Study of the Faith of Our Fathers and the Work of Our Mothers*, Gilman singles out for special praise the play *A Bill of Divorcement* as an example of art illustrating a 'vivid and beautiful instance of woman's power...wherein a modern girl, finding that there was hereditary insanity in her family, broke with her lover. She did not offer him a birth-controlled, childless life, but left him free to raise a family; she was a social hero'.[9] The analogues of sexually transmitted disease put on display Gilman's social villains, men who knowingly infect woman and blight future generations with their pursuit of self-gratification at the expense of the whole of humanity.

The female analogue can thus, broadly, be said to be concerned with the future of the human race and the positive disruption of existent patterns of social organisation, and, whilst the male analogue is also inevitably concerned with the future because it has the power to affect the social health, it can be constructed as being in thrall to the past and the continuation of the status quo. The 'Past' is often the subject of vilification in Gilman's work; in her story 'Freed' the most positive development imaginable is that 'From the world without and the world within had utterly vanished The Past.'[10] The presence of literal infection in the body of the past is one of Gilman's most effective tropes, communicating as it does the depth and the power of the social malaise which lies unseen and insulated from change by the enduring practice of enforcing female sexual ignorance as one of the means by which to sustain the male hegemony.

Gilman's analogues, in their recurrence, actually represent her attempt to redefine and extend nothing less than the province of fiction as it has existed in the past. In her discussion of 'Masculine Literature' in *The Man-Made World; or, Our Androcentric Culture*, serialised in *The Forerunner* between 1909 and 1910, and published in a single volume by Gilman's Charlton Company in 1911, she classifies literature as being traditionally concerned only with war or love and goes on to offer five new areas of interest for creative artists:

First the position of the young woman who is called upon to give up her career – her humanness – for marriage, and . . . the middle-aged woman who at last discovers that her discontent is social starvation – that it is not more love that she wants, but more business in life; Third the inter-relation of women with women – a thing we could never write about before, because we never had it before, except in harems and convents; Fourth the inter-action between mothers and children; this is not the eternal 'mother and child,' wherein the child is always a baby, but the long drama of personal relationship; the love and hope, the patience and power, the lasting joy and triumph, the slow eating disappointment which must never be owned to a living soul – here are the grounds for novels that a million mothers and many million children would eagerly read; Fifth the new attitude of the full-grown woman, who faces the demands of love with the highest standards of conscious motherhood.[11]

These models are substantially those which are utilised by Gilman in her work both singly and in combination and are the basis for those stories which I describe as her female analogues.[12] Whilst the generally up-beat nature of her prescription for the writing of innovative fictions here seems to preclude the other half of my representative story equation – the sexually transmitted disease tale – it does not, in fact, as can be illustrated by looking briefly at Gilman's novel, *The Crux*, serialised in *The Forerunner* in 1910 and published separately by Gilman's own Charlton Company in 1911. *The Crux* actually enacts all of the precepts of Gilman's model fictions in having the heroine, Vivian Lane, make a decision about her future based not on her feelings of love for Morton Elder, who has venereal disease, but for the children she may have. Similarly, Jane Bellair trains as a doctor instead of continuing with her marriage and does so in order to help other women and their children avoid the pain and bitterness of the disease with which she has been infected. Additionally she acts in despite of the 'professional honor' which is felt by her male medical colleague, answering the higher call of female solidarity by letting Vivian know that Morton is contaminated in order to protect both her and her children. ' "Marriage is motherhood" ' is Jane Bellair's creed and the core of the narrative her admonition: 'Beware of a biological sin, my dear; for it there is no forgiveness' ".[13] So *The Crux* is the perfect model of a story which contains all the constituents of a Gilman analogue and encompasses both male and female versions simultaneously. The majority of the short stories do not enact the same process in quite such an inclusive manner but are either concerned with female health or male disease. The fictions which have what the local women in 'The Unnatural Mother' euphemistically term 'the bad disease' at their heart are the most naked and unadorned of awful warnings in Gilman's moral fictions, and the pieces I will be looking at in detail here are 'Wild Oats and Tame Wheat', published in 1913,[14] and 'The Vintage', published in October 1916.[15] Whilst these are representative of the analogue of the sexually transmitted disease, the story of such infections permeates much of Gilman's work, lurking unseen but not unsuspected in as many stories as male bodies.

Gilman deliberately invokes the past in 'Wild Oats and Tame Wheat' through the use of archaic vocabulary and syntax. It is a very precisely and carefully structured and articulated piece which pays close attention to the differences not only between the upbringing of men and women but also the language which invokes the parameters of their worlds. When describing the man and his youthful exploits Gilman's syntax is stylised because she is writing about a representative 'Certain Man who followed the habits of his kind' in a parabolic strain. However, she is simultaneously manipulating the standard understanding of the man who has sown his 'wild oats' and has subsequently reformed toward the depiction of a situation which does not allow of reform, the acquisition and passing on of sexually transmitted diseases. In this brief parable Gilman complicates both the genre and an otherwise dead metaphor, as she did in 'Two Storks', wrenching signification away from complacency about the reform of past conduct, the usual point of any tale about 'wild oats', and re-opening questions laden with whole cultural importance about the future. The man here, having exercised his 'freedom', 'free association', his *'Wanderlust'*, has a past and retains this past. The woman is emblematic of the restrictive practices of the past, being communicated, in archaisms, as an epigone: 'a damsel young, innocent, in the bloom of maidenhood, knowing not man'; she is a relic from a chivalric tale waiting to accomplish 'her one hope – a husband'. The language which evokes the life of the 'damsel' is the language of confinement: 'shelter', 'walled', 'veiled and guarded', 'limited'; she is defined by what she does not know and by what she cannot do. Gilman moves, however, from noting the words which define male and female worlds of freedom and restraint to the exploration of words which are the same but actually signify radically different things in the context of gendered lives:

> Her world was not his world, and her language was not his language. For him to be bold was right and honorable; for her to be bold was an offence. Freedom to him was the breath of life, liberty his high ideal. Freedoms and liberties were known to her only as insults fraught with danger.

Bold men are brave and dynamic, bold women are shameless and lewd; men have freedom and liberty to choose their course of life, women who wait only for a new 'owner' are vulnerable to having liberties and freedoms taken with them as forms of violation. This analogue weighs freedom against liberty in a number of ways and not the least of these is in the differentiation of a male language which speaks of licence and a female language which speaks only of constraint. The oppositions invoked and sustained throughout are then brought to a climax in the final lines of the parable: 'Nevertheless she knew little, even of the life of him she lived with, though he shared with her what he thought fit, including his diseases'. Gilman does not fall into the trap of simply rewriting her female characters into archetypal male attributes or roles; she is more sophisticated in her interrogation of the generic conventions of the 'wild oats' tale. She undermines the usual conclusion of such a tale through the revelation of the concomitant, usually hidden features of the standard story, features unrevealed by the standard practice of the genre of parable.

'Wild Oats and Tame Wheat' is crucial as an informing text to Gilman's vision of the whole-cultural value system which allows the sexually transmitted disease to rage unchecked. The man with a past is valued, esteemed even, as a superior mate for a girl carefully nurtured in ignorance of what he might bring back from his travels for her. The girl is in no position to judge, having been sheltered quite specifically from real knowledge: 'vice, license, and bad habits she but vaguely knew were in the world. And of all the things she knew not, especially she knew not man'.[16] The woman trapped in the middle ages by a language and a system of morality which is predicated on the maintenance of her ignorance gets no enlightenment, the analogue of the sexually transmitted disease is a story without end for as long as the status quo remains unchanged. This story and the other male analogue I propose to discuss here,

'The Vintage', play with language and form in order to reinforce theme, the latter opening with a refutation of generic boundaries which concomitantly rejects spatial limits: 'This is not a short story. It stretches out for generations'.[17] Whilst Gilman is concerned with the ruin of the particular lives which are the immediate concern of the narrative the whole thrust of the analogue of sexually transmitted disease is with its continuing, even endless, nature, with its insidious and persistent endurance in the face of medical and moral injunctions against it. Unlike the woman doctor in *The Crux*, who breaks professional secrecy in order to tell her friend what the consequences of her marriage to an infected man will be, the doctor in 'The Vintage' is a rival for the affections of the woman in question, Leslie Montroy, and so is compromised into silence.

The emphasis in this analogue is upon the contrast between before and after as regards marriage and the woman's health.[18] Gilman purposefully overstates the physical and genealogical perfection of the single girl who is Leslie Vauremont Barrington Montroy, superior in strength and endurance as she is to her future husband, Rodger Moore: 'Everywhere she carried the joy of her splendid vigor, the beauty of abounding health.' The purity of Leslie's mind and body is offered in sharp contrast to Rodger's knowing moral and physical infection but, notwithstanding his wilful refusal to give up the idea of marrying, Gilman does not paint him as a villain; indeed she addresses her audience directly in order to press the point about the reasons behind his decision to continue: 'He was a determined man. This brief black incident in his past had long since been buried by that strong will, and he would not allow it to rise now like a skeleton at the feast. Understand – he did not really in cold blood decide to offer such a risk to the women [sic] he loved. He refused to admit that there was a risk'. Charlotte Perkins Gilman constructs and articulates her culture in terms of its ignorance of its own profound sickness and thus its need to take the radical measures which would both prevent and cure.

Perhaps the central trope of her vision of the derelict moral and physical condition of the western world is predicated in the scene where Dr Howard Faulkner is present as a silent onlooker at the wedding of his two dear friends: 'So he held his tongue, and saw the woman he had loved so long, all white and radiant in her bridal glory, marry the man with the worst of communicable diseases'. The bride, symbolising everything constructed as womanly in the culture – purity, innocence, love, devotion, faithfulness, imminent maternity – is joined to the man with the timebomb of concealed infection which will explode all her hopes for the future, and who is, withal, aided in the maintaining of his secret by a male solidarity expressed here as 'professional honor'. In focusing on this spectacle, the supposed culmination of a woman's destiny, Gilman actually foregrounds it as the decisive moment at which the woman passes from health to sickness. The presence of the disease makes literal the passage between a healthy girlhood and an ailing womanhood; Leslie has had faith in the fact that she has been given sufficient information – that delivered by romantic love – to make a choice between suitors, but this misplaced faith leads to physical destruction of the most cataclysmic kind, of her own health and that of her children.

Time is crucial in micro- and macrocosm in Gilman's analogues of sexually transmitted disease. 'The Vintage' opens with the endlessness of the story of such infection: 'Its beginning was thousands of years ago, and its end is not yet in sight. Here we have only a glimpse, a cross-section, touching sharply on a few lives'; thus Gilman offers this particular 'cross-section' as one among many, in other words, as an analogue. Rodger Moore refuses to take the 'time' for tests which would establish the extent of the disease, time brings one crippled child but many more 'blasted buds'; as time passes, Leslie sickens and her husband watches 'the proud clean beauty of the woman he adored wither and disappear' and the time comes when she is 'taken away in the prime of her womanhood'. There is a larger time scale in operation here, however, and that is the one that contains the moral climate in which Dr Faulkner's higher duty is to secrecy than to explication, in which Rodger Moore's first thought is for the inconvenience of cancelling the wedding rather than the fatal infection of his wife and future children and, finally, in which a suffering woman can die ignorant even of that which has killed her: 'She did not know what was the matter with her, or with her children. She never had known that there was such a danger before "a decent woman", though aware of some dark horror connected with "sin", impossible to mention'. Silence is the real enemy and in making this story an analogue, telling it over and over again, Gilman is breaking silence.

In her story 'The Unnatural Mother', as I have said above, it is made plain that Esther Greenwood's understanding of her own body and matters of public health makes her able to exercise an informed choice about marriage and also to understand the nature of the commitment. It is this understanding, however, that damns both her and her father in the eyes of the local community: "He taught that innocent girl about – the Bad Disease! Actually!" "He did!" said the dressmaker. "It got out, too, all over town. There wasn't a man here would have married her after that".[19] For speaking out about what a man might hide when he comes a-courting of a fair 'damsel' there is no reward except ostracism; no-one tells Leslie what she has been afflicted with, not even the man who gave it to her and who, apparently, holds her in high esteem and love. The fact that Rodger marries the woman who he constructs as above all else *'clean'* in the full knowledge of his own contamination is the clearest illustration of the analogue of selfish individualism; for Gilman the highest love is always the love of the race, of the future, not personal, romantic love. Whilst the stories which repeat the principles of communitarianism occupy different positions on the scale of change from the minor adjustment to housekeeping to major revolutions in the social organisation, all have certain features in common, chief amongst which is the narrative drive toward finding solutions, not, as in the analogues of infection, toward reiterating the perils of the status quo.

The majority of the stories which I want to discuss as female analogues are collected in Carol Farley Kessler's volume, *Charlotte Perkins Gilman: Her Progress Towards Utopia and Selected Writings*, and, with the exception of 'Aunt Mary's Pie Plant' which featured in *Woman's Home Companion* in June 1908, they were originally published in *The Forerunner*, between 1909 and 1913. Kessler describes Gilman's Utopian fiction as her 'primary locus for culture-creation or cultural work...proclaiming the belief that the female half of humanity not be confined to one traditional mode of being – wife/motherhood, but fill as varied social roles as male counterparts, that the female work of society be valued equally with that of the male',[20] and she divides the fiction into different stages of development of Gilman's Utopian thematic. In moving between the family as the 'lowest level of social organization', through 'society as a whole' to the 'woman-centered' or 'futuristic'[21] text, Kessler charts how Gilman's ideas about social organisation and the best means of communicating them develop. I will be in very similar territory in my discussion and will be focusing on the relationship between the analogues of social reform, on their consonance whether they feature as a part of a tiny change in the domestic arrangements of a single household or as major ideological revolutions which affect large numbers of people. As well as 'Aunt Mary's Pie Plant', I will be looking at 'Three Thanksgivings', published in *The Forerunner* in 1909, 'Her Housekeeper', January 1910, 'Her Memories', August 1912, 'Maidstone Comfort', September 1912, 'Forsythe and Forsythe', January 1913, 'The Cottagette', August 1910 and 'Mrs Hines' Money', April 1913.

There are principles which are enacted and re-enacted in these stories which signal inclusion rather than exclusion for a wide variety of people in the revised social order, for men as well as women and children and which, somewhat surprisingly, valorise the marriage plot as an intrinsic part of the working out of the organisation of the new world. There are stories where the exclusion or refutation of the marriage plot is as important as the inclusion – namely 'Mrs Hines' Money', 'Three Thanksgivings' and to a lesser extent, 'Bee Wise', but in all the others, the accomplishment of a male–female partnership negotiated on radical new principles of domestic equality is a powerful and oft-repeated analogue. In 'Her Housekeeper', 'The Cottagette' and 'Forsythe and Forsythe' the same solution is offered for both romantic and domestic difficulties and the male protagonist is as active, if not more active, in procuring the solution than the woman, although in all cases the original scheme of re-ordered living is developed and implemented by the woman. These three analogues repeat principles of community living, where each person has their own autonomous space but is in receipt of a professionalised housekeeping service to clean, cook and deliver food of a high standard. They repeat situations where the protagonists have experience of previous relationships or living arrangements with intractable or opinionated partners or lovers They also have stories reiterated within stories which tell of the good health and clean living of the men: the effortless strength of Mr Olmstead and his refusal to smoke in 'Her Housekeeper', new abstemiousness as regards smoking from James Jackson as well as his avoidance of his wife's frivolous pursuits and disappointment in her refusal to have children in 'Forsythe and Forsythe' and, in 'The Cottagette', there is a clear reference to the analogue of sexually transmitted disease in Malda's pæon to Ford Mathews' purity: ' "He is strong and well – you can read clean living in his eyes and mouth." Ford's eyes were as clear as a girl's, the whites of them were clear. Most men's eyes, when you look at them critically, are not like that. They may look at you very expressively, but when you look at them, just as features, they are not very nice'.[22]

In all three cases the agreement between future spouses on the principle of housekeeping as a business to be conducted by others, on their behalf, is the principle that facilitates courtship and subsequent harmony. Mr Olmstead organises his personal and his professional life around the business of arranging a domestically untrammelled existence for Mrs Leland, Ford Mathews insists that Malda give up cooking if she is to be his wife and James Jackson undertakes to 'begin again'[23] ideologically in order to share a life with Clare Forsythe. The objections which Mrs Leland has to marriage are based on her first, unsuccessful attempt and Gilman threads details of her life with her first husband, where she was confined and deprived of economic and personal autonomy, throughout the story of her courtship by Mr Olmstead as a simple means of illustrating differences between men. The story of escape or the hard-won transformation of a repressive marriage is another familiar analogue, being instrumental in the plot of 'Mrs Hines' Money', 'The Widow's Might', and 'Maidstone Comfort' as well as 'Old Mrs Crosley' (1911), 'Mrs Elder's Idea' (1912) and 'Mrs Beazley's Deeds' (1916) the latter four featuring husbands who are still alive but have their exclusive control of the family economy removed by a variety of measures.

The three communitarian analogues that are also tales of courtship have in common a primary point of emphasis: the woman's career and the conditions necessary to its continuation. Mrs Leland, Malda and Clare Forsythe can only, it is made plain, follow their acting, designing and engineering careers if freed from the obligations of running a home and it is this primary shift in domestic responsibility from the woman to the man or the partnership between them that is the backbone of this analogue. Gilman exerts herself to emphasise the manliness of these men, Mr Olmstead's physical prowess is frequently invoked and he is characteristically described as 'clean' with 'solid strength';[24] Ford Mathews is 'a man with a big view and grip – with purpose and real power'[25] and James Jackson's masculinity is never in doubt. Gilman, whilst not quite homophobic, is nevertheless eager to press home the point that there is nothing effeminate about these men; her overall point is a humanist one – that no-one is genetically programmed to organise or perform household tasks, but she is sometimes overdeterminate in the defensive transparency of her didactic purpose.

The courtship stories are concerned with small-scale alterations, with the relationship between two people and the private but significant changes to the usual forms of domestic organisation they can make within their own lives. The three female analogues which focus on the amelioration or the refusal of marriage, 'Three Thanksgivings', 'Maidstone Comfort' and 'Mrs Hines' Money' are concerned with making improvements to the individual life, establishing some sort of autonomy but achieving this through working for the public good. All three of the women at the heart of these narratives crave independence from men, Mrs Hines from her husband and those who would continue to enforce his rules and constraints even after his death, Mrs Morrison from her landlord's proposal that she redeem her mortgage by marrying him, and Sarah Maidstone from her repressive and self-absorbed husband whose main pleasure is apparently to be found 'in opposing his wife'.[26] The public solution to a problem which is also personal is very distinctly a female solution, women are concerned in the establishment of Mrs Morrison's house as the Women's club, women provide ideas and finance for 'Maidstone Comfort' and Mrs Hines chooses her own mentors, does her own research. All these schemes are conceived, facilitated and carried out by women and in many ways duplicate the patterns for women's work amongst projects for social improvement which Gilman experienced at Hull House, Jane Addams' settlement house in Chicago.

As Carol Farley Kessler demonstrates in her discussion of Gilman's Utopian fictions in her *Charlotte Perkins Gilman: Her Progress Toward Utopia With Selected Writings*, Gilman's letters to her daughter Katharine from Hull House during her period of residence there in 1895 provide outlines of organisational principles and facilities which translate almost untouched into her fictions of improvement. To take 'Mrs Hines' Money' as representative, this analogue contains a series of other mini-analogues which recur again and again in Gilman's writing, some of which also make their appearance in her letters to Katharine from Hull House. Structurally this story moves from female sickness to health and the nature of the sickness is such that whilst it reaches its climax in an accident which needs to be recuperated from, more significant than the injuries sustained by Mrs Hines is the necessity to recover from years of oppression by her husband. Health and well-being are here, as elsewhere in Gilman's work, associated with individual autonomy, independence of thought and action combined with the opportunity for the individual to establish a mutually beneficial relationship with the community. Mrs Hines has been kept on a tight rein by her husband, Jason, a tightness both financial as well as physical.

These constraints upon her are communicated by Gilman as completely unnecessary considering the wealth which Jason Hines actually possesses, but, because of his economic control of their lives, he can entrap his wife in financial dependence and thus in aesthetic and physical confinement. So, she is, after his death, 'the middle-aged woman who at last discovers that her discontent is social starvation – that it is not more love that she wants, but more business in life;' as predicated as a model in Gilman's formula for fiction. On a smaller scale she is also able to indulge her predi-liction for discussing the practice, a simple practice but referred to so often in Gilman's letters, autobiography and stories that it is clearly a contentious matter, about sleeping with the window open: 'How gently the curtain waved in a soft current of air! Mrs Hines preferred the window open. Jason had preferred it shut'.[27]

The freedom to sleep with one's window open to just the right degree, a complaint actually made by Gilman because of over-crowding at Hull House in letters to Katherine,[28] is as much an analogue as the repeated warning within other stories that men who are smokers are more likely to be dissolute, men with red faces have been bon viveurs and are therefore to be regarded with suspicion, hot baths in porcelain tubs are vital to a civilised existence, long hair on women is time-wasting, unhygienic and frivolous and that tight clothing, skirts without pockets and high heels disable women in the business of living. Such analogues thus employed in the fictions at large are synechdochic, they are telling parts of the human or social body which are made to represent the larger whole of a social malaise which manifests itself in matters of health and illness, fashion, patterns of consumption – especially of food, drink and tobacco and, of course, sex. More constructively, however, the analogues which hold the formula for both remedy and reform also feature in 'Mrs Hines' Money' and these owe a more positive debt to Hull House where the design and function of Mrs Hines' community building closely imitates the facilities on offer at Hull House. As Mary Hill says in her discussion of

Gilman's stay in the settlement house and what she learned from it, the principles of Hull House informed and underpinned most of her solution-orientated fiction. Both ideological and practical elements of Jane Addams' regime are affirmed in Gilman's fiction, here enumerated by Hill:

> In point of fact, many of the practical reform suggestions that appeared in her later utopian novels, how-to-do-it articles, and even larger analytic works, were ones originally designed and tested in Ward Nineteen. She would recast them to be sure; sometimes her proposals were more radical, more uncompromising, some would say bizarre (e.g. kitchenless houses). But for the most part they paralleled Hull House projects she had seen. She suggested, for instance, that professionals be hired to prepare healthy family meals; Hull House had a public kitchen. She advocated professionally run day-care centers to free woman for outside work; Hull House had already established one. She wrote about co-operative living and training centers for working-class women and domestic servants; Hull House had a cooking school, a kindergarten training program, a self-supporting cooperative for women factory workers. She wanted community recreational centers; Hull House provided one – with music, art, a library, a theater, a gymnasium, the works. She wrote articles on "Making Towns Fit to Live In," on problems of city dirt, political graft and corruption, unemployment, child labor – all major Hull House concerns.'[29]

'Mrs Hines' Money' is used to establish a model 'community recreational center', and as with all Gilman's communitarian schemes, it is a model which turns in a profit. Mrs Morrison's Women's Club makes sufficient money to pay off her mortgage and entertain her children for Thanksgiving. Like so many of the grown-up children in Gilman's fiction the Morrison offspring are waiting in the wings to do their duty, take their mother in, to cramped and confining quarters, and support her into her old age. This familiar scenario, yet another analogue, is one which engages directly with the tendency of the culture to discount the older woman, to cast her aside as having served her purpose having been married and raised children, what Gilman calls an 'Ex-Mother'[30] in the story 'A Partnership', published in *The Forerunner* in June 1914. 'Old Mrs Crosley', 'Mrs Elder's Idea', 'The Widow's

Might', 'Three Thanksgivings' and 'Mrs Hines' Money', as well as 'A Partnership', all these tales take the woman who is deemed by those around her to be past use or even pleasure and transform her into the active agent who re-invigorates both the individual and the social body. In telling the story of the woman's re-entry into the social world after marriage and motherhood Gilman is providing another analogue which offers a solution, one which demonstrates that it is never too late, that change can come no matter how many wasted years have passed. In addition to the re-habilitation of the 'Ex-Mother' Gilman also provides instances of other women whose lives have been dedicated to the care of others. In 'The Jumping-Off Place', dating from _The Forerunner_ of April 1911,[31] Gilman brings a middle-aged spinster back from the brink of suicide – another familiar mini-analogue in the fiction – into a reinvigorated career as the proprietor of a boarding-house.

The stories which have women reordering the social world at the beginning of their lives, perhaps the most hopeful and positive amongst Gilman's communitarian analogues, are the most incorporated of the stories here discussed, in that they demonstrate an inclusive ideology of reform. 'Aunt Mary's Pie Plant', 'Her Memories' and 'Bee Wise': the first set in an ordinary small town, New Newton, constructed by the narrator at the outset as 'narrow-minded', 'poor' and 'slow'[32] but, in the new order of things, transformed, largely at the instigation of a single man, the Reverend James Exeter Curtis, into a community which is both co-operative and mutual in its organisation; the second a retrospective look at 'Home Court' a self-contained community with a perfect balance of public and private spaces and amenities; and the third a purpose-built new town, which, as Carol Farley Kessler notes, treats 'all of the "fresh fields of fiction"'[33] which Gilman offered to her public in _The Man-Made World; or, Our Androcentric Culture._ Although committed to whole-scale changes in the social organisation these three tales, interestingly, parallel the small-scale reform tales which have courtship as a prominent theme in that they incorporate an idealised married state as an intrinsic part of the new world order. Gilman, as has been often noted by Ann Lane, Mary Hill and Carol Farley Kessler amongst others, was in many ways, deeply conservative and, on some questions, like that of race, reactionary even by the standards of her time. Monogamous marriage was one of the features of the social order to which she adhered as an unchanged principle of organisation and which, as she says in _Women and_

Economics, is 'the form of sex-union best calculated to advance the individual and society'.[34] Her idea of marriage in the idealised community, however, is in a superior stage of development, that predicated as an objective in *Women and Economics*: 'Although made by us an economic relation, it is not essentially so, and will exist in much higher fulfilment after the economic phase is outgrown'; [35] the men who live in New Newton and Bee Wise do so on the basis of ideological and moral affinity not economic or professional superiority.

The chief focus of the story, 'Her Memories', is of the generic over the specific, the species over the individual; the story is full of 'babyhood and motherhood' not babies and mothers, with specific examples given to support Gilman's perennial argument that some women are cut out for mothering small babies and others are not, that it is possible to live in a close community without having one's privacy or autonomy challenged and that city dwellers can make their environment as pleasant and healthful as those who live in the country. Like Gilman's novel, *Moving the Mountain*, published in *The Forerunner* in 1911, this analogue has a male narrator who needs to have the principles of community living explained to him; his resistance, like John Robertson's in the novel, thus provides the dialogic structure which moves the tale forwards. The figure of the initially sceptical outsider in 'Aunt Mary's Pie Plant' and 'Bee Wise' is ameliorated somewhat in that in both cases a woman reporter with a previous connection with the leading lights of the new communities comes to town, undergoes a willing conversion and remains to 'sit and write in a big, cool comfortable house in the country – laundry sent out, meals sent in, sweeping by the day'[36] in New Newton and to propagandise the achievements of the inhabitants of Beewise and Herways.

In naming her communities Gilman takes care to acknowledge the Utopian ambitions of previous settlers; what was once a New Town becomes New New Town, made over by that most traditional of American ethical positions, that taken on the dignity of work. The names of Herways and Beewise, as Gilman explains, come from the Biblical text: 'Go to the ant thou sluggard; consider her ways, and be wise'[37] but she adapts it through the double e spelling to include the principle of swarming as the means by which they will expand. So, rather than allowing their community to grow too large: 'Now we'll swarm like the bees and start another.... And they did, beginning another rational paradise in another beautiful valley, safer and surer for the experience behind them'.[38] The dominating theme within this analogue is that of work; the models of their endeavour from the natural world are the ant and the bee. The founders of the community are introduced as having already formed their identities amongst their friendship group at college by the professions they intend to adopt. As well as 'Mother', 'Teacher', 'Nurse', three traditional female roles quickly disposed of by Gilman in her introduction to the future social engineers: 'Then there was the "Minister", the "Doctor", and the far-seeing one they called the "Statesman". One sturdy, square-browed little girl was dubbed "Manager" for reasons frankly prominent, as with the "Artist" and the "Engineer". There were some dozen or twenty of them, all choosing various professions, but all alike in their determination to practice those professions, married or single, and in their vivid hope for better methods of living. "Advanced" in their ideas they were, even in an age of advancement, and held together in especial by the earnest words of the Minister, who was always urging upon them the power of solidarity'.[39] Gilman's ideal community is populated only by 'working people – there were no other',[40] and this is established early in the tale as the most fundamental principle of a happy, productive life. The women who define themselves at the outset according to their chosen field of professional endeavour gain not only economic control of their own destinies but control over the health of their own bodies.

As mentioned earlier, the men who seek to join the 'rational paradise' are 'selected' on grounds of good health as well as ideological commitment and for this reason the profession least needed is that of the medical practitioner: 'There was a sanitarium, where the Doctor and the Nurse gathered helpers about them, attended to casual illness, to the needs of child-birth, and to such visitors who came to them as needed care.'[41] The only sick people in this new 'Eden' are 'visitors'; from the beginning it is plain that the inhabitants of the new community lead such healthful, productive lives, wearing only comfortable clothing, which they make themselves, shoes and sandals 'that fitted the human foot, allowed for free action', that they are never sick. As Carol Farley Kessler says, all of Gilman's prescriptions for new subjects are enacted within 'Bee Wise' but the text also contains all the negative analogues from her fiction. The danger of sexually transmitted disease and dissolute masculine living are acknowledged within the good health test which the men must undergo and the injunction that 'every citizen must be clean physically and morally'; the exclusion of women from purposeful professional work in the world outside is acknowledged in the device of the legacy which makes the founding of the community possible, nowhere else in the existing social order could these women practise the professions they wish to follow without resistance. The pursuit of profit over all other goals is addressed through the fact that the community prospers sufficiently to break even and then re-duplicate itself; artists dedicating themselves to the making of 'beauty for the use of their neighbours' refute the aesthetic of art for art's sake, the only valid aesthetic here is one of use; and the drudgery of housework and servanting is vehemently rejected by making cookery into a science: 'Food was prepared in clean wide laboratories, attended by a few skilled experts, highly paid, who knew their business, and great progress was made in the study of nutrition, and in the keeping of all the people well'.

As ever in Gilman's writing it is nothing less than the social health that is at issue in every detail; every point of principle ends with the reiteration of the fact that it is the distinct Beewise practice that keeps people well. The reasons for the refusal of too much growth in the town is because to allow more people to settle there would mean the development of 'the disease of cities',[42] a debilitating disease which Gilman catalogues throughout her work, both in telling tales of its presence and tales of its absence in the fictions where she proposes solutions. In her novel *Benigna Machiavelli*, published in *The Forerunner* in 1914, the narrator, Benigna herself, says: 'I see how absurd it is for novelists to try to "end" a story. There is no end to anybody's story, until they are dead, and some people think that is only the beginning'.[43] Gilman's analogues are without end, through iteration and reiteration, they break the silence which might otherwise be unchallenged. Nowhere is that silence more catastrophic than in the tale of the endless cycle of sexually transmitted disease and nowhere is the silence more repeatedly and resoundingly contested than in the stories of female community, Gilman's analogues of 'health, peace... prosperity... human happiness beyond measure'.[44]

Notes

1. Rosen, Ruth *The Lost Sisterhood: Prostitution in America, 1900–1918* (Baltimore: The Johns Hopkins University Press, 1982), p. 54.
2. 'Bee Wise' was originally published in *The Forerunner* of July 1913, and is reprinted in Kessler, Carol Farley *Charlotte Perkins Gilman: Her Progress Toward Utopia with Selected Writings* (Liverpool: Liverpool University Press, 1995), pp. 211–19.
3. Showalter, Elaine *Sexual Anarchy: Gender and Culture at the Fin de Siècle*, 1990, (London: Bloomsbury, 1991), pp. 196–7.
4. Glasgow, Maude 'On the Regulation of Prostitution, with Special Reference to Paragraph 79 of the Page Bill', *New York and Philadelphia Medical Journal*, 42 (1910), p. 2. Cited in *The Lost Sisterhood: Prostitution in America, 1900–1918*, p. 53.
5. *The Lost Sisterhood: Prostitution in America, 1900–1918*, p. 12.
6. *The Lost Sisterhood: Prostitution in America, 1900–1918*, p. 53.
7. Rosenberg, Rosalind *Divided Lives: American Women in the Twentieth Century* (London: Penguin, 1993), p. 65.
8. *The Lost Sisterhood: Prostitution in America, 1900–1918*, p. 53.
9. Gilman, Charlotte Perkins, *His Religion and Hers: A Study of the Faith of Our Fathers and the Work of Our Mothers*, 1923 (New York: Hyperion reprint, 1976), pp. 273–4.
10. 'Freed' was originally published in *The Forerunner* of March 1912 and reprinted in Knight, Denise D. (ed.) *'The Yellow Wallpaper' and Selected Stories of Charlotte Perkins Gilman* (London, Associated University Presses, 1994), pp. 206–9.
11. Gilman, Charlotte Perkins *The Man-Made World; or, Our Androcentric Culture* (New York: Charlton Co., 1911), Chapter 5.
12. Carol Farley Kessler makes this point about the Utopian stories satisfying Gilman's injunctions for a new type of fiction in an enlightening discussion in her chapter 'Writing to Empower Living', in *Charlotte Perkins Gilman: Her Progress Toward Utopia with Selected Writings*. I am seriously indebted to Kessler's work in this area, to her bibliographical as well as her critical endeavour in putting together her volume of stories and criticism.
13. Ann J. Lane (ed.) *The Charlotte Perkins Gilman Reader* (London: The Women's Press, 1981), pp. 121–2.
14. 'Wild Oats and Tame Wheat' originally published in *The Forerunner* of May 1913 and reprinted in *'The Yellow Wallpaper' and Selected Stories of Charlotte Perkins Gilman*, pp. 218–19.
15. 'The Vintage', originally published in *The Forerunner* of October 1916 and reprinted in *'The Yellow Wallpaper' and Selected Stories of Charlotte Perkins Gilman*, pp. 104–11.
16. *'The Yellow Wallpaper' and Selected Stories of Charlotte Perkins Gilman*, p. 218.
17. *'The Yellow Wallpaper' and Selected Stories of Charlotte Perkins Gilman*, p. 104.
18. For an extended discussion of marriage and health in Gilman's fiction see my essay, 'Charlotte Perkins Gilman and Women's

Health: the "long limitation"', in a collection forthcoming from the University of Liverpool Press.

19. *The Charlotte Perkins Gilman Reader*, p. 62.
20. *Charlotte Perkins Gilman: Her Progress Toward Utopia with Selected Writings*, pp. 6–7.
21. *Charlotte Perkins Gilman: Her Progress Toward Utopia with Selected Writings*, p. 59.
22. *The Charlotte Perkins Gilman Reader*, p. 50.
23. *Charlotte Perkins Gilman: Her Progress Toward Utopia with Selected Writings*, p. 202.
24. *Charlotte Perkins Gilman: Her Progress Toward Utopia with Selected Writings*, p. 155.
25. *The Charlotte Perkins Gilman Reader*, p. 49.
26. *Charlotte Perkins Gilman: Her Progress Toward Utopia with Selected Writings*, p. 187.
27. 'Mrs Hines' Money', originally published in *The Forerunner* of April 1913 and reprinted in *Charlotte Perkins Gilman: Her Progress Toward Utopia with Selected Writings*, pp. 203–10.
28. Carol Farley Kessler includes an extract from Gilman's last letter to Katharine in *Charlotte Perkins Gilman: Her Progress Toward Utopia with Selected Writings*: 'Things are happening now quite vigorously – at least I am happening! I happen to be visiting around at present; because I don't like to stay at Hull House and sleep in half a room. They are so full that three rooms are double bedded and double inhabited and as I am but a transient guest I was one of these doublers. But I didn't like it because the other occupant was not accustomed to as much air as I – only one window open for two people! One of my possible roommates raised her's [sic] about a foot – that didn't suit me at all. The other opened her's fairly wide, but she read in bed, by the light of a large lamp, until midnight, and I liked that still less', pp. 92–3.
29. Hill, Mary A. *Charlotte Perkins Gilman: The Making of a Radical Feminist, 1860–1896* (Philadelphia: Temple University Press, 1980), p. 277.
30. Shulman, Robert (ed.) *'The Yellow Wallpaper' and Other Stories* (Oxford: Oxford University Press, 1995, p. 257.
31. *'The Yellow Wallpaper' and Other Stories*, pp. 148–58.
32. *Charlotte Perkins Gilman: Her Progress Toward Utopia with Selected Writings*, p. 118.
33. *Charlotte Perkins Gilman: Her Progress Toward Utopia with Selected Writings*, p. 211.
34. Gilman, Charlotte Perkins *Women and Economics*, 1898, reprinted. Carl N. Degler. (New York, Harper Torchbooks, 1966), p. 25.
35. *Women and Economics*, p. 213.
36. *Charlotte Perkins Gilman: Her Progress Toward Utopia with Selected Writings*, p. 128.
37. *Proverbs*, 6:6.
38. *Charlotte Perkins Gilman: Her Progress Toward Utopia with Selected Writings*, pp. 218–19.

39. *Charlotte Perkins Gilman: Her Progress Toward Utopia with Selected Writings*, p. 213.
40. *Charlotte Perkins Gilman: Her Progress Toward Utopia with Selected Writings*, p. 218.
41. *Charlotte Perkins Gilman: Her Progress Toward Utopia with Selected Writings*, p. 217.
42. *Charlotte Perkins Gilman: Her Progress Toward Utopia with Selected Writings*, p. 218.
43. *The Charlotte Perkins Gilman Reader*, p. 163.
44. *Charlotte Perkins Gilman: Her Progress Toward Utopia with Selected Writings*, p. 219.

9

'The Yellow Wallpaper' on Film: Dramatising Mental Illness

In 1988 a ninety-minute adaptation of 'The Yellow Wallpaper' by Charlotte Perkins Gilman was made for BBC television; filming took place in the autumn of that year and it was ready for broadcasting in January 1989 although it was not actually shown until January 1992. The project had been initiated by the producer, Sarah Curtis, who invited the dramatist, Maggie Wadey, to write the screenplay.[1] Whilst the adaptation was almost entirely the work of Maggie Wadey a number of decisions about the way in which the text would be approached and also how to shoot and edit the film were made collaboratively between dramatist, producer and the director, John Clive.

I became interested in the idea of writing about the film version of the story when working on this book because it seemed to offer an example of the multiplicity of the type of engagement which it is possible to have with 'The Yellow Wallpaper' and one which, although creative, actually parallels the enormous critical endeavour to read, interpret and contextualise the story which has taken place over the past 20 years. Wadey's screenplay, whilst not an academic exercise, is the same kind of expansive undertaking as the critical endeavour: picking up, emphasising and developing themes, tropes and structural devices in order to build the story into a substantial drama which reverberates with wider signification. Through reading in detail, exploiting every figurative and referential opportunity, Wadey turns the interior monologue of a woman descending into madness into a drama which makes explicit both the private and public conditions of existence for the woman who desires something beyond marriage and motherhood. It tells the story which lies behind every other tale or theory constructed by Gilman; 'The Yellow Wallpaper' enacts the degradation and decline of the female of the species, from physical and mental health to dependance and incapacity. The story of the post-partum breakdown told here is the driving force behind Gilman's analogues, behind her manipulation of the generic, behind her writing life, and the dramatisation of that story seems to me to carry Gilman's purpose to inform and enlighten the widest possible audience to a beautiful, logical climax.

The film of 'The Yellow Wallpaper' is noteworthy for a number of reasons, not least of which is in its extension of the usual audience for Gilman's work. Perhaps the most striking thing about the conversion of the printed text into the screen version is in the dramatic explication of the social conditions which lead to the psychological breakdown of the woman who is the centre of consciousness in the original text. This broadening of the picture is not achieved at the expense of diluting Gilman's original intensity of setting; all the action, until the very end when we see John giving a speech in London, takes place in and around the house. The 'ancestral halls',[2] hired for the express purposes of effecting a cure, are, in the film, even more obviously a monolithic trope for the domestic confinement of women, and the whole apparatus which ensures the social control of women is on display within the confines of the individual household. Wadey here effectively dramatises not only mental illness but the context for mental illness, demonstrating, in a manner absolutely consonant with the author's declared purpose in writing the tale, that the conditions which lead to what Gilman describes in her autobiography as '...painful mental sensation, shame, fear, remorse, a blind oppressive confusion, utter weakness, a steady brainache that filled the conscious mind with crowding images of distress.... Absolute incapacity. Absolute misery.'[3] are socially remediable.

One of the earliest decisions taken by Wadey and Curtis together was to underplay the potential for interpretation as a gothic text which 'The Yellow Wallpaper' undoubtedly offers. They both felt that to exploit the gothic elements in the text in a filmed version of the story would have the effect of reducing its power as a disturbing and moving portrait of the mental breakdown of an intelligent, promising young woman. Whilst Wadey's 1986 dramatisation of Jane Austen's *Northanger Abbey* overstates and sends up the gothic elements in the novel in order to mirror Austen's ridicule of the reading public's taste for the lurid and fantastic, such overstatement also makes the serious point that the constraints upon young women entering polite society at the time –

as regards their manners, appearance and even their companions – were kept in place by fear of trespass, of transgression of social codes, codes which they often did not fully understand. Such fear expresses their true position of powerlessness in a situation where reputation could be made or broken by rumour, where social invisibility could signify disgrace or failure and the consequences of any breach of social decorum could carry a penalty of exclusion as damaging as literal incarceration. So whilst the scenes of mock-gothic terror in the dramatisation of *Northanger Abbey* ironise the melodramatic imagination of the heroine they also point to the very real limits of her worldly knowledge and the extent to which her trust could and would be abused.

Elements of gothic resonate throughout the text of 'The Yellow Wallpaper' and the effect thus achieved has been extensively discussed[4] in critical responses to the story and Gilman's two other overtly gothic fictions, 'The Giant Wistaria'[5] and 'The Rocking Chair',[6] both of which can be considered more straightforwardly as ghost stories than 'The Yellow Wallpaper'. The decision to omit from the dramatic text and the film style of 'The Yellow Wallpaper' any suggestion of supernatural intervention and, indeed, to exclude from the visual text any ambiguity as to the origins or cause of the mental breakdown, means that the drama focuses unremittingly on the social circumstances of the woman driven to madness. The breakdown is psychic but the context for and circumstances of the descent into madness are physically demonstrable in the conditions of the everyday life of the woman concerned.

Another early decision by the dramatist was to name the protagonist Charlotte, the transparency of the autobiographical reference in the story – and in all Gilman's pronouncements upon its reason for being – making the identification between the protagonist and Gilman herself an enabling factor in the grounding of the text in the social, and particularly the medical, culture of the time. The majority of the research undertaken by the dramatist was, in fact, into the treatment of mental illness in the late 19th century. In particular Wadey found Elaine Showalter's *The Female Malady: Women, Madness and English Culture, 1830–1980*[7] invaluable for both its discussion of the treatments most commonly used on women with severe depression or mental breakdown and the ideology which informed the development and use of such therapeutic regimes.

To avoid the dangers of cross-referencing or the over-academicising of the dramatic text Maggie Wadey's preliminary research put the piece into its cultural context but did not look extensively at the writer's life and other works. As a working method Wadey generally prefers to look at secondary texts once her first draft has been written thus generating the dramatic impetus from the story alone rather than allowing references to other works to influence the adaptation. The symbolism, the motifs and dramatic structure of the film thus evolve from Wadey's sense of the metaphoric richness of 'The Yellow Wallpaper' in aesthetic if not cultural isolation and whilst Gilman scholars can see patterns of imagery, figurative language and themes which recur throughout the whole body of Gilman's fiction and non-fiction in the film, the dramatist has actually achieved this command of Gilman's tropes and lexis through an intense concentration upon the story and its interaction with the social and medical conventions of the time. Whilst this speaks of the richness of this individual text and the insightfulness of the dramatist it is also a reminder that the language of health and illness which features in so dominant a manner in 'The Yellow Wallpaper' reverberates unremittingly throughout the whole body of her published work; Gilman never ceased to express herself through configurations of the social health.

The dramatic version of the text thus incorporates all sorts of thematic patterns – both ideological and autobiographical – from Gilman's lifelong work which speak to those who know the extent and purpose of Gilman's achievement as a writer whilst not detracting from the impetus of the straightforward narrative which enacts the descent into madness. The film incorporates Gilman's use of the limited point of view in the story where the reader knows as much as the narrator, but it also provides scenes where Charlotte is not present either as point of view or participant and these, without exception, provide reinforcement of the themes which dominate in both the visual and printed text, most powerful of which is the hard fact of the gender divide. Issues which endlessly absorb Gilman in her writing: the features of women's lives which confine and restrict them unnecessarily, like the manner of their dress and hairstyle, the limitation of their forms of exercise and virtual exclusion from formal education here take shape as the dramatic structure of 'The Yellow Wallpaper'. The whole drama is predicated on the consequences that arise from the differentiation between men and women's relationships with the world outside the home, in Gilman's view the most crippling amongst the myriad of handicaps that women had to contend with in their adult lives.

An event threatened in the story and enacted in the screenplay, which can, additionally, be seen as paradigmatic of the manner in which Wadey expands the drama beyond the limits of the original text, depicts the doctor called in by Charlotte's husband to give a second opinion delivering moral as well as medical advice to his patient:

Let me repeat what I told you two months ago: I cannot answer for your good health, physical or mental, unless you undertake to lay aside your writing. Your child, your husband, your home, cannot be laid aside and the energy of the human body is finite.
(HE NOW PROCEEDS TO EXAMINE CHARLOTTE'S EYES, PULLING THE LOWER LID DOWN WITH HIS THUMB)
What nature expends in one direction she must economise on in another. The young woman who makes too much intellectual effort risks decline into a delicate, ailing woman whose future – allow me? (HE OPENS HER GOWN) – is more or less suffering. A lesson I should not like to see experience teach you, Charlotte.
I see your dressmaker has already begun to help you conceal your loss of weight. You must put on flesh, my dear. Surely I can appeal to your vanity if nothing else?
(HE CLOSES HER GOWN AGAIN)
But there's nothing gravely wrong with you – we may reassure poor John on that point!
(HE LIGHTLY TOUCHES ONE OF HER EARRINGS WITH HIS FINGER-TIPS)
Charming earrings, my dear. (pp. 125–6)[8]

Contained within the doctor's pronouncements about the recovery and maintenance of good health are allusions to matters which Gilman considered instrumental in the oppression of women and which are also discussed as significant by Elaine Showalter in the management of female mental illness at the end of the 19th century. With regard to women's capacity for intellectual work Showalter cites manifold pronouncements by male doctors on the limited capacity which women have for study and the deleterious effects which scholarship would have upon their reproductive capacity.[9] In her autobiography Gilman repeats the advice she was given by Silas Weir Mitchell, her physician, ' "Live as domestic a life as possible. Have your baby with you all the time. Lie down for an hour after each meal. Have but two hours intellectual life a day. And never touch pen, brush or pencil as long as you live."'.[10] In the dramatisation Wadey actually paraphrases Henry Maudsley, the Victorian psychiatrist, when Dr Stark invokes the order of the natural world as authority for the physical and cerebral inferiority of women. The example of the natural world, as Charlotte Perkins Gilman constantly tells us, is often used as proof by those eager to establish the lesser status of the female and the selective nature of the evidence thus offered is critiqued throughout her writing by direct reference and also by her own decision to make use of equally selective references to species where the female is dominant.[11]

On the subject of dress and adornment Showalter discusses Maudsley's abjuring of his fellow practitioners to be vigilant in the detection of those women who would seek to conceal their emaciation: '"Those in whom the organs are wasted invoke the dressmaker's aid in order to gain the appearance of them; they are not satisfied unless they wear the show of perfect womanhood."'.[12] Gilman herself returned again and again throughout her fiction and non-fiction to the exaggeration of the sex characteristics of the woman in the fashionable clothing of her day, here in *Women and Economics*: 'In garments whose main purpose is unmistakably to announce her sex; with a tendency to ornament which marks exuberance of sex-energy, with a body so modified to sex as to be grievously deprived of its natural activities; with a manner and behavior wholly attuned to sex-advantage, and frequently disadvantageous to any human gain; with a field of action most rigidly confined to sex-relations; with her over-charged sensibility, her prominent modesty, her "eternal femininity", – the female of genus homo is undeniably over-sexed.'[13] When dressing for the occasion of the visit of her mother-in-law – another dramatic expansion of a passing reference in Gilman's text: 'John thought it might do me good to see a little company, so we just had mother and Nellie and the children down for a week.'[14] – Charlotte talks to Jennie about how 'indecent' (p. 106) a thing the bustle is, calling her and John 'hypocrites' (p. 107) for dressing her up in clothes designed to accentuate the woman's sexual parts in order to be exhibited as a well woman to the visitors.

Wadey further substantiates the matters raised in the doctor's pronouncements upon the causes of Charlotte's continuing ill health with a conversation between her husband and his fellow practitioner, where they discuss therapies used with mentally ill women specifically designed to appeal to their vanity. All the while they are discussing such treatments Jennie is singing at the piano, demonstrating yet another of the accomplishments that makes her the perfect wife-in-waiting. She is, however, ignored completely by the men absorbed in the detail of a professional practice which objectifies women and makes the sex-relation merely a constituent of the pathology of female mental illness. In writing a larger role in the drama for Jennie, Wadey does not lose the sense that there is a complicity between John and his sister to restrain Charlotte but she does develop the portrait of Jennie to a point where the treatment meted out to her by her brother and Dr Stark – who she is clearly hoping to impress with her womanly skills – provides dramatic reinforcement for Charlotte's claims that she is never listened to, that her opinions and achievements are ignored and her life is one that is deemed irrelevant to the business of high professional endeavour reserved for the male of the species.

Jennie, in both the original – 'She is a perfect and enthusiastic housekeeper, and hopes for no better profession.'[15] – and the adaptation, is John's accomplice in enforcing the rest cure. The part played by Jennie and the brief but horrifying appearance of John's mother provide substance for another of Gilman's perennial arguments, that women are complicit in perpetuating the system which keeps them subordinate. However, the inclusion in the film of additional goals for both John and Jennie, alters the balance of the drama, again extending the support for attributing Charlotte's breakdown to the social organisation rather than an individual predisposition to 'nervousness' or any other euphemism. John and Jennie and the narrator all share the same ambition in Gilman's text, the restoration to health of the central protagonist, although, they differ, of course, on the best method of achieving this end. In addition to the effecting of Charlotte's recovery in the film John and Jennie are given individual, professional ambitions – house-keeping here being designated as the only 'profession' ever con-sidered by Jennie – John, to make an impressive debut at the Royal Society and his sister to practise being a wife and attract Dr Stark. The end of the dramatic version thus shows the woman driven mad in isolation but extends the sense of failure and disillusionment beyond the individual to the concomitant disappointment of Jennie and John's personal and professional ambitions; Jennie fails to attract a suitable man and John fails cataclysmically in his attempt to cure Charlotte. The drama therefore makes it more obvious that the whole of society is implicated in the psychological disorder of the individual; that it is a sick society in Gilman's terms, which wastes the talents and aspirations of all its members by making the task of limiting and confining one half of the population a compulsory part of the duties which must be performed by all in preservation of the status quo.

The difference between the youthful aspirations of the young Charlotte and the reality of her life as a married woman are figured forth in the visual text through dialogue, where she talks to Jennie, her husband's sister, about the ambitions she had to manage her own magazine and adds: 'But of course what happened when I grew up was, I met John. A doctor! It made my ideas seem very trivial.' (p. 43); when she asks Jennie what her own ambitions for her adult life were; and in a series of conversations with her husband which position his professional importance against the failure of all her ambitions. The repeated motif in the film of John's departure for work being signalled by the closing of a large gate and his walking away down the lane from the house also reinforces the separation between the woman's sphere, the house, where Charlotte is confined, and the masculine world of external endeavour and freedom. The fact that women's lives are controlled by men is plain enough in Gilman's text where John is both husband and doctor, two awesomely powerful authority figures in one, but in the dramatic text one of the most sinister and indiscriminately damaging features of this control is made much more explicit through the presentation of sexual relations between John and Charlotte.

Ann J. Lane, in her biography of Gilman, talks about the smell which the narrator of 'The Yellow Wallpaper' identifies as emanating from the paper itself: 'It is, she says, "the most enduring odor I ever met," and perhaps it is, even if Gilman did not recognize it, the dreaded smell of sex, a sensual smell, excretion of the night'.[16] The fear of sex which Lane recognises in Gilman's writing: 'I wake up in the night and find it hanging over me.'[17] is made explicit in the dramatic text in a number of forms. When talking to Jennie Charlotte expresses directly one of the reasons why she would want to avoid sexual relations: 'He is such a sweet baby, but – it still makes me so nervous to be with him. I – I worry in case there should be another one, and then -' (p. 75), a fear which

Jennie ignores. The distress which is evident in Charlotte's explanation to John of her reasons for needing to leave the house is interpreted by him in the exigencies of his own need, to be a cry for physical attention not the intellectual stimulation she is pleading for:

> And you know, when I'm away from you, it's such a joy to know exactly what you're doing. At one o'clock I can imagine you lying here in bed.
> (HE TURNS BACK TO CHARLOTTE)
> At three, I know that James has come in to play with you. What a charming picture that is! At six I can imagine you dressing for dinner.
> (HE SLIPS THE SLEEVE OF HER DRESS DOWN FROM HER SHOULDER WHICH HE KISSES)
> But how much better it is to be here beside you. How adorable you look this evening! Dearest Lotta!
> (CHARLOTTE THROWS AN ARM UP OVER HER EYES TO HIDE HER TEARS)
> Don't hide! You needn't be ashamed with me. There are times I wish to God I could cry as easily as you do. Tears one moment, smiles the next. So give me a smile, won't you? Please, my sweet. That's better. (p. 99)

Wadey makes plain the connection between Charlotte's helpless despair and John's desire through both dialogue and action. The timetable of her day, the control which he exerts over her every movement in his absence, another infantilisation to add to the confining of her within the nursery and forbidding of certain activities, is shown to be an intrinsic part of the way in which he eroticises her. As he visualises her in the process of following the schedule he has prescribed so he feels his power; the place in which he confines her is the place where, as he says, 'I've been looking forward to being alone with you again. In our nursery. Like another world.' (p. 54). The pressing nature of his attentions in the film, making love to her on the nailed down bed in a furtive manner – not undressing or expecting any response but mere compliance – communicates a powerful sense of the claustrophobia, powerlessness and physical distress felt by her. The scene where John makes love to Charlotte does not celebrate or sensationalise sex, it is painful and oppressive, providing further evidence of a social order in which only one sex is allowed full expression of its desires, whether sexual or professional. When Charlotte reacts to the final articulation of the spiteful insincerity of John's mother: 'You do John credit, my dear.' (p. 119) by choking and fainting, tearing at her clothes, she is making the only effective protest she can against her many constrictions.

Whilst Charlotte is chastised for thinking and for talking about her 'feelings' (p. 121) the conversation between the two doctors as they look at photographs of women being treated for mental breakdown is unashamed in its subjectivity, male subjectivity being acceptable as a basis for judgement:

> Initially she was diagnosed as melancholic, but she's tormented with a sense of guilt and punishes herself with fasting. She's become very weak, her menstrual periods have stopped, she hallucinates occasionally and sometimes talks of suicide. There's something intensely feminine and appealing about her, don't you think? (p. 135)

The pictures which the men handle in the film are some of those which Showalter uses in *The Female Malady* to illustrate her instructive discussion of Jean-Martin Charcot's use of photographs in the treatment of hysteria at the Salpêtrière clinic in Paris in the late 19th century. As Showalter says: 'Charcot's hospital became an environment in which female hysteria was perpetually presented, represented and reproduced...photographs...were given subtitles that suggested Charcot's interpretation of hysteria as linked to female sexuality, despite his disclaimers "amorous supplication", "ecstasy", "eroticism". This interpretation of hysterical gestures as sexual was reinforced by Charcot's efforts to pinpoint areas of the body that might induce convulsions when pressed. The ovarian region, he concluded, was a particularly sensitive hysterogenic zone'.[18] The right to interpret both woman and illness is thus reserved for the practitioner; the woman becomes the supplicant and the doctor the arbitrator of meaning beyond the doctor–patient relationship. The division of the organisation of the treatment of hysteria into antagonistic parts, that is, into doctor and patient, artist and subject, master and subordinate, man and woman, is represented in Gilman's text and Wadey's screenplay in both structural and thematic terms. The intimate link between the breakdown of the narrator's health and the birth of her child, between the sexual act and the prostration and weakness of the woman and between medical intervention and her enduring state of helplessness is borne in upon Charlotte in every aspect of her life as it reinforces her status as decorative, subordinate, intellectually inferior and, most shamefully in the eyes of the ouside world, a failure as a mother.

Above all else the dramatisation makes plain what is intimated in every line of Gilman's writing, that the essentialist argument that keeps women in their place as subordinate to men has its foundation in an authority which constantly breaches the distinction between the objective and subjective and which flaunts that subjectivity as a means of oppression: 'Charming earrings, my dear.' The way in which John as husband and as doctor communicates with Charlotte in the adaptation is consonant with his tone in the original text and, as both lover and professional, one minute intimate and the next distant, occupier of private space and enacter of public opinions, he expresses the all-embracing nature of the authority which is brought to bear on the woman in the home. The central principle of development in the story is the descent into madness but what determines the course of that development is the treatment the protagonist receives. The narrative, both textual and visual, follows the transformation of woman into child then a creature beyond reason, and it is the therapeutic regime, at once intimate, in Gilman's words: ' "Bless her little heart!" said he with a big hug, she shall be as sick as she pleases!" '[19] and distant: 'John says if I don't pick up faster he shall send me to Weir Mitchell in the fall.'[20] that finally impresses the truth of her powerlessness and therefore lack of personhood upon the narrator. Charlotte's last coherent speech in the film concerns the realisation of her failure as a professional, or at least as a member of an identifiable group:

The strange thing about it is – when I started out, I thought I was joining a community, a brotherhood of writers, living and dead. But I found I was always alone. I seem to have drifted further and further away into a world of my own, and strangest of all, the more it's become my own, the less control I have over it. The more I talk to myself the less I understand what's being said. (p. 139)

In being treated as sick – infantilised, subjected to the linguistic and ideological impositions of the masculine world – she has lost her sense of relatedness, becoming first an isolate and finally nothing. The treatment she receives annhilates her, in becoming a wife she takes on subject status, in becoming a mother she is expected to focus even more narrowly on one thing, even to become that thing, a baby – 'I'm getting dreadfully fretful and querulous. I cry at nothing, and cry most of the time.'[21] – and in becoming ill she becomes nothing, nothing but a failure. As Showalter says: 'Mental breakdown, then, would come when women defied their "nature", attempted to compete with men instead of serving them, or sought alternatives or even additions to their maternal functions.';[22] it is the essentialist argument which divides and rules without mercy.

Wadey's introduction of the writing and delivery of John's speech to the Royal Society as another means by which the dramatic action is propelled is a further substantiation of the dialectic which reigns throughout the drama between public and private, home and work and men and women. The gender divide fuels the action and it is expressed in every scene and motif, reaching a climax as the film cuts between the final stages of Charlotte's madness and John's delivery of the speech to his fellow physicians. As John descends to the auditorium, Charlotte wrenches out the nails which hold the bed to the floor; as he opens his lecture notes before an audience, she clears surfaces, moves furniture and overturns the wardrobe; as John holds forth on the benefical effects of recreation in reducing instances of ill health amongst the poor, turning the pages of his lecture, so Charlotte rips the paper from the walls. The camera registers the attentiveness of John's audience as he delivers his speech whilst the camera in Charlotte's bedroom is positioned so that it looks at her from inside the newly bare wall. As she crawls, demented, around the room in pursuit of a single idea, he receives the congratulations of his peers for the effective expression of his many ideas and theories.

The visual contextualisation of Charlotte's breakdown in the midst of John's professional debut as a public speaker foregrounds the difference between public and private texts as well as lives. John's prominent position in the medical establishment enacts a straightforward contrast between his place in the outside world and Charlotte's obvious isolation from anyone who cares about the stuff of the imagination or the writer's craft. As he becomes more public so she is forced into greater seclusion and internality, as she says in her lament for the loss of her sense of 'community'.

The sequence of scenes which show Charlotte writing in her forbidden notebook culminates in her being viewed from outside the bedroom window; the window frames the shot and the visual image is of the writer behind bars, imprisoned for practising her art. A number of exchanges between John and Charlotte in the dramatisation make plain their epistemological divergence, Wadey setting up a dialectic between scientific and poetic truth, between imagination and fact and between varieties of textual authority.

The dramatisation also makes more obvious the difference between private and public texts. Charlotte's notebook, kept in a concealed pocket and written in secret, is a covert text; the schedule which says at what time she must do everything during the course of the day is a public, prescribed text. As her writing in the notebook is curtailed by Dr Stark's discovery of her 'secret vice' (p. 18) and she is also forbidden access to the library, so the only text she has to read and to inscribe herself upon is the wallpaper, the only replacement for her notebook to which she can gain access. As the doctor makes a physical examination of Charlotte, so he discovers her hidden pocket; in marriage the location of her hidden pocket by her husband is the cause of her past and present misery and the continued scrutiny of all her private places the surest sign of its continuance. As Dr Stark leaves her she sits beside the wallpaper, scrutinising it for its hidden pockets of meaning; it becomes the text she has both to decipher and to get behind, to study and to find her own meaning or hiding place within.

As Annette Kolodny says in her essay, 'A Map for Rereading: or Gender and the Interpretation of Literary Texts': 'the narrator progressively gives up the attempt to *record* her reality and instead begins to *read* it – as symbolically adumbrated in her compulsion to discover a consistent and coherent pattern amid "the sprawling outlines" of the wallpaper's apparently "pointless pattern".'23 Once the realisation dawns upon her that her only resource is the wallpaper then she accedes to the opportunity it seems to offer for complexity rather than the simple truth of childish punishment and reward offered by John's cure. She has been placed in the nursery for the purpose of effecting that cure; John has offered it as semiotically one-dimensional, the uncomplicated baby-place in which to grow stronger, to mature and face one's proper responsibilities. She makes her own semiotic landscape out of the nursery, however, by converting the wallpaper into a complex and multi-faceted text which speaks of the nether side of the process of childbirth and baby-rearing. Its smell is its essence; it smells not only of sex but of custom and practice – 'the subtlest, most enduring odor I ever met'.[24] It registers the disgust of the woman at her own adult smell as well as the processes which, in spite of her intellectual capacities, her body is capable of, as the wallpaper gives birth to her and others like her: 'I wonder if they all come out of that wall-paper as I did'.[25]

Ann J. Lane talks about the nightmarish version of parturition in the figurative language of the story's climax: 'She is both child and mother. She is the child in the mother. Frantically she peels off the paper and sees "all those strangled heads and bulbous eyes and waddling fungus growths", imagery which brings to mind dead babies'.[26] The blank white page of girlhood, the clean page of her notebook, are made sordid and stale by the adult business of sex and procreation. Hymen, the Greek God of marriage, wears a saffron robe; the hymen is broken and all that purity of body and of intention is made stale, dirty and decadent. Prior to the appearance in the film of the crawling woman in yellow, Wadey has Charlotte look with envy and admiration at the figure of a girl, usually dressed in white, on a bicycle, riding on the grass behind the house. Identified in the dramatisation as 'the gardener's daughter', she appears and reappears to us as we look out from the house from Charlotte's point of view. That she exists on a literal as well as metaphorical level in the dramatisation is made plain when Jennie answers Charlotte's query as to why she has disappeared with 'No! She's quite the young lady now. No more bicycle riding.' (p. 130); as the youthful freedom, energy and ambition she symbolises is relinquished so she is consigned to the constraints of being 'quite the young lady'. Her penultimate appearance is, in the words of Wadey's stage directions: 'The girl on her bicycle crosses left to right, balancing on the saddle on one hand – very cheeky.' (p. 61) as an acrobat, making concrete the dramatist's sense of the closure of female youthful daring and physical potential whilst forging a connection with Gilman's own declaration in her autobiography, 'With right early training I could easily have been an acrobat, having good nervous coordination, strength, courage, and excellent balancing power'.[27] The last appearance of the girl, however, shows her, once again in white, riding the bicycle down a long slope into an area of darkness beyond.

Like the girl on the bicycle and her replacement, the crawling woman, there are a number of motifs in the film all of which make literal the gender divide. We see the opening and closing of the garden gate each time John leaves for work, he calls for the 'boy' in order to part from him, throwing him into the air as the ritualised and limited contact that the father has with his child is demonstrated. Such repetitions establish and support a dialectic structure between male and female lives, but they also reinforce the divide between female health and illness and girlhood and maturity. As Charlotte retreats into herself so the wallpaper takes on a life of its own, hissing and creaking; as the camera tracks around the room it becomes plain that Charlotte is following the line of her own mark or 'smooch' (p. 173) upon it. The house, provided in order to restore her to health, keep her in enforced seclusion – in other words to reinforce, by its isolation, the limits of her world – is the place wherein the ceaseless round of the domestic routines of the family house are enacted. As Jennie sorts towels, folds linen, chooses material, orders the meals, and administers the therapeutic regime in John's absence, so the over-mighty weight of the household presses in upon Charlotte. In her one illicit visit to the library she strokes and smells the volumes on the shelves, she takes some to her room and lies on her bed surrounded by a surfeit of the printed page as she opens books and architectural plans. She dips into a variety of different texts with the camera above her, emphasising the totality of her absorption in her reading as she lies, perfectly still, until her sense of being watched, spied on, returns and she looks suspiciously at the wallpaper.

At an early point in the dramatic version of 'The Yellow Wallpaper' Charlotte responds to John's recital of her daily schedule by asking the question 'Is silence consent?' (p. 27). The film makes evident the silence which greets Charlotte when she tries to talk about her writing, her feelings, her imagination, her ambitions, sex, clothes, leaving the house or anything other than meals, rest and recovery but also shows her own decline into silence as she uses fewer and fewer words, alone and turning ever inward, secretive about the last of her ambitions, to find the time and space to strip the bedroom of its hidden meaning. Charlotte Perkins Gilman felt herself to be isolated from the thinkers and doers of the world as a young wife; as a mature woman she was convinced that if the seclusion of the domestic life of women could be broken then that would achieve dramatic social improvements which would bring benefit to every member of society: man, woman and child. The film of 'The Yellow Wallpaper' enacts the drama of isolation, re-telling the story of the individual woman driven by the whole-cultural imperatives which would make her one-dimensional into becoming so, a creature ultimately confined to that most one-dimensional of planes, a wall. As the camera moves behind the wall so the stark horror of the point of view from behind the paper is revealed. The film of 'The Yellow Wallpaper' does not replace the original story, it is yet another renewal of the tale which Gilman wrote, after all, with the express intention that it should 'save people from being driven crazy'.[28]

Notes

1. I am very grateful to Maggie Wadey for her help; without her assistance it would not have been possible to write this account of 'The Yellow Wallpaper'.
2. Gilman, Charlotte Perkins *The Yellow Wallpaper*, 1872 (London: Virago Press, 1973), p. 9.
3. *The Living of Charlotte Perkins Gilman*, pp. 90–1.
4. See especially Juliann E. Fleenor, 'The Gothic Prism: Charlotte Perkins Gilman's Gothic Stories and Her Autobiography', pp. 139–158 in Erskine, Thomas L. and Connie L. Richards (eds) *Charlotte Perkins Gilman: 'The Yellow Wallpaper'* (New Jersey: Rutgers University Press, 1993).
5. Gilman, Charlotte Perkins 'The Giant Wistaria', first published in *New England Magazine*, No. 4 (June 1891), pp. 480–5.
6. Gilman, Charlotte Perkins 'The Rocking Chair', first published in *Worthington's Illustrated*, I (May 1893), pp. 453–9.
7. Showalter, Elaine *The Female Malady: Women, Madness and English Culture, 1830–1980* (London: Virago Press, 1985).
8. All page references in the text are to the screenplay of 'The Yellow Wallpaper' by Maggie Wadey.
9. *The Female Malady*, p. 126.
10. *The Living of Charlotte Perkins Gilman*, p. 96.
11. For example, in the first chapter of *Women and Economics*, 1898, reprinted. Carl N. Degler (New York, Harper Torchbooks, 1966), Gilman argues that 'We are the only animal species in which the female depends upon the male for food, the only animal species in which the sex-relation is also an economic relation.' (p. 4) and goes on to discuss a variety of other species.
12. *The Female Malady*, p. 125; the quotation is taken from Maudsley's *Responsibility in Mental Disease* (2nd edn London: Kegan Paul, 1874), p. 40.
13. Gilman, Charlotte Perkins *Women and Economics*, pp. 53–4.
14. *The Yellow Wallpaper*, p. 18.
15. *The Yellow Wallpaper*, pp. 17–8.

16. Lane, Ann J. *To* Herland *and Beyond: The Life and Work of Charlotte Perkins Gilman* (New York, Meridian, 1991), p. 129.
17. *The Yellow Wallpaper*, p. 29.
18. *The Female Malady*, p. 150.
19. *The Yellow Wallpaper*, p. 24.
20. *The Yellow Wallpaper*, p. 18.
21. *The Yellow Wallpaper*, p. 19.
22. *The Female Malady*, p. 123.
23. Golden, Catherine (ed.) *The Captive Imagination: A Casebook on 'The Yellow Wallpaper'* (New York: The Feminist Press, 1992), p. 156.
24. *The Yellow Wallpaper*, p. 29.
25. *The Yellow Wallpaper*, p. 35.
26. *To* Herland *and Beyond*, p. 127.
27. *The Living of Charlotte Perkins Gilman*, p. 64.
28. Gilman, Charlotte Perkins 'Why I Wrote "The Yellow Wallpaper" ' *The Forerunner*, 1913, reprinted in *The Captive Imagination*, pp. 51–2.

Conclusion

I hope that this book will open up as many questions for further debate as it answers in terms of the work of the three writers here discussed. Whilst I have endeavoured to offer a number of thematic or generic readings which have critical concerns in common, I am very conscious of the fact that I have left relatively untouched any rigorously comparative approach to their work. My justification for this omission lies in the rich variety of the fiction of Chopin, Wharton and Gilman within the limits of their own pages, wherein I have been absorbed by their own individual intra-mural connections, correlations and developments. Additionally, in embracing another constraint, confining myself to consideration of their work in the short story, I have been able to raise questions about both the limitations and the licence on offer to these practitioners in the genre, to look at the wider cultural context of the publication of their work, to examine thematic continuities and also to re-define some of the terms of engagement which are appropriate to the scrutiny of their short fiction.

Short fiction in general perhaps receives a smaller portion of critical notice than it deserves and this is reflected particularly in the limited availability of stories by these writers, although Gilman seems at last to be receiving greater attention, with recent outstanding work by scholars like Denise Knight and Carol Farley Kessler making more of her work available to scholars and general readers alike. The full range and diversity of her writing, beyond 'The Yellow Wallpaper', is gradually becoming more accessible and, as critical bias against didactic fiction is further eroded, Gilman's work will, I am sure, be more widely discussed in the context of work by fellow social reformers like Jane Addams, and also in relation to developments in both American realism and naturalism at the turn of the century.

Kate Chopin, Edith Wharton and Charlotte Perkins Gilman were all professional writers who had, in their work, to negotiate a space for themselves in the artistic and economic marketplace; they did this on their own terms for their own purposes although there is no doubt that Chopin and Gilman did it less profitably than Wharton. All three made creative interventions in traditions of both genre and theme through their fiction and all made a distinct and dynamic difference to the American short story.

Bibliography

Ashcroft, Bill, Gareth Griffiths and Helen Tiffin *The Empire Writes Back: Theory and Practice in Post-colonial Literatures* (London: Routledge, 1989).

Banta, Martha 'The Ghostly Gothic of Wharton's Everyday World', *American Literary Realism*, Vol. 27 (1), 1994, pp. 1–10.

Beer, Janet (ed.) *A Shameful Affair and Other Stories* (London: Pheonix Paperbacks, 1999).

Beer, Janet *Edith Wharton* (Tavistock: Northcote House, 2002).

Beer, Janet (ed.) *The Reckoning and Other Stories* (London: Pheonix Paperbacks, 1999).

Beer Goodwyn, Janet *Edith Wharton: Traveller in the Land of Letters* (Basingstoke: Macmillan Press Ltd., 1990).

Bell, Michael Davitt *The Problem of American Realism: Studies in the Cultural History of a Literary Idea* (Chicago: University of Chicago Press, 1993).

Bell, Millicent (ed.) *The Cambridge Companion to Edith Wharton* (New York: Cambridge University Press, 1995).

Bendixen, Alfred & Annette Zilversmit (eds) *Edith Wharton: New Critical Essays* (New York: Garland Publishing Inc., 1992).

Berthoff, Warner *American Trajectories: Authors and Readings 1790–1970* (University Park: Penn State Press, 1994).

Boren, Lynda S. & Sara deSaussure Davis *Kate Chopin Reconsidered: Beyond the Bayou* (Baton Rouge: Louisiana State University Press, 1992).

Brodhead, Richard *Cultures of Letters: Scenes of Reading and Writing in Nineteenth-Century America* (Chicago: University of Chicago Press, 1993).

Campbell, Donna M. 'Edith Wharton and the "Authoresses": the Critique of Local Color in Wharton's Early Fiction', *Studies in American Fiction*, Vol. 22 (2), Autumn 1994, pp. 169–83.

Chopin, Kate *The Awakening and Selected Stories*, introduction by Sandra Gilbert (London: Penguin Books, 1984).

Chopin, Kate *The Complete Works of Kate Chopin*, Per Seyersted (ed.) (Baton Rouge: Louisiana State University Press, 1969, repr. 1993).

Cranny-Francis, Anne *Feminist Fiction: Feminist Uses of Generic Fiction* (London: Polity Press, 1990).

de Crèvecoeur, J. Hector St John *Travels in Pennsylvania and New York*, 1801.

Dock, Julie Bates *'The Yellow Wallpaper' and the History of Its Publication and Reception* (University Park: The Pennsylvania State University Press, 1998).

Dock, Julie Bates with Daphne Ryan Allen, Jennifer Palais and Kristen Traug. '"But One Expects That": Charlotte Perkins Gilman's "The Yellow Wallpaper" and the Shifting Light of Scholarship', *PMLA*, Vol. 111, 1, January 1996, pp. 52–65.

Elliott, Emory (ed.) *The Columbia History of the American Novel* (New York: Columbia University Press, 1991).

Erlich, Gloria C. *The Sexual Education of Edith Wharton* (Berkeley and Los Angeles: University of California Press, 1992).

Erskine, Thomas L. & Connie L. Richards (eds) *Charlotte Perkins Gilman: 'The Yellow Wallpaper'* (New Jersey: Rutgers University Press, 1993).

Ewell, Barbara C. *Kate Chopin* (New York: The Ungar Publishing Company, 1986).

Fedorko, Kathy A. *Gender and the Gothic in the Fiction of Edith Wharton* (Tuscaloosa: University of Alabama Press, 1995).

Freeman, Mary Wilkins *Pembroke*, 1894 (New Haven: College and University Press, 1971).

Freeman, Mary E. Wilkins *The Winning Lady and Others* (New York, Harper and Brothers Publishers, 1909).

Fusco, Richard *Maupassant and the American Short Story: The Influence of Form at the Turn of the Century* (University Park: The Pennsylvania State University Press, 1994).

Gilman, Charlotte Perkins *Women and Economics*, 1898, reprinted. Carl N. Degler (New York: Harper Torchbooks, 1966).

Gilman, Charlotte Perkins *The Man-Made World; or, Our Androcentric Culture* (New York: Charlton Co., 1911).

Gilman, Charlotte Perkins *His Religion and Hers: A Study of the Faith of Our Fathers and the Work of Our Mothers*, 1923 (New York: Hyperion reprint, 1976).

Gilman, Charlotte Perkins *The Living of Charlotte Perkins Gilman, 1935* (Madison: University of Wisconsin Press, 1990).

Golden, Catherine (ed.) *The Captive Imagination: A Casebook on 'The Yellow Wallpaper'* (New York: The Feminist Press, 1992).

Golden, Catherine J. & Joanna Schneider Zangrando (eds) *The Mixed Legacy of Charlotte Perkins Gilman* (London: Associated University Presses, 2000).

Goodman, Susan *Edith Wharton's Women: Friends and Rivals* (Hanover: University Press of New England, 1990)

Gough, Val & Jill Rudd (eds) *A Very Different Story: Studies on the Fiction of Charlotte Perkins Gilman* (Liverpool: Liverpool University Press, 1998).

Gough, Val & Jill Rudd (eds) *Charlotte Perkins Gilman: Optimist Reformer* (Iowa City: University of Iowa Press, 1999).

Hill, Mary A. *A Journey From Within: The Love Letters of Charlotte Perkins Gilman 1897–1900* (London: Associated University Presses, 1995).

Hill, Mary A. *Charlotte Perkins Gilman: The Making of a Radical Feminist, 1860–1896* (Philadelphia: Temple University Press, 1980).

Hill, Mary A. *The Journey from Within: The Love Letters of Charlotte Perkins Gilman, 1897–1900* (Lewisburg: Bucknell University Press, 1995).

JanMohamed, Abdul R. 'The Economy of Manichean Allegory: The Function of Racial Difference in Colonialist Literature', *Critical Enquiry*, Vol. 12, (1) Autumn 1985, pp. 59–87.

Jewett, Sarah Orne *The Country of the Pointed Firs* (Boston and New York: Houghton Mifflin, 1896).

Jones, Anne Goodwyn *Tomorrow is Another Day: The Woman Writer in the South, 1859–1936* (Baton Rouge: Louisiana State University Press, 1981).

Joslin, Katherine & Alan Price (eds) *Wretched Exotic: Essays on Edith Wharton in Europe* (New York: Lang, 1993).

Kaplan, Amy *The Social Construction of American Realism* (Chicago: University of Chicago Press, 1988).

Kessler, Carol Farley *Charlotte Perkins Gilman: Her Progress Toward Utopia with Selected Writings* (Liverpool: Liverpool University Press, 1995).

Kilcup, Karen L. (ed.) *Soft Canons: American Women Writers and Masculine Tradition* (Iowa City: University of Iowa Press, 1999).

Knight, Denise D. (ed.) *The Diaries of Charlotte Perkins Gilman*, 2 Volumes, (Charlottesville: University Press of Virginia, 1994).

Knight, Denise D. (ed.) *'The Yellow Wallpaper' and Selected Stories of Charlotte Perkins Gilman* (London: Associated University Presses, 1994).

Knights, Pamela (ed.) *The Awakening and Other Stories* (Oxford: Oxford University Press, 2000).

Kundera, Milan *The Book of Laughter and Forgetting*. tr. Aaron Asher (London: Faber and Faber, 1996).

Lane, Ann J. *To Herland and Beyond: The Life and Work of Charlotte Perkins Gilman* (New York: Meridian, 1991).

Levy, Andrew *The Culture and Commerce of the American Short Story* (Cambridge: Cambridge University Press, 1993).

Lewis, R.W.B. *Edith Wharton* (London: Constable & Co., 1975).

Lewis, R.W.B. & Nancy Lewis (eds) *The Letters of Edith Wharton* (London: Simon and Schuster, 1988).

Lohafer, Susan *Coming to Terms with the Short Story* (Baton Rouge: Louisiana State University Press, 1983).

Lohafer, Susan & Jo Ellyn Clarey (eds) *Short Story Theory at a Crossroads* (Baton Rouge: Louisiana State University Press, 1989).

Peel, Ellen 'Semiotic Subversion in "Desiree's Baby"', *American Literature*, Vol. 62, 2, June 1990.

Ramsden, George *Edith Wharton's Library: A Catalogue* (York: Stone Trough Books, 1999).

Raphael, Lev *Edith Wharton's Prisoners of Shame: A New Perspective on her Neglected Fiction* (New York: St Martins Press, 1991).

Rosen, Ruth *The Lost Sisterhood: Prostitution in America, 1900–1918* (Baltimore: The Johns Hopkins University Press, 1982).

Rosenberg, Rosalind *Divided Lives: American Women in the Twentieth Century* (London: Penguin Books Ltd., 1993).

Ryu, Chung-Eun 'The Negro as a Serious Subject in Kate Chopin's Fiction', *English Language and Literature*, Vol. 36, (4), 1990, pp. 659–78.

Sedgwick, Ellery *A History of the Atlantic Monthly 1857–1909: Yankee Humanism at High Tide and Ebb* (Amherst: University of Massachusetts Press, 1994).

Seyersted, Per *Kate Chopin: A Critical Biography* (Baton Rouge: Louisiana State University Press, 1969).

Seyersted, Per & Emily Toth (eds) *A Kate Chopin Miscellany* (Natchitoches: Northwestern State University Press, 1979).

Showalter, Elaine *The Female Malady: Women, Madness and English Culture, 1830–1980, 1985* (London: Virago Press, 1987).

Showalter, Elaine *Sexual Anarchy: Gender and Culture at the Fin de Siècle, 1990* (London: Bloomsbury, 1991).

Showalter, Elaine 'Smoking Room', *Times Literary Supplement*, 16 June 1995, p. 12.

Shulman, Robert (ed.) *'The Yellow Wallpaper' and Other Stories* (Oxford: Oxford University Press, 1995).

Singley, Carol *Edith Wharton: Matters of Mind and Spirit* (New York: Cambridge University Press, 1995).

Solomon, Barbara H. Herland *and Selected Stories by Charlotte Perkins Gilman* (New York: Penguin Books Signet Classic, 1992).

Taylor, Helen *Gender, Race and Region in the Writings of Grace King, Ruth McEnery Stuart and Kate Chopin* (Baton Rouge: Louisiana State University Press, 1989).

Taylor, Helen 'Walking Through New Orleans: Kate Chopin and the Female Flâneur', *Symbiosis*, Vol. 1, No. 1, April 1997, pp. 69–85.

Todorov, Tzvetan *Genres in Discourse* (Cambridge: Cambridge University Press, 1990).

Todorov, Tzvetan *The Fantastic: A Structural Approach to a Literary Genre* (Ithaca: Cornell UP, 1975).

Toth, Emily *Kate Chopin* (London: Century, 1990).

Waid, Candace *Edith Wharton's Letters from the Underworld* (Chapel Hill: University of North Carolina Press, 1991).

Walker, Nancy A. *Kate Chopin: A Literary Life* (Basingstoke: Palgrave, 2001).

Wegener, Fred (ed.) *Edith Wharton: The Uncollected Critical Writings* (Princeton: Princeton University Press, 1996).

Wharton, Edith *A Backward Glance*, 1934 (London: Constable, 1972).

Wharton, Edith *Ethan Frome*, 1911 (London: Constable, 1976).

Wharton, Edith *French Ways and Their Meaning* (New York: D. Appleton & Co., 1919).

Wharton, Edith *The Age of Innocence* (New York: D. Appleton & Co., 1920).

Wharton, Edith *Hudson River Bracketed* (New York: D. Appleton & Co., 1929).

Wharton, Edith *Madame de Treymes: Four Short Novels* (London: Virago Press, 1995).

Wharton, Edith *The Collected Short Stories of Edith Wharton*, introduction by R.W.B. Lewis, 2 Vols. (New York: Charles Scribner's Sons, 1968).

Wharton, Edith *Roman Fever and Other Stories* (New York: Charles Scribner's Sons, 1964).

Wharton, Edith *The Ghost Stories of Edith Wharton* (New York: Charles Scribner's Sons, 1973).

Wharton, Edith *The Writing of Fiction* (London: Charles Scribner's Sons, 1925).

White, Barbara A. *Edith Wharton: A Study of the Short Fiction* (New York: Twayne Publishers, 1991).

Wood, Ann Douglas 'The Literature of Impoverishment: The Women Local Colorists in America 1865–1914', *Women's Studies*, Vol. 1, 1972, pp. 3–45.

Wright, Sarah Bird *Edith Wharton A–Z* (New York: Checkmark Books, 1998).

Ziff, Larzer *The American 1890s: Life and Times of a Lost Generation* (London: Chatto and Windus, 1967).

Index

Note: works appearing in single quotes refer to short stories and articles.

Addams, Jane, 187, 189, 214
Arabian Nights, 168, 173
Ashcroft, Bill, Gareth Griffiths and
   Helen Tiffin, 25, 38
Atlantic Monthly, 3, 28, 43, 64, 129
Austen, Jane, 198

Banta, Martha, 118, 143
Barbe, Waitman, 10–11
Bates Dock, Julie *et al.*, 21
Beecher, Lyman, 173
Bell, Michael Davitt, 18, 23
Berry, Walter, 9
Berthoff, Warner, 12, 22
Brodhead, Richard, 55, 64, 129–30
Brownell, William, C. 9
Burlingame, Edward, L. 2, 9

Cable, George Washington, 13–14
Campbell, Donna, 143
Cather, Willa, 84
Century Magazine, 2, 10, 11, 129
Charcot, Jean-Martin, 206
Chopin, Kate – Works
 'An Idle Fellow', 82
 'As You Like It', 4–5
 'At Chênière Caminada', 52–4
 At Fault, 1, 10, 67
 'Athénaïse', 28, 31–2, 37, 42–5
 'At the 'Cadian Ball', 59–60
 'Aunt Lympy's Interference', 35
 Awakening, The, 1, 6, 10, 12, 18,
   29, 41, 66, 67, 85
 Bayou Folk, 11, 29, 62
 'The Bênitous' Slave', 35, 70–1,
   73, 76, 84–5
 'Beyond the Bayou', 35
 'Boulôt and Boulotte', 82–4
 'Croque Mitaine', 87–8
 'Désirée's Baby', 12, 30, 36–7,
   48

'Doctor Chevalier's Lie', 74–7
'A Dresden Lady in Dixie', 32–7,
   72
'A Gentleman of Bayou
   Têché', 54
'The Godmother', 14–17
'A Harbinger', 77–8, 80
'Her Letters', 41, 45–8
'Emancipation: A Life Fable',
   67–70
'For Marse Chouchoute', 35
'In and Out of Old
   Natchitoches', 54–8
'In Sabine', 42, 54–5
'In the Confidence of a Story-
   Writer', 10
'Is Love Divine?', 40, 47
'Juanita', 78–80
'La Belle Zoraïde', 13, 26–8, 37
'A Little Free-Mulatto', 70, 73–4,
   88–9
'Mamouche', 30
'A Matter of Prejudice', 29–30
'Mrs Mobry's Reason', 2, 6
'Neg Creol', 35
'The Night Came Slowly', 67, 78,
   80–2
Night in Acadie, A, 6
'A No-Account Creole', 11, 42
'Odalie Misses Mass', 35
'Old Aunt Peggy', 28, 70–3, 85
'Ozème's Holiday', 35
'A Respectable Woman', 48, 50–1
'Ripe Figs', 87
'Tant' Cat'rinette', 35
'A Shameful Affair', 48–50
'The Storm', 40–1, 59–62
'The Story of an Hour', 28, 32, 42,
   45
'A Turkey Hunt', 85–7
'Two Portraits', 47, 58–9

'Two Summers and Two Souls', 41, 51–2
'A Very Fine Fiddle', 72, 84–5
'A Vocation and a Voice', 47
'The Western Association of Writers', 41
'Wiser than a God', 24
'With the Violin', 24
Young Doctor Gosse, 1
Clive, John, 197
Cranny-Francis, Anne, 20, 23, 148
Critic, 41
Curtis, Sarah, 197–8

de Crèvecoeur, J. Hector St John 12, 25, 38
Dix, Dr Morgan, 8
Dreiser, Theodore, 3

Elliott, Emory, 146
Ellis, Nancy, 53
Erlich, Gloria, 113, 134, 143
Ewell, Barbara, 35, 38

Fedorko, Kathy, 117, 136, 143
Fleenor, Juliann E., 212
Forerunner, The, 3, 4, 147–9, 152, 154, 157, 159, 175, 178–9, 184–5, 189–91, 193
Fowles, John, 150
Freeman, Mary Wilkins, 120–3, 144
Fusco, Richard, 42, 63, 83–5

Garland, Hamlin, 11
Gilbert, Sandra, 26, 38
Gilder, R.W., 11
Gilman, Charlotte Perkins – Works
'Aunt Mary's Pie Plant', 184–5, 190
'Bee Wise', 175–6, 190–3
'Being Reasonable', 163
Benigna Machiavelli, 193
Concerning Children, 4
'The Cottagette', 185–6
Crux, The, 179, 182
'Forsythe and Forsythe', 185–6

'Freed', 168–71, 178
'The Giant Wistaria', 199
'Her Housekeeper', 185–6
Herland, 149, 152–3, 175
'Her Memories', 185, 190–1
His Religion and Hers: A Study of the Faith of Our Fathers and the Work of Our Mothers, 147, 150, 153, 178
Home: Its Work and Influence, The, 4
Human Work, 4
'If I Were a Man', 157, 168–70
'Improving on Nature', 154, 159–62
'Joan's Defender', 162, 167
'The Jumping-Off Place', 190
'Lady Oyster', 154, 157–9
Living of Charlotte Perkins Gilman, The 3, 21, 210
'Maidstone Comfort', 185–7
'Making a Change', 162, 165, 168
'Mr Peebles' Heart', 162–3, 166–8, 174
'Mrs Beazley's Deeds', 186
'Mrs Elder's Idea', 186, 189
'Mrs Hines' Money', 185–90
'Old Mrs Crosley', 186, 189
'A Partnership', 189–90
'The Rocking Chair', 199
'Similar Cases', 171
'A Strange Land', 149
'Three Thanksgivings', 187, 189–90
'Turned', 162–6, 168
'Two Storks', 154–7, 159, 180
'The Unnatural Mother', 152–4, 170, 174, 180, 183
'The Vintage', 180, 182–4
'Unpunished', 165
'When I Was a Witch', 157, 168–70
'Wild Oats and Tame Wheat', 180–2
'With a Difference (Not Literature)' 150–1
'The Widow's Might', 162, 166–8, 186, 189–90

Gilman (*contd*)
  Women and Economics, 4, 105, 154,
    190, 202
  'The Yellow Wallpaper', 3, 6,
    19–20, 197–212, 214
Gilman, Houghton, 18
Glasgow, Maude, 176, 194
Golden, Catherine, 21
Goodman, Susan, 123, 143–4
Goodwyn Jones, Anne, 13, 22
Grand, Sarah, 176
Grant, Robert, 7

Hardy, Thomas, 11
Hawthorne, Nathaniel, 120–1,
    133–4, 137, 145
Hearst, William Randolph, 3
Heterodoxy, 177
Hill, Mary A., 188–9, 190, 195
Hull House, 187, 189, 195

Impress, 4, 21

James, Henry, 2, 117, 131
JanMohamed, Abdul R., 28, 30,
    36–7, 38
Joslin, Katherine, 143

Kaplan, Amy, 117, 118, 126, 142,
    143
Kessler, Carol Farley, 150, 184, 187,
    190, 192, 194–5, 214
Knight, Denise, 214
Kolbenheyer, Dr Frederick, 11
Kolodny, Annette, 209
Kundera, Milan, 62–3, 65

Lane, Ann J., 18, 21, 147, 162, 171,
    173, 190, 204, 210
Leary, Lewis, 90
Lewis, R.W.B., 6, 21–2, 99
Lohafer, Susan 63–4, 67, 89

Maudsley, Henry, 202, 212
Maupassant, Guy de, 11–12, 31, 42,
    48, 83
Missouri Historical Society, 22
Mitchell, Silas Weir, 20, 201, 207
Moods, 78

New England Magazine, 3, 21
New Orleans Times-Democrat, 3, 48,
    52
New York Suffragist
    Association, 177
*Man-Made World: Or Our Andro-
    centric Culture, The*, 178, 190,
    194

Orne Jewett, Sarah, 120, 123

Parrington, Vernon, 21
Peel, Ellen, 36–7, 39
Philadelphia Musical Journal, 24
Price, Alan, 143

Raphael, Lev, 112–13
Ringe, Donald, 90
Rosen, Ruth, 89, 176–7, 194
Rosenberg, Rosalind, 89, 177
Ryu, Chung-Eun, 22–3

Schuyler, William, 13, 66
Scudder, Horace, 3, 43–4
Sedgwick, Ellery, 43, 64
Seyersted, Per, 14, 22, 58, 68
Showalter, Elaine, 2, 21, 176, 194,
    199, 201–2, 206, 208, 212
Singley, Carol, 121, 144
Stowe, Harriet Beecher, 148, 149

Taylor, Helen, 13, 22
Todorov, Tzvetan, 134, 145, 157,
    169
Toth, Emily, 2, 13, 21, 40, 43, 54, 60,
    67, 85, 89
Twain, Mark, 12
Two Tales, 3, 54, 60

Vogue, 3, 26, 28, 36, 40, 45, 48, 51,
    74, 87

Wadey, Maggie, 197–212
Waid, Candace, 120, 144
Ward, Mrs Humphrey, 11, 66
Wharton, Edith – Works
  Age of Innocence, The, 106, 119,
    129, 130
  'All Souls', 116, 122, 133, 137–43

'The Angel at the Grave', 116,
    126–30, 142
Backward Glance, A, 9, 120
'Bewitched', 116–17, 119, 122,
    133–7, 142
Crucial Instances, 116
Custom of the Country, The, 99
Ethan Frome, 116, 119–22, 126,
    135, 136
*French Ways and Their
    Meaning,* 110, 114–15
'Friends', 116, 122–7, 142
Fruit of the Tree, The, 7
Ghosts, 7, 116, 142
Here and Beyond, 116
House of Mirth, The, 6, 9, 119, 125
Madame de Treymes, 1, 91–3, 97,
    107–12
Marne, The, 20

'Mrs Manstey's View', 2
Old New York, 91
Sanctuary, 1, 91–108
Summer, 116, 119–20, 122, 125,
    136
'The Triumph of Night', 122
Touchstone, The, 1, 91–108
Valley of Decision, The, 123
Writing of Fiction, The, 7
'The Young Gentlemen', 116,
    130–3, 142
White, Barbara, 7, 22
Whitman, Walt, 81
Writer, The, 13, 66

Youth's Companion, The, 116, 123

Ziff, Larzer, 22
Zola, Emile, 11